THE MAGNIFICENT COLLIE

THE MAGNIFICENT COLLIE

by **PATRICIA ROBERTS STARKWEATHER**
with **JOHN BUDDIE**

Doral Publishing, Inc.
Wilsonville, Oregon
1997

Published by Doral Publishing, Inc
8560 Salish Lane #300, Wilsonville, Oregon 97070-9612.
Order through Login Publishers Consortium, Chicago, Illinois.

Printed in the United States of America.

Edited by Luana Luther.
Cover design by Mark Christian Smith, Graphica Pacific Design
Cover photographs: Front - Ch. Glen Hill Top of the Line, Patty Fitzgerald photographer. Back: top right - four-week-old puppies by Ch. Glen Hill Knight O' Round Table bred by Kristi Alford, photo by Lasting Impression Photography; lower right - Ch. Bellevue Spring Sir Lance at eight weeks, photo courtesy of Sayuri Harami; lower middle - Glen Hill Really Regal at five weeks bred and photographed by Diana Stearns; lower left - Smooth Ch. Foxbride's Nut 'N Honey at four months, bred by Lynne Fox and Barbara Kilbride, photo courtesy of Foxbride Kennels.

Library of Congress Number: 97-065309.
ISBN: 0944875-34-3

Starkweather, Patricia Roberts.
    The magnificent collie: history, breeding, care of & multiple capabilities of the breed/ Patricia Roberts Starkweather with John Buddie.
    320 p. cm.
    Includes index.
    1. Collie.
1. Title.
SF429.C6.573 1997
636.7'3

To my brother, Admiral W. E. Roberts, USNR,
his wonderful children, Don, Kate, Judith and Dave,
and his grandsons Jaxon and Thomas.

And to my good friend Tom Jones,
who makes all things possible.

Acknowledgements

I wish to thank the people who have so graciously given of their time and energy in helping me produce *The Magnificent Collie.*

First of all, no one could have been more devoted to its progress than my great friend, John Buddie. He was in consultation all the way. I applaud his diligent research in putting together the fascinating data in his "Dominating the Decades." It is and shall remain an unmatched source of information on the development of the Collie.

Next, but certainly equal, is Gayle Kaye's contribution to the information contained in the Magnificent Collie. Her remarkable tracing of "Collie Origins and History" will be the standard reference work on this subject, probably definitively and forever.

How Doris Werdermann, ex-president of the Collie Club of America could have assembled all the material on the Smooth Collie is a mystery. Out of her busy life she found time to gather important data and wonderful pictures that will make the Collie fancy and the public in general aware of the great qualities of the smooth collie.

Lois Russell has written and contributed a fascinating account: "A Brief History of the Collie as a Herding Dog." She has supplied many exciting pictures. This well-rounded account will present a new look at the Collie as a herder and companion. Interest in the herding phase of the breed is rapidly growing.

Jean Levitt, president of the American Working Collie Association has interestingly told of the many titles that can be won by Collies (in conjunction with their trainers), in many different endeavors. Such accomplishments as service dog, backpacking, carting, and many more, are of new interest to fanciers,

Carol Knock, Collie Club of America Obedience Training Committee Chairman, has supplied up-to-the-minute information on Collie Obedience work. This field has changed—for the better— and Carol Knock introduces us to what is going on in the '90s. Her submitted pictures show the agility and versatility of the Collie.

Dr. Cindi Bossart is a leading veterinarian in the Fort Lauderdale area. She also does consulting work for her alma mater, University of

Pennsylvannia Veterinary School. She is the proud owner of Ch. Affenloch The Silver Laser, and several champions by him.

Bill Cleek is half of the well-known Loch Laren Collies with his wife Barbara Cleek. He put immense time and effort into getting the book onto computer disks—I thank him.

Veasey Jones, is to be thanked for her help in getting this book underway.

Thanks to Libby Lewitt for taking a whole day to take pictures for my section on "Grooming."

Chip and Pat Atkins were very kind to send information on the unique Quarter Century Club, which they head so artistically.

Thanks to all the others who have contributed so generously to the contents of *The Magnificent Collie*.

CONTENTS

PART I.
INTRODUCTION TO THE COLLIE

Ch. Glen Hill Ultra Violet Ray HIC, one of five champions by Ch. Affenloch The Silver Laser ex Glen Hill Pipi Longstocking. Bred by Pat Starkweather and Mary Dritsas.

The Collie Standard as written by the Collie Club of America and approved by the American Kennel Club (The Complete Dog Book, 17th Edition)

Rough

General Character — The Collie is a lithe, strong, responsive, active dog, carrying no useless timber, standing naturally straight and firm. The deep, moderately wide chest shows strength, the sloping shoulders and well-bent hocks indicate speed and grace, and the face shows high intelligence. The Collie presents an impressive, proud picture of true balance, each part being in harmonious proportion to every other part and to the whole. Except for the technical description that is essential to this Standard and without which no standard for the guidance of breeders and judges is adequate, it could be stated simply that no part of the Collie ever seems to be out of proportion to any other part. Timidity, frailness, sullenness, viciousness, lack of animation, cumbersome appearance and lack of overall balance impair the general character.

Head — The head properties are of great importance. When considered in proportion to the size of the dog, the head is inclined to lightness and never appears massive. A heavy-headed dog lacks the necessary bright, alert, full-of-sense look that contributes so greatly to expression. Both in front and profile view the head bears a general resemblance to a well-blunted lean wedge, being smooth and clean in outline and nicely balanced in proportion. On the sides it tapers gradually and smoothly from the ears to the end of the black nose, without being flared out in backskull ("cheeky") or pinched in muzzle ("snipy"). In profile view the top of the backskull and the top of the muzzle lie in two approximately parallel, straight planes of equal length, divided by a very slight but perceptible stop or break. A mid-point between the inside corners of the eyes (which is the center of a correctly placed stop) is the center of balance in length of head.

The end of the smooth, well-rounded muzzle is blunt but not square. The underjaw is strong, clean-cut and the depth of skull from the brow to the under part of the jaw is not excessive. The teeth are of good size, meetings in a scissors bite. *Overshot or undershot jaws are undesirable, the latter being more severely penalized.* There is a very slight prominence of the eyebrows. The backskull is flat, without receding either laterally or backward and the occipital bone is not highly peaked. The proper width of backskull necessarily depends upon the combined length of skull and muzzle and the width of the backskull is less than its length. Thus the correct width varies with the individual and is dependent upon the extent to which it is supported by length of muzzle. Because of the importance of the head characteristics, *prominent head faults are very severely penalized.*

Eyes — Because of the combination of the flat skull, the arched eyebrows, the slight stop and the rounded muzzle, the foreface must be chiseled to form a receptacle for the eyes and they are necessarily placed obliquely to give them the required forward outlook. Except for the blue merles, they are required to be matched in color. They are almond-shaped, of medium size and never properly appear to be large or prominent. The color is dark and the eye does not show a yellow ring or a sufficiently prominent haw to effect the dog's expression. The eyes have a clear, bright appearance, expressing intelligent inquisitiveness, particularly when the ears are drawn up and the dog is on the alert. In blue merles, dark brown eyes are preferable, but either or both eyes may be merle or china in color without specific penalty. A large, round, full eye seriously detracts from the desired "sweet" expression. *Eye faults are heavily penalized.*

Ears — The ears are in proportion to the size of the head and, if they are carried properly and unquestionably "break" naturally, are seldom too small. Large ears usually cannot be lifted correctly off the head, and even if lifted, they will be out of proportion to the size of the head. When in repose, the ears are folded lengthwise and thrown back into the frill. On the alert they are drawn well up on the backskull and are carried about three-quarters erect, with about one-fourth of the ear tipping or "break-ing" forward. *A dog with prick ears or low ears cannot show true expression and is penalized accordingly.*

Neck — The neck is firm, clean, muscular, sinewy and heavily frilled. It is fairly long, carried upright with a slight arch at the nape and imparts a proud, upstanding appearance showing off the frill.

Body — The body is firm, hard and muscular, a trifle long in proportion to the height. The ribs are well-rounded behind the well-sloped shoulders and the chest is deep, extending to the elbows. The back is strong and level, supported by powerful hips and thighs and the croup is sloped to give a well-rounded finish. The loin is powerful and slightly arched. *Noticeably fat dogs, or dogs in poor flesh, or with skin disease, or with no undercoat are out of condition and are moderately penalized accordingly.*

Legs — The forelegs are straight and muscular, with a fair amount of bone considering the size of the dog. A cumbersome appearance is undesirable. *Both narrow and wide placement are penalized.* The forearm is moderately fleshy and the pasterns are flexible but without weakness. The hind legs are less fleshy, muscular at the thighs, very sinewy and the hocks and stifles are well bent. *A cowhocked dog or a dog with straight stifles is penalized.* The comparatively small feet are approximately oval in shape. The soles are well padded and tough, and the toes are well arched and close together. When the Collie is not in motion the legs and feet are judged by allowing the dog to come to a natural stop in a standing position so that both the forelegs and the hind legs are placed well apart, with the feet extending straight forward. Excessive "posing" is undesirable.

Gait — Gait is sound. When the dog is moved at a slow trot toward an observer its straight front legs track comparatively close together at the ground. The front legs are not out at the elbows, do not "cross over", . (sic) nor does the dog move with a choppy, pacing or rolling gait. When viewed from the rear the hind legs are straight, tracking comparatively close together at the ground. At a moderate trot the hind legs are powerful and propelling. Viewed from the side the reasonably long, "reaching" stride is smooth and even, keeping the back line firm and level.

As the speed of the gait is increased the Collie single tracks, bringing the front legs inward in a straight line from the shoulder toward the center line of the body and the hind legs inward in a straight line from the hip toward the center line of the body. The gait suggest (sic) effortless speed combined with the dog's herding heritage, requiring it to be capable of changing its direction of travel almost instantaneously.

Tail — The tail is moderately long, the bone reaching to the hock joint or below. It is carried low when the dog is quiet, the end having an upward twist or "swirl." When gaited or when the dog is excited it is carried gaily but not over the back.

Coat — The well-fitting proper-textured coat is the crowning glory of the rough variety of Collie. It is abundant except on the head and legs. The outer coat is straight and harsh to the touch. *A soft, open outer coat or a curly outer coat, regardless of quantity is penalized.* The undercoat, however, is soft, furry and so close together that it is difficult to see the skin when the hair is parted. The coat is very abundant on the mane and frill. The face or mask is smooth. The forelegs are smooth and well feathered to the back of the pasterns. The hind legs are smooth below the hock joints. Any feathering below the hocks is removed for the show ring. The hair on the tail is very profuse and on the hips it is long and bushy. The texture, quantity and the extent to which the coat "fits the dog" are important points.

Color — The four recognized colors are "Sable and White," "Tricolor," "Blue Merle" and "White." There is no preference among them. The "Sable and White" is predominantly sable (a fawn sable color of varying shades from light gold to dark mahogany) with white markings usually on the chest, neck, legs, feet and the tip of the tail. A blaze may appear on the foreface or backskull or both. The "Tri-color" is predominantly black, carrying white markings as in a "Sable and White" and has tan shadings on and about the head and legs. The "Blue Merle" is a mottled or "marbled" color predominantly blue-gray and black with white markings as in the "Sable and White" and usually has tan shadings as in the "Tricolor." The "White" is predominantly white, preferably with sable, tri-color or blue-merle markings.

Size — Dogs are from 24 to 26 inches at the shoulder and weigh from 60 to 75 pounds. Bitches are from 22 to 24 inches at the shoulder, weighing from 50 to 65 pounds. *An undersize or an oversize Collie is penalized according to the extent to which the dog appears to be undersize or oversize.*

Expression — Expression is one of the most important points in considering the relative value of Collies. Expression, like the term "character" is difficult to define in words. It is not a fixed point as in color, weight or height and it is something the uninitiated can properly understand only by optical illustration. In general, however, it may be said to be the combined product of the shape and balance of the skull and muzzle, the placement, size, shape and color of the eye and the position, size and carriage of the ears. An expression that shows sullenness or which is suggestive of any other breed is entirely foreign. The Collie cannot be judged properly until its expression has been carefully evaluated.

Smooth

The Smooth Variety of Collie is judged by the same Standard as the Rough Variety, except that the references to the quantity and the distribution of the coat are not applicable to the Smooth Variety, which has a short, hard, dense, flat coat of good texture, with an abundance of undercoat.

Approved May 10, 1977

INTRODUCTION TO THE COLLIE

As far back as human history goes, the Collie has been man's companion. Legend has it that when the first Roman legions crossed Europe and invaded the British Isles, the Collies or their antecedents were with them. An invading army must carry its own provisions, and Romans brought with them cattle and sheep to use as food on the way—also to establish herds for future use. The Collie of today doubtless descends from those sturdy marchers of the past.

While many of us are involved in the Collie as a show dog, many, many more have them as pets. The breed is especially well adapted for this purpose. The love and devotion that Collies give their human companions are legendary. The breed, having been developed over the centuries to take care of sheep and other helpless creatures, is gentle by nature. The Collie puppy may frisk and play about, but the adult Collie is a sweet, reserved creature. This makes the dog ideal as a companion for children as well as adults. When a kennel-raised Collie first spies a child one can see an immediate magnetism develop. The Collie wants to run to the child, and be held and fondled by him. The child, in turn, is drawn to this wonderfully gentle affectionate animal.

The Collies recorded in the earliest stud books, were smaller than today's dog. Some were reputed to be only about 14 inches at the shoulder, which would make quite a small Shetland Sheepdog of today. These dogs were usually black or tricolor (black, white and tan). There are various theories regarding how the name Collie came to be. The first I heard was that the breed was called "coalie" because of its black coat. That was in the early 1950s. Older fanciers, English and Scotsmen, used that term.

Another theory has it that the Collie was named after the "colley" sheep of Scotland, which they herded. Thus came the often-heard expression "colley dogs." One still hears that expression occasionally.

The color has also produced a legend that may or may not be true. Since the breed was black at the time of origin, something certainly happened to bring the sable color (gold to red to mahogany), which has come to dominate the breed. The most widely held theory is that the Irish Setter was bred into the Collie breed to produce the reddish color. That theory should not produce concerns regarding the purity of the breed. It is widely known that nearly every breed has been mixed with others to introduce changes thought to be beneficial. Many Collies to this day, including many champions, show speckles of brown or black on the white of the forelegs—perhaps this harks back to setter blood in the distant past.

Some people have said to me that their homes were too small for a big dog like a Collie. My answer is that a big dog lying still takes up less

Collies and babies love each other from the "git go!"

A child and a Collie—a natural and joyous combination.

room than a small dog running around! The Collie is a reserved dog who loves to lie at his master's feet. The best time in the world for a Collie is that time spent in his master's company. This grand dog is easy to be around. He does not annoy the owner by constantly begging for attention. A quiet word and a pat on the head will satisfy most Collies.

Books and movies have extolled the devotion and bravery of Collies. When I was a child, I read books by Albert Payson Terhune that filled my mind with dreams of owning such a Collie. These books are well written and well plotted, and they led me to become a Collie breeder. I have devoted my entire, long life to this pursuit. Some of the great books by Albert Payson Terhune are: *Lad a Dog, Further Adventure of Lad, Lochinvar Luck, Wolf,* and many more. These books are out of print so far as I know. However, I sometimes see them in used book stores and in out-of-print collections. They were written in the early twenties.

Probably more familiar to present day readers will be the book *Lassie Come Home.* This book and the movies and television series that followed found a great audience. Most children were brought up with the idea that Lassie (who happened to be male!) was the greatest dog on the planet. The exploits of Lassie were exciting, and Lassie was a great pet as well as wonderdog. All this, is a true reflection of the character of the breed.

The Collie can be counted on to guard only in non-aggressive ways. The Collie will bark and give a warning when a stranger approaches, but he will be very unlikely to bite the invader. Most Collies would not be willing to attack a human. They will look after children and will stand between a child or even an adult and danger. Many a Collie has been cited for bravery for pulling a child from the approaching wheels of a car. In today's extreme litigious culture, it is best to have a dog that will bark but not bite. One can even be sued by an intruder who is bitten by the owner's dog on his own ground. So, the Collie is particularly suitable to today's way of living. I have heard police officers say that a barking dog is the best deterrent to break-ins—better than a biting dog.

The Collie is easy to train and must be trained with a soft hand. The gentle appearance truly represents the gentle heart within. A Collie will respond readily to a soft word of reprimand. Some Collies will almost die of contrition at the simple word "no." The best way to get a Collie to learn what not to do is to raise a finger and sternly say, "NO." Do not ever strike a Collie, especially not around the head or face. Such treatment will cause the dog to become headshy. This is a very unattractive quality in a pet, and a ruinous one in a show dog.

Some Collies, especially when young, will jump up on people because they want attention. This is an annoying trait that should be

A Clarion puppy doing what Collies do best— adoring his owner.

stopped. The best way to handle this problem is to push the dog back gently with your knee when he jumps up. A few experiences of this will quickly train the dog to stay down. It does not hurt the dog and saves your clothes. When the dog does something right, like greeting you on all fours, be sure to give the dog praise.

In fact, the use of praise is extremely important in training the Collie. This dog is one that almost lives for praise from his master. He won't beg for it but will revel in praise when it happens. It is the old story that honey gathers more flies than vinegar. The Collie will be obedient and joyous in his work if treated with love. He will become sullen and withdrawn if treated roughly.

Collie As A Protector

Each year, one hears tales of bravery and the protective qualities of the Collie. I have one experience engraved on my memory forever. A woman who was working for me in my kennels told me this story:

She was about to enter the pen of one of my young (8 months) puppies when she heard the pup start to growl. She told me she had never heard a Collie growl before so she stopped. The puppy was wildly exited and kept looking at her and then at the ground, while dancing around and barking. She started to open the gate and the dog went into a fit of barking, and jumped against the gate to close it. Finally, my helper looked down. She saw a poisonous snake coiled and ready to strike. If she had opened the gate, she would have stepped right onto the venomous viper. This puppy saved her from a possibly mortal attack. He was a tricolor Collie, later famous as Ch. Glen Hill Knight O' Round Table—a Westminister winner!

It has been said by truly uninformed people that the Collie is unintelligent due to his narrow head. This has been disproved again and again by the accomplishments of Collies.

Some year ago, I saw a team of Collies engaged in a basketball game against some Dobermans and other breeds. The Collies were wildly joyful while playing and beat the other teams. Collies enjoy a challenge, but become bored rapidly when faced with repetition. Most Collies, for instance, can master the moves of obedience work, but are not eager to do it. I am sure they say to themselves: "I've done this, why must I do it again." For this reason, it behooves those who want to train Collies in obedience work to create a bouncy attitude toward the work and use lavish praise when the dog is right.

I am happy that agility work is gaining popularity. The main reason that I admire agility trials is that dogs love them. To see happy dogs doing work they love is a great and fulfilling experience.

A dog that can herd sheep has to be a dog that can think for himself. He must be a dog that can make decisions, and that is a true test of intelligence. Herding cannot be done by rote; it must be thought out. Even Collies that never before have seen stock

A Collie looks lovingly at her owner while demonstrating heeling with attention. The obedience work builds a bond between a Collie and mistress, or master. The dog is U-CD Sunrise Diane Duo Delight UD. (Photo courtesy of Mrs. Alan A. Cummings)

can, in many cases, herd on the first exposure. We, who breed Collies, are happy that the instinct has not died out of the breed.

At a Herding Instinct Certification contest held by the Collie Club of America (CCA), I had wonderful proof that this instinct lives. I entered a blue merle puppy at exactly six months of age. This event was staged with geese to be herded. My puppy, which had never seen such animals before, took to it like a duck (goose?) to water.

He passed and received his Herding Instinct Certificate. Later, only a few months later, this beautiful dog finished his championship. He is Ch. Glen Hill Ultra Violet Ray. When he looks at me, intelligence shines from his lovely, dark, properly shaped and sized eyes. He is a dog that deserves to be exposed to every challenge the dog world holds.

The rough and the smooth Collies share the same heredity. They share the sweet, charming, slightly mischievous attitude toward life. They both make superb pets—with the smooth being somewhat easier to maintain coatwise.

For the pet owner, be advised that the male rough will usually shed either about his birthday, or at the advent of hot weather near his birthday. The female usually sheds after each season. Collie females are likely to have about an eight-month cycle between seasons. Some are longer—some shorter.

In order to keep the shedding to a minimum, it is important that at shedding time all the loose hair be removed. A small implement called a "rake" is good for removing clumps of hair. Also, a pin brush may be used. The hair should be brushed against the grain, toward the head. This will enable you to get out all the loose hair. The whole shedding process may take up to a week. Then the new coat will start to grow and shed-

Ch. Kings Valley Back T' Th' Future shown enjoying fulfilling his natural instinct for herding. (Photo courtesy of Leslie and Eva Rappaport)

ding will be finished until next shedding season.

It is best not to bathe the dog often. Bathing will dry out the skin and coat. The dog can be kept clean with weekly brushing and an occasional application of corn starch as a dry shampoo.

To keep the dog mat-free, a weekly brushing is necessary. Most important of all is the area behind the ears. That is an area of very silky hair that mats easily. If your Collie becomes very matted, it will be best to go to a professional groomer for help.

COLLIE ORIGINS AND HISTORY
By Gayle Kaye

Unfortunately, it is a sad but true fact, that the Collie's exact origins are shrouded in obscurity. On several occasions they have been the subject of much research and speculation. A famous 18th Century naturalist was of the opinion that the Collie was one of the oldest breeds in the canine family. However, it has never been proven that the Collie was in fact a descendant of the ancient sheepdog. The word "Collie" is as obscure as the breed itself. Over a period of time the name has been spelled many different ways: Coll, Colley, Coally and Coaly. Generally, the most accepted origin of the word is "Coll," the Anglo-Saxon word for black. The black-faced sheep of Scotland came to be called colleys and the dogs that guarded them soon became "colleys." Regrettably, unless new information turns up, this part of our breed's heritage will never be known. Whatever the origins, around 1875 the name "Collie" became firmly in place.

In the 18th Century, the Collie's natural home was in the highlands of Scotland, deep in the hills and the mountains, where he had been used for centuries as a sheepdog. The dogs were bred with great care in order to assist their masters in the herding and guarding of their flocks. These people were totally dependent on their pastoral pursuits, so the dogs were bred for strength, endurance, intelligence, devotion and loyalty. Physical characteristics included a thick coat, an active, graceful outline, alert eyes and keen ears—all important traits for a highly successful guardian of the flock. Most of these early specimens were either tri-color or blue merle. The absence of white markings was a prized characteristic and indicated purity of the stock. By today's standards, they were a smaller dog, with heads on the coarse side, with heavier ears and less coat.

Up until 1860, these dogs were used almost exclusively as working sheepdogs, but this would soon change upon Queen Victoria's trip to Scotland in the early 1860s. She was so impressed with the beauty, intelligence and faithfulness of these sheepdogs that several soon joined her "Royal Kennels." This was a historic epoch in the breed's history. From this point on, Collies' popularity grew rapidly and they soon became very fashionable.

Development as a Show Dog

While the breed, as we know it, may have originated in Scotland invariably we think of England as the true home of the breed. For without a doubt, it is to the English fancy of the late 1800s that the breed owes its development as a popular show dog.

Collies were first exhibited in 1860 at the Birmingham, England, dog show in the generic class "Scotch Sheep-dogs." Five Collies were benched at this show. By 1862, the breed had its own class for "Scotch-Colleys." Birmingham continued for years to be the center of great Collie activity and produced some of the best dogs in the history of the breed. This is where the true history of the show Collie begins.

By the 1870s, the breed had caught the eye of several English dog men who would go on to develop and refine it. Among the early pioneers in the breed were the Rev. Hans Hamilton (Woodmansterne) who was the first president of the English Collie Club, C.H. Wheeler (Edgbaston), Mr. A.H. Megson, Mr. Tom Stretch (Ormskirk), Mr. R.H. Lord (Seedley), Hugo Ainscough (Parbold), W.E. Mason (Southport), J. and W.H. Charles (Wellesbourne) and H. E. Packwood (Billesley). These are the breeders who took the ordinary sheepdog and began the process of developing him into the breed we know today as the Collie.

The stock that laid the Collie's original foundations were dogs such as, Bess, Old Mec, Old Hero, Carlyle, Trefoil, Tartan, Tricolour, Tramp, Marcus, Scott, Duncan, Hunt's Lassie and Brackenbury's Scott. Almost nothing is known of their pedigrees except that most came from a strain of working sheepdogs.

One of the first show Collies was a dog named **Old Cockie** (1868). He was a major influence on the early development of the breed. Not only was he the greatest show dog of his day, but he was the first show Collie to distinguish himself as a sire. He is also the dog that is credited with introducing the sable color. Although he left no sons to carry on, his daughters produced remarkably well when bred to the tricolor, **Trefoil**. This is where the Collie pedigree chart begins. From Trefoil, whelped in 1873, the Collie chart progresses right down to the present day dogs. Coming down through Trefoil's son, **Charlemagne** (1879), we come to his grandson, **Metchley Wonder** (whelped in 1886). He was a typical Collie of his day and was a tremendous improvement over his predecessors. He was a big winner and a prolific sire. It was at this point that English breeders began making rapid progress in developing the show Collie. They went to work

Eng. Ch. Charlemagne, 1879. (Photo courtesy of Gayle Kaye)

Eng. Ch. Metchley Wonder, 1886.
(Photo courtesy of Gayle Kaye)

Eng. Ch. Christopher, 1887.
Ch. Metchley Wonder ex
Peggie II. One of the first influ-
ential Collie sires. (Photo cour-
tesy of Gayle Kaye)

creating a bigger dog, with more refinement of head and thicker coats, topped off with flashy white markings. Over the years, the breed has undergone numerous changes, but it was between the years 1861 and 1900, that the greatest strides were made.

In 1887, one of the breed's greatest progenitors was whelped. He was a great-grandson of Trefoil, descending in tail male line. His name was **Ch. Christopher** and he was considered the best-headed dog up to that point—known far and wide for his beautiful coat and fashionable markings. He was mated to some of the best bitches in England, with the end result that he produced many top winners of the day. In the history of the breed there have been certain key dogs of tremendous influence and Christopher ranks high on the list of importance! It is through his two English sons, whelped on the same date in 1888, that all Collies trace. These two sons, **Stracathro Ralph** and **Edgbaston Marvel**, were by different dams. Each was responsible for two sharply defined lines of progression from which all present day Collies descend. Through Ralph, we come down to **Ch. Squire Of Tytton** whelped in 1904. The other line progresses from Marvel to **Ch. Parbold Piccolo**, whelped in 1899. Piccolo and Squire were among the first foundation sires imported to America.

Other English show Collies, all important in future pedigrees, were Ch. Ormskirk Emerald, Ch. Wishaw Clinker, Ch. Southport Perfection, Ch. Wellesbourne Counsellor, and Ch. Wellesbourne Conqueror. All the above mentioned are males, which leads one to believe the only dogs of great importance in the early days were sires. While this wasn't necessarily the case, it is true that bitches weren't as highly thought of nor was their history as well documented. In some instances, male puppies were highly prized, while the female puppies were destroyed at birth. Males will always have more opportunities at limitless influence on a breed and therefore will always receive greater credit. Especially in the early days, Collie studs received top billing.

The Collie Comes To America

At about this same time, the breed was also becoming popular in this country. The only difference was our Collies

Ch. Squire Of Tytton, 1904. Ch. Balgreggie Baronet ex Belle Of Boston. (Photo courtesy of Gayle Kaye)

had not made the strides toward perfection that the English dogs had made. Prior to 1880, Collies in this country were a pretty ordinary lot. However, the situation was about to change dramatically.

In 1879, the first English Collie was imported to this country by a Mr. Allen Apgar. After one of his imported dogs won an impressive dog show in New York, other breeders followed suit and the great importing craze began. Little did anyone realize it would initiate a practice that would continue for almost 50 years and would have tremendous influence on the development of the American Collie. Indeed, it is from England that we find the famous pillars of the breed from which American fanciers sought not only their next big winner, but also their foundation stock. American importers followed the winning bloodlines in England and yesterday's top English winner soon made his way to our shores. Most of the early imports were of indifferent quality, especially when compared to the excellence of later imports. In addition to Mr. Apgar, other prominent exhibitors of the time were James Watson, Thomas Terry of Hempstead Farm Kennels, W. Atlee Burpee & Company, and J.B. Van Schaick, the first president of the CCA which was organized in 1886.

One of the leading importers of this era was Mitchell Harrison of the Chestnut Hill Kennels in Philadelphia. Ch. Christopher was among the numerous quality dogs imported by this kennel. J.L. Behling of Bon Ami Collies, at one time or another imported some of the greatest Collies of the time. J.P. Morgan, the famous financier, joined the ranks of Collie breeders and exhibitors. He began his Cragston Kennels in 1888 and didn't waste any time in accumulating some of the best Collies this country had ever seen. He was one of the first American breeders to import blue merle Collies. He completely dominated the show ring for many years with his imports, but he could never develop his own breeding program. He remained a prominent force in Collie circles until his retirement in 1908.

While it may be true that his breeding program did not bring overwhelming success, he did much to help popularize the breed in this country. Another well-known importer was Samuel Untermyer of Greystone Collies. He and Morgan were arch rivals in the show ring, as well as the purchasing department. They competed vigorously for years, paying top dollar for the latest English winners. It quickly drove overall prices up, putting most of the really good dogs out of the reach of the ordinary person. It was a time in which "buyers" completely dominated the market, for it was easier to buy a good Collie than to breed one. However, in spite of spending great sums of money and importing only the best, breeding progress was slow in this country. The situation wouldn't change for several years until the buyers lost interest, leaving the true fanciers to pick up the pieces. At that point, the dedicated breeders were able to acquire good stock at more reasonable prices. Ultimately, the quality of the dog became more important than the "rumored" purchase price.

Although he was an English breeder and exhibitor, W.E. Mason of Southport Collies traveled frequently between the two countries. For a short time, he resided in this country, establishing a kennel in New Jersey. He was an important person in the early history of the breed for several reasons. He was a breeder, exhibitor and conditioner "extraordinaire." Most importantly, he was responsible for bringing more high-quality Collies to this country than any other single individual. Today, he might be considered a broker, but he was really much more than that. He was a true fancier and an inveterate Collie fan. Some of the greatest Collies in the beginning of this century were either owned, bred or sold by him. He is the person that wealthy Americans contacted regarding the purchase of top English dogs. He was a successful breeder in his own right, but his true value was in negotiating deals that brought such dogs as Ch. Anfield Model, Ch. Squire Of Tytton, Ch. Parbold Picador and Ch. Southport Sample all to this country. He and the early history of the American Collie are practically inseparable.

The Turn Of The Century

By the turn of the century, the American Collie was still in a state of development, leaving much to be desired. On the other hand, the breed continued to flourish in England. British dogs were still finding their way to our shores by the droves. Unfortunately, due to the overall lack of quality, the American-bred Collies simply could not compete. Show prizes were completely dominated by the British imports. In the long run, the breed benefited immensely from these importations. Some felt it actually encouraged the English to breed better dogs in order to supply the demand. Americans were in the market for the best dogs money could buy. The English used certain dogs to great advantage and when they had sons and daughters to carry on, they sold the parents to this country. Dogs changed hands frequently for record sums of money. As a result of the imports, the breed made rapid progress between 1900 and 1920. These dogs built the foundations upon which the present-day Collie is based.

Shortly after 1920, the import frenzy reached its peak and the American Collie began to emerge from being a rather ordinary, farm-type specimen to the modern show type, similar to those seen in the ring today.

The Early Influential Imports

Ch. Parbold Piccolo (1899) was an important dog in the early history of the breed, although his story is both sad and ironic. He was imported in 1904 by Mr. J.L. Behling of Bon Ami Collies who purchased him

Right: Ch. Parbold Picador, 1910. Master Willie ex Moss Hill Vera; Below: Eng. Ch. Anfield Model, 1902. Ch. Parbold Piccolo ex Bellfield Beauty. He was felt to be the breed standard in head, eye and expression. (Photos courtesy of Gayle Kaye)

at one of the highest prices ever paid for a Collie. In England, Piccolo had accomplished some impressive siring, so expectations were high that he would make major contributions when bred to American bitches. Regrettably, he never got the opportunity. After the dog's arrival, Behling took him for a walk and turned him off leash. Piccolo immediately ran off and was never seen again. Fortunately, he had already sired two influential sons in England, Ch Anfield Model and Parbold Pierrot. One can only wonder what he might have produced in this country had he not been lost to the fancy.

One of the most important events of the new century was the birth of the beautiful sable and white **Ch. Anfield Model** (1902). He was imported by William Ellery of Valverde Collies in Napa, California. Ellery had amassed one of the greatest collection of Collies ever seen in this country. He undoubtedly would have made significant contributions to the sport of dogs were it not for a disgruntled ex-employee who preferred charges against him to the American Kennel Club (AKC). The dispute developed into a suspension, which Ellery did not appeal. Consequently, Model made little if any impact after his arrival in this country. Fortunately, his best siring had already been done in England. Although he was controversial because of the shyness that plagued him and his descendants, he was one of the most important of the early sires. He was a beautiful specimen and his excellent photograph was used repeatedly to exemplify correct Collie type. It was felt for years that he was the living standard in head, eye and expression. Model remained a dominant tail-male sire well into the 1920s, thanks to his three sons, Ch Parbold Peacock, Parbold Prior and Master Willie. However, in the long run, his greatest contribution would be on the distaff side of pedigrees.

Ch. Squire Of Tytton (1904) was descended eight generations, tail male from Ch. Christopher. He was imported to this country by the famous American attorney, Samuel Untermyer of Greystone Collies. Squire was a sensational winner and was used extensively at stud in both countries. He had many admirers and was known for his outstanding temperament. His influence is strong through two of his sons, Grimsby Squire and Seedley Squire.

Ch. Ormskirk Foxall (1907) descended through the Piccolo son, Parbold Pierrot. Because of Anfield Model's temperamental nature, breeders tried to find other bloodlines with which to work. Foxall provided a different outlet from the Model line of influence. Unfortunately, Foxall's line produced a different kind of temperament problem. They weren't shy, but could be overly aggressive. Ultimately, he did not provide the other sire line as hoped, but he does remain prominent in bitch bloodlines through his descendants, Ch. Seedley Stirling and Ch. Magnet.

Ch. Southport Sample (1909) had a sensational show career in both countries. He was brought to this country when his owner, W.E. Mason of Southport Collies, established an American branch of his prestigious kennel. Sample was a beautiful specimen, excelling in overall type and a profuse coat. In the days when many Collie temperaments were questionable, he excelled and, in fact, was known for his wonderful disposition. He proved to be a popular sire in both countries and sired nine American champions—a record held for many years. Despite this achievement, he did not produce a surviving sire line. However, he remains an important influence in bitch pedigrees through his son, Ch. Southport Sceptre and his granddaughter, Laund Lily, the dam of Laund Limit.

Ch. Parbold Picador (1910) was heavily linebred on Model, as were most dogs of the day. He was imported by one of the first prominent American breeders, Dr. O.P. Bennett of Tazewell Collies. Picador was a consistent sire of quality stock and an essential ingredient in the progress of the American Collie. His influence was lasting through his son, Ch. Laund Limit and his daughter, Southport Seal, the dam of Ch. Magnet. Upon Picador's death, Dr. Bennett, one of the great authorities on the breed, felt no other sire had done more for the advancement of the Collie.

Ch. Seedley Stirling (1911) was bred by the talented R.H. Lord of Seedley Collies, who provided a seemingly endless supply of good dogs to this country. Stirling was imported by Thomas Hunter of Knocklayde Collies, who was quickly becoming one of the shining lights in the American Collie world, until struck down by a heart attack in the prime of life. Stirling was considered by many early breeders to be one of the finest examples of correct Collie type. He was known for his wonderful head, eye and expression and his well-fitting coat. He had many admirers and expectations ran high that he would have a great career at stud. However, years later he was deemed a failure simply because he left no surviving sire line. This was an unfair assessment because thanks to his influence bitch lines flourished. He sired six bitches and at least three males that played a significant role in the development of the American Collie. He remains today one of the most important sires for the distaff side of pedigrees.

Ch. Laund Limit (1912) has been one of the most underrated sires in the history of the breed, when actually he was one of the most influential. Bred in England by W.W. Stansfield of Laund Collies, he was imported by Edwin L. Pickhardt of Sterling Collies. Limit's sire was Ch. Parbold Picador. Limit was not only his best son, but his best producing, as well. His dam was Laund Lily, whose pedigree was linebred on the beautiful Ch. Southport Sample. Limit was beautifully balanced, with an enormous coat. Not only was he stylish, but he was very sound. He was one of the first Collies to combine these two attributes successfully. He just happened to be a contemporary of another great dog named Ch. Magnet. The two of them through their descendants would help change the direction of the American Collie.

Much of the breed's rapid progress after 1920 was the direct result of numerous crossings of the progeny of these two dogs. These successful crosses provided the groundwork for the top American kennels of the 1920s, 1930s and beyond. Limit's influence is significant through his numerous quality producing sons and daughters: Ch. Bellhaven Laund Logic, Ch. Alstead Laund Luminous, Ch. Laund Laureate, Ch. Laund Laird and Eden Emily.

All of this leads to a major turning point in the development of the Collie—the birth in 1912 of a sable-and-white male sometimes referred to as the "Sire Supreme." The title of Sire Supreme applies to only a few studs in any breed. **Ch. Magnet** truly deserved this accolade, as he proved to be a sire of major influence. He was imported to this country at the age of nine by Eileen Moretta of Glen Rose Collies. His importation was incidental to his success as a sire here, because he had already made his mark in England. Several of his good sons actually preceded him across the pond. He was descended 13 generations from Ch. Christopher. His pedigree was based extensively on Ch. Anfield Model, with a cross to Ch. Ormskirk Foxall. It is a safe assessment that almost all of today's American Collies trace in tail male to Ch. Magnet. He played an important part in the distaff side of pedigrees as well. He came along at a time when certain attributes were desperately needed—attributes he just happened to possess and pass on with great frequency. At first he was not held in high esteem by all who saw him.

Fortunately, certain breeders realized his potential and his ability to upgrade almost any bitch bred to him. His head was very refined at a time when many Collies were coarse headed. His head qualities were of the lasting kind, an important factor in his success at stud. Many of the major American lines were not aging well and his influence helped to reverse this trend. He was known for his sweet expression. His most important quality however, was his wonderful disposition; a trait he passed on regularly to his puppies. Due to the influence of certain early sires, Collie temperaments had become a problem; either they were too timid or overly aggressive.

Magnet helped change this. However, not everyone was a fan. There were those who felt he was too refined—to the point of being "bitchy." Some breeders felt he was too rangy and slab-sided, lacking in substance. While still others felt the quality of his eyes and ears left much to be desired. In any case, at the time he was definitely what the breed needed. In every breed, timeliness is a tremendous factor in the success of any sire. It is ironic that for all of Magnet's eventual influence, he was the sire of only two American champions, neither of which made any impact on the breed. It was through his English sons and grandsons that he really made his impact. This was especially true when his descendants were bred to daughters and granddaughters of Ch. Laund Limit. At that point, Magnet's dominance became almost overwhelming. It is through three sons, Ch. Poplar Perfection, Laund Legislator and Ch. Seedley Supremacy that his strongest influence would be felt. Most prolific of the three was Ch. Poplar Perfection, whose sire line remains dominant to this day.

One of the most important Collies ever to be imported to this country was **Ch. Eden Emerald,** whelped in 1922. He provided a major turning point for the American breeder. His sire was Ch. Poplar Perfection and his dam was the beautiful bitch, Ch. Eden Elenora, a Ch. Laund Limit granddaughter. Emerald was imported by Mrs. Lunt of Alstead Collies in 1923, shortly after finishing his English championship. Perhaps his greatest claim to fame was that he was one of the few English imports that did not sire their best stock in England. In fact, he did some of his best siring right here in this country. This was a welcome change for American breeders, who were hoping to halt the British influx. Not only did Mrs. Lunt use Emerald wisely, but many of the day's foremost kennels, such as Arken, Arrowhill, Tokalon and Tazewell used him to great advantage. Many of these breedings produced the dogs that would carry on for the next 70 years.

Emerald, and all the great dogs before him, paved the way for the next era in Collie history when the American breeders began to import less and finally began breeding quality dogs of their own. Once Emerald's American descendants got established, the American breeders never looked back. This is the point at which the American breeders successfully established the breed in this country. Finally the American Collie emerged in all its glory.

Foundation American Kennels

Tremendous credit is owed to those early American breeders who played a role in establishing the American Collie. Most of them overcame formidable obstacles, setbacks and major disappointments. Through initiative and fortitude, they stayed with the sole objective of creating a better Collie. Many of them purchased dogs from England at tremendous prices. A great number of the dogs were not the quality as represented, while others proved barren or a huge disappointment in the producing department. Kennels battled such things as distemper, rabies and other diseases, in the days before vaccinations and antibiotics. There was no such thing as "premium dog food." Dog food was mostly cooked from scratch, using table scraps. Dog shows and travel were an ordeal at best—this in the days when the main method of shipping was by railroad. Shipping a bitch to a stud was a feat in itself, that most people simply could not afford. It was not uncommon for many dogs to die en route. We will never know all the sacrifices and ordeals these people endured in their quest to create the perfect Collie. They had one common goal—to breed and own the very best Collies possible.

Any treatise on the Collie's early beginnings in this country has to begin with Alstead Collies, for this kennel is the whole key from which the American Collie emerged. It was owned and operated for more than 50 years, from 1902 to 1953, by Mrs. Clara Lunt of New Jersey. Not only did she appear on the scene in the initial years of the Collie's development, but she endured through most of its critical periods. She is someone who has never been given sufficient credit for helping to establish the Collie in America—which is especially surprising because she did it almost single-handedly. She bred numerous high-quality champions and imported more good English dogs than almost any other individual. When she obtained what she wanted in her own breeding program, she passed the dogs along to someone else, thereby sharing in the wealth. However, without a doubt, her most important contribution was that Alstead was the source upon which most of the early American kennels were based. She was responsible for several importations and key breedings that helped shape the destiny of the American bloodlines. She put together a family of Collies, at a time when most fanciers were only interested in importing their next big winner. Ultimately, her family of dogs blended well with almost every major American line. Not only did she have a wonderful eye for a dog, but she was someone with great insight who excelled in timing.

In the early years, she acquired: the good producing bitch, **Knocklayde Queen Bud**; the top winning American-bred bitch **Ch. Ardshiel's Wendy**; the English winner, **Ch. Alstead Laund Luminous**; the top producing bitch, **Ch. Alstead Seedley Queen**; and the aforementioned, Ch. Alstead Eden Emerald. She used all judiciously in her breeding program and when she was done, she created a family of Collies with quality type, that would last forever.

Most of the early American breeders drew from her bloodlines and all the important kennels of the 1920s and 1930s had Alstead in their pedigrees. To say that she was the whole key to the turn of events is no exaggeration. Every major kennel from that point on utilized the best that Alstead had to offer.

The next breeder of note, Dr. O. P. Bennett of Tazewell Collies, was right on the heels of Mrs. Lunt. For years, he was considered the world's greatest authority on Collies. He was an important breeder, judge and writer for over 40 years. By 1910, he had imported and was offering at stud some of the top Collies of the day, Ch. Seedley Squire, Parbold Prior and Parbold Proclamation. Years later, he added the successful sires **Ch. Parbold Picador** and **Ch. Cock Robin Of Arken**. He felt the sire was the most important element in correct breeding. Ironically, none of his males left a surviving sire line, but the distaff influence of his dogs is everywhere. His bitches produced well and blended wonderfully with the top bloodlines of the day. He was devoted to the Collie and never tired of helping other breeders. He wrote scores of articles for various magazines. Two of his books, *The Collie* and *Famous Collies*, are highly sought after by collectors of Collie literature.

For more than 50 years, Edwin Pickhardt of Sterling Collies was a prominent breeder, exhibitor and judge. His Sterling Collies began in 1914. Like most serious breeders of the day, he imported many top English dogs—most notably **Ch. Laund Limit.** His kennel came into full bloom in the 1930s and 1940s. Among his important dogs, to which all future Collies would trace, were **Ch. Sterling Stardust, Ch. Sterling Syndicate**, and **Ch. Sterling Starmist.** Many future breeders based their kennels on dogs with a Sterling prefix. Mr. Pickhardt was highly respected for years with his top winners and producers.

Hertzville Collies began in 1907 by a Chicago banker, Mr. Henry Hertz. Within a few years, he gave up the Collies and transferred ownership to Chris Cassleman, a co-worker who shared his love for the breed. Along the way, Chris and Tom Halpin joined in partnership. Most of their foundation stock had been imported from England, to which Brighton and Tazewell were incorporated. The result was a dominant family of Collies that really came into their own in the 1930s and 1940s. Some of the famed characteristics were beautiful heads, combined with soundness and outstanding showmanship. Some of their big winners and producers were **Ch. Hertzville Headstone, Ch. Hertzville However,** and **Ch. Hertzville Historian.** Both Halpin and Cassleman were popular judges and true students of the breed. Many of their dogs went on to influence other American kennels in the 1940s and beyond. **Ch. Hazeljanes Bright Future**, the sensational winner in the early 1950s, was almost solid Hertzville breeding. Even though he met with an untimely death at the age of six, he holds the breed record for four consecutive Best Of Breeds at the National Specialty.

Fred and Madge Kem, along with their son Oren created one of the most prominent kennels in the Midwest, Lodestone Collies. They made tremendous contributions in almost every area of the fancy, through breeding, judging, writing and stock work. Their first Collie was purchased

Ch. Sterling Starmist, 1940. Sterling Select ex Sterling Starnymph. This dog is behind nearly every American Collie of today. (Photo courtesy of Gayle Kaye)

Ch. Hertzville Headstone, 1939. Lodestone Landmark ex Hertzville Blue Heatherbelle. (Photo courtesy of Gayle Kaye)

in 1920, as a pet for Mrs. Kem. Because of this dog, they became enamored of Collies and soon began to raise them. The dog that put them on the map was **Lodestone Landmark**, whelped in 1929. He was one of the first important American-bred sires to make an impact. He not only became the foundation sire for their kennels, but for others as well. Other significant dogs were Lodestone Landstar, Lance of Lodestone, Lodestone Live Oak, and Star of Lodestone. The contributions of the Lodestone bitches were equally as impressive. Several would play key roles in the development of later kennels, such as Parader. Though not known as a "showing" kennel, they produced stock regularly used by other breeders. Since Lodestone was located on a farm, they shared an interest in the working Collie. Their dogs were sold all over the country to farms, ranches and stock yards. Another area of major contribution was in the field of education. Both Fred and Oren were gifted writers and shared their knowledge for years, through various magazines and periodicals.

Bellhaven was one of the most famous of the old-time kennels. Florence Ilch of Bellhaven did it all. She had an excellent eye for a quality dog that was evidenced repeatedly for over 40 years. She was one of the few early breeders who had a successful breeding program, while continuing to import some of the biggest winners of the day. She started in 1919, with a pet Collie. Deciding she wanted to breed and show with the best of them she began acquiring some of the best Collies available. Like many of the day's breeders, she turned to Alstead for her foundation stock. Early acquisitions were Ch. Alstead Allysum, Ch. Alstead Attractive and Ch. Starbat Strongheart. Along with Strongheart came the greatest Collie handler, exhibitor, and conditioner to ever live—Mike Kennedy. It's no exaggeration that much of Bellhaven's success over the years was a result of Mike Kennedy's natural abilities with the dogs. Bellhaven was located on the Shrewsbury River, in Red Bank New Jersey, in one of the world's truly fantastic canine establishments. In its heyday, it housed close to 125 Collies, producing more than 130 champions, 89 of which were homebred.

The Bellhaven breeding program was an integral part of the formative years of the American Collie. With her start of the Alstead bitches, she added the blood of various imports such as Ch. Bellhaven Laund Logic. Among those housed in her kennels were her favorites, Ch. Bellhaven Black Lucason and Laund Loyalty of Bellhaven, the only Collie to go Best In Show at Westminster. In addition to the remarkable stud force, several top bitches held producing records for many years, Ch. Eden Edith of Bellhaven, Ch. Bellhaven Seedley Snowdrop and Ch. Bellhaven Seedley Solution. Many of the Bellhaven dogs remain in today's pedigrees through the influence of two other American kennels, Arken and Honeybrook. Mrs. Ilch loved the Collie and devoted her entire life to improvement of the breed. As a result, her influence will always be an important part of the breed's history.

About the same time that Bellhaven was beginning its influence, another breeder of note was establishing her kennel on a sloping hillside, in upstate New York. Mrs. Elisabeth Browning and her Tokalon Collies were quickly ascending the ladder of Collie fame and success. Although, she started in the 1920s, her dogs really came into their own in the 1940s. To this day, her dogs are greatly admired for their outstanding type, elegance, beauty, overall balance and tremendous coats. Mrs. Browning was one of the early breeders to use Ch. Eden Emerald in her breeding program. The result, in succeeding generations, was the production of the gorgeous tri-color, **Ch. Tokalon Storm Cloud**, the sire of 13 champions. He headed a successful sire line that lasted for years. She also utilized the blood of the great Ch. El Troubadour of Arken, producing Ch. Tokalon the King's Choice, the sable and white who headed her other great line of

Ch. Tokalon Storm Cloud, 1941. Ch. Tokalon Blue Eagle ex Tokalon Aileen. (Photo courtesy of Gayle Kaye)

Ch. Honeybrook Big Parade, 1934. Ch. Future Of Arken ex Honeybrook Helen. A leading sire in the 1930s. (Photo courtesy of Gayle Kaye)

Collies. Tokalon would have a profound effect on future breeders and bloodlines, that lasts to this day, some 60 years later.

W.R. Van Dyck began his Honeybrook Collies in the early 1900s, but his kennel did not come to prominence until the 1930's. The dog that put him on the map was the great **Ch. Honeybrook Big Parade**, whelped in 1934. His pedigree was very carefully based on the best of Alstead, with a liberal infusion of Bellhaven. He was a magnificent, heavily coated sable and white, who was a true "natural" showman. Not only was he the top winner of his day, but he went on to become a top producer. He was one of the first sires to produce 17 champions—a distinguished record held for many years. Among his many champions was a beautiful sable puppy who won the 1940 CCA futurity and later became **Ch. Silver Ho Shining Arrow**. He in turn sired the incomparable **Ch. Silver Ho Parader**. In essence, Big Parade could be considered the grandfather of a future family of dogs—Parader. It is a bloodline that continues to dominate to this day. Van was also a popular writer, educating hundreds of Collie fanciers through his writings in all the top magazines.

Although Arrowhill Collies actually started in 1910, Florence Cummings didn't reach prominence until many years later, thanks to various setbacks. She started over in Collies three different times. Twice she was wiped out by rabies and distemper. She started over for the third and final time in 1940 with the purchase of Ch. Arrowhill Admiral O'Silver

Ho (a full younger brother to Shining Arrow) and the bitch Ch. Arrowhill Silver Ho Of Glamis. She bred these two together and this was the beginning of the Arrowhill dogs known far and wide today. Her best producing dog was **Arrowhill Ace High**, who went on to sire 16 champions. Among his sons was Ch. High Man of Arrowhill, the sire of the top Smooth sire of all time, **Ch. Black Hawk Of Kasan**. Other important sires include Ch. Arrowhill Oklahoma Redman and Ch. Arrowhill Oklahoma Tornado. Many kennels in the 1940s and 1950s incorporated Arrowhill dogs in their bloodlines.

The next kennel of note was one of tremendous influence. If Alstead was the beginning of the American Collie, then Arken was where everything came together. While other kennels were busy importing their latest winners, Arken was attempting to establish its own successful family of dogs. They utilized the best of Alstead—dogs that included Alstead Eden Emerald, Ch. Alstead Seedley Queen, Alstead Aviator, and Ch. Alstead Adjutant. Arken is bar none, one of the most important of the early kennels. They had one of the most successful sire lines in the history of the breed-a line that remains dominant to this day. At the same time, they had a kennel full of prolific bitches. Arken was and is the "Quintessential" American kennel. Owned and operated by Charles and Lillian Wernsman, they started showing Collies in 1919.

However, the true beginning of Arken was in 1925 with the purchase of the great Ch. Halbury Jean Of Arken. She was the catalyst that would set everything in motion. She not only founded the Arken family of dogs, but founded a major line of productivity. She was one of the few bitches in the early history of the breed who combined a successful show career with an even more successful career in the whelping box. Her importance to the American Collie can never be over estimated. She produced five litters that included 6 champions, a breed record for many years. She was also the dam of an influential male (sired by Eden Emerald), who was never shown due to an injury to his nose. His name was El Capitaine of Arken, best known for his production of the top sire **Ch. El Troubadour Of Arken**. Many of Jean's descendants went on to become top winners and producers themselves. Among her champion daughters was the National Specialty Best Of Breed winner, **Ch. Nymph Of Arken**. Nymph also played a prominent role in the creation of the sire line that remains dominant to this day.

When she was bred to Jean's grandson, Ch. El Troubadour of Arken, the resultant litter produced one of the most important sires in the breed's history, **Ch. Future Of Arken**. This is another pivotal dog in the history of the breed. Though he only sired five champions, two of his sons Ch. Sterling Stardust and Ch. Honeybrook Big Parade, would produce

Ch. El Troubadour Of Arken, 1930. El Capitaine Of Arken ex Gailley Arrayed Of Arken. One of the breed's foundation sires. (Photo courtesy of Gayle Kaye)

two important sire lines. Ch. Cock Robin Of Arken, was a full brother to Future and unfortunately would forever live in his shadow. In spite of this, he was an accomplished sire in his own right and produced well for owner Dr. Bennett. He went on to sire five champions and would be especially influential in bitch pedigrees. The Arken dogs were almost always sable in color, with brilliant orange-gold coats, combined with flashy white markings. They were known for their overall beauty, great coats and superb head details, along with beautiful eye and expression. They continued an unbroken line of successes for close to 30 years, until the death of Mr. Wernsman in 1952. Much of the success of Arken rested on Halbury Jean's shoulders, but the ultimate choices of her breedings were made by the Wernsmans and obviously they chose very wisely. It is easy to see why Arken was in the thick of everything, for it is here that everything came together.

One of the leading lights in the Collies' early years, was Albert Payson Terhune and his Sunnybank kennels. Although not a foundation kennel nor a major influence on Collie bloodlines, Mr. Terhune did enormous public relations work by promoting the Collie in the 1920s and

1930s. He bred and owned numerous champions such as **Ch. Sunnybank Sigurd, Ch. Sunnybank Sigurdson, Ch. Sunnybank Explorer** and the sensational winner, **Ch. Sunnybank Thane**.

Ch. Sunnybank Sigurdson, 1922. Owned and bred by the famous author, Albert Payson Terhune. (Photo courtesy of Gayle Kaye)

However, his true place in Collie history is assured through the many books and articles he wrote during that time. Thanks to his prolific pen, he did more to help popularize the Collie than any other individual. For decades, his dog stories charmed the entire nation. He was a Collie fanatic and his deep love for the breed shone through in everything he penned. There is no way to estimate how many people have been influenced by his writings and became involved in the world of purebred dogs. His books continued to keep the Collie in the limelight for years following his death in 1942. Some books, such as *Lad, A Dog*, are still in print to this day. He was the Collie's most staunch defender.

All of the above mentioned breeders and kennels played a most important role in the creation of the American Collie.

The era of the big kennel, though still very much in existence, was slowly coming to an end. Following in the steps of the foundation breeders were the next generation of fanciers. Although sometimes their successes and accomplishments overlapped with the foundation kennels, these were the breeders who followed once the building blocks had been laid. These breeders drew from the above kennels and their wealth of resources and knowledge. Many of the early kennels' successes were interwoven. Sometimes it becomes difficult to separate them, as all relied on one another and used each other's dogs to great advantage.

The Second Stage In American Development

For some 40 years, the name Noranda, owned by Dorothy Long, was a name to contend with. At Noranda, Collies were a family affair and a large number of dogs were never kept in the kennel. Mrs. Long mostly concentrated on bitches, although she did produce some top-winning males. She utilized the top bloodlines of the day to help establish her family of dogs. Noranda has the unique distinction of finishing Collies in all four colors. It all began in 1924 with the purchase of a pet Collie from Albert Payson Terhune. However, the true beginning of Noranda was in 1929 with the purchase of Ch. Lodestone Lute, a litter sister to the famous Landmark. Lute was not only a big winner in her day, but was also trained for stock work. Among Mrs. Long's top winners were Ch. Cadet of Noranda, Ch. Ink Spot of Noranda and years later, Ch. Noranda Daily Double. Continuity played an important part in her breeding program. When **Ch. Noranda Daily Double** won Best Of Breed at the 1967 National Specialty, he traced back in unbroken lineage to the original foundation bitch, some 40 years later. Many people are not aware that her dogs played a significant role in the development of the Parader family.

The beautiful Ch. Silver Ho Shining Arrow was half Noranda through his dam, Silhouette of Silver Ho. Silhouette was also the dam of Florence Cumming's Ch. Arrowhill Admiral of Silver Ho. Mrs. Long's interests in Collies were numerous and varied and not necessarily limited to the show ring. She was one of the first people in this country to become active in obedience. She owned and trained the first champion CDX Collie, **Master Lukeo of Noranda**. Further involvement's included co-founding Dogs For Defense during World War II. She was also active in a program to help blind children train dogs. She strongly believed in the Collie's versatility and utilized him to every advantage. Thanks to people like Mrs. Long, the Collie has been perceived over the years as an extremely service-oriented dog.

By 1936, the Cainbrooke Collies were becoming firmly established. They were an extremely small operation in the home of Dr. James McCain and his wife Gertrude. They started with a bitch called Tazewell Tidiness, who was bred to Ch. Cock Robin Of Arken. This breeding produced Corogal Joan, who when bred to Royal Majesty II (Alstead and Arken breeding) produced the top-producing bitch, **Ch. Cainbrooke Clear Call**. For close to 30 years, Clear Call held the breed record for top-producing dam when she produced seven champions. Overall, Cainbrooke Collies were known for their good heads, combined with beautiful coats and sound temperaments. Although they finished a lot of males, they relied heavily on bitches. The Cainbrooke influence would be felt for generations to come through many of their dogs and bitches. Dr. McCain was especially interested in the care and raising of puppies. His article, "Conservation of Puppies," was a very informative and popular essay for many years. The highly respected doctor was one of the most popular judges of the day, which was quite an achievement for an African-American, who was born a son of a slave. Tragically, it all came to an end in 1956 upon his death from cancer.

Grace and James Christie had Collies since their marriage in 1903. However, it would be many years down the road before the dream of the Saint Adrian kennel "Aristocrats-All," would be fully realized. In 1932, under the guidance of Mrs. Lunt they began their quest to start a kennel. One of their first purchases was the top winner Ch. Major Lukeo. They imported Eden Eureka, in whelp to Eng. Ch. Laund Lieutenant. This breeding produced four champions. One of their most popular Collies was **Ch. Saint Adrian Fifan Farrant**, whose picture graced the official CCA's brochure as an example of the ideal Collie. It was one of the few kennels, along with Bellhaven who continued to draw from the English dogs. During WWII and because of the war, they were able to purchase several dogs from Mrs. George of Beulah Collies in England. In 1941, Ch. Beulah's Silver Don Mario of Saint Adrian arrived on one of the few convoy ships that wasn't torpedoed. Many kennels of the 1940s drew heavily from Saint Adrian stock.

The Poplar kennels of Lloyd and Mary Beresford was built on a strong Tokalon base, since Mary was Elisabeth Browning's daughter. Lloyd had actually been around Collie circles since the 1920s. However, the true start of Poplar began upon the marriage of Lloyd and Mary. Upon leaving home, Mary acquired several of the Tokalon Collies. Unfortunately, the split from Tokalon was not amicable, but Poplar did manage to have its own successes. Among their top winners were Ch. Poplar Golden Opportunity, Ch. Poplar Star's Opportunity and the CCA winner, Ch. Poplar Pencil Stripe. One of the top sires produced by their kennel was the tricolor dog **Poplar By Storm**, who would have a tremendous influence on the Gaylord-Brandwyne Collies in the 1950s and 1960s. Probably Poplar would have gone on to bigger and better things had it not been for the untimely death of Mary Beresford in 1955. Nonetheless, Poplar had a profound impact on Collies in succeeding years.

During World War II, out of necessity, breeding and showing activities slowed down. Not only were dog shows restricted, but traveling to them was curtailed due to gas rationing. Food supplies were rationed and many people went off to war. For four years during the war, breeding activity was seriously reduced. Ironically, the next kennel of importance began during the war years. Fortunately for the Collie, nothing deterred this individual from his goals and dreams of becoming a top Collie breeder. He is one of the few people whose influence would forever change the Collie scene. Around 1940, Steve Field of Parader fame began searching for a good Collie bitch to start his kennel. The rest, as they say, is history. His contributions are so significant that they will be dealt with in a separate section under kennel stories. Suffice it to say the breed would never be the same.

So ends the part of the Collie's history up to 1950. After 1950, the Collie scene changed dramatically. Starting in the 1950s, many smaller kennels emerged and bloodlines became less concentrated. The large kennel was a thing of the past. Many of the old-time breeders had either died or were becoming too old to maintain the pace. It ended a wonderful era in the history of the Collie, the likes of which we will never see again.

Ch. Clarion Color My World at 12 weeks. 'Nuf said! (Photo courtesy of J. Evans)

CHOOSING A SHOW-QUALITY COLLIE PUPPY

Perhaps the single most important skill in breeding dogs lies in choice of puppies. Some say the *eye for a dog* is a built-in factor that cannot be acquired. I personally doubt that as I have watched people learn over a period of time and observation. True, there are others who never seem to learn to select the right pups. To me that is a mystery. I find that when I look at a litter, the best pups seem to jump out of the box into my eyes. I remember one time I was distressed to find I could not decide which was the best of four pups in a liter of mine. I never did decide, but it really did not matter too much. All four became champions.

First of all, one must learn to look at the overall dog. Many breeders become so hung up on details of head that they cannot see the whole picture. Head is important—no Collie is a good Collie without a good head. However, the dog runs from nose tip to tail tip, and it is all important.

I would suggest, in selecting puppies, that they be at least eight weeks old, preferably nine weeks, before serious decisions can be made. By that time, the pups will be up on their legs and running around. At this age, you will be able to see if some pup or pups are high headed, with nice reach of neck. Some pups may stand nice and square with feet pointing forward on all fours. You will hope to see solid body structure, with well-

Can you pick out who's smooth and who's rough? We'll give you a clue— there's only two smooths. (Photo courtesy of Lynne Fox and Barbara Kilbride of Foxbride Kennels)

rounded rib cage, nice broad loin, well-developed, well-rounded bone in the fore and hind legs. The body proportions will remain the same at maturity. You want a body slightly longer than it is high. You will look for a well-rounded croup. This should assure you of a good tail carriage, which

Same look on all three—rough and smooth.

is carried below the level of the back. (Some call it below the horizon—that is "dog talk.")

An important factor in selection is coat. What I am speaking of here is a rough. Coat is the only factor that is different between selecting a rough and a smooth. A voluminous coat is going to show up early. There will be a fuzzy undercoat down close to the skin. Then, hopefully, there will be long guard hairs that stand off away from the body in all directions. The only exception to this description of the Collie coat is poor coat inheritance, or poor health. If a puppy is thin and wormy he will not show a healthy coat. That is true of adults as well.

The ears on a puppy will be anywhere from perfectly on top of the head, to "every which way." Some Collies seem to be miraculously born with perfect ear carriage, which is on top of the skull and softly bent forward. The fact is that unfortunately few of them are like that by nature, so man has intervened. The ears of most show prospects are taped into position from about seven or eight weeks onward. In another section, this taping will be described. Be warned however, that there are two poor types of ears that may never become right.

First, the more common: This is the small pointed "prick" ear. Because it is small and usually thin in leather, it is hard to train such ears to tip. And tip they *must.* The better ear has heavier leather and a rounded tip.

The other difficult ear is the low ear. This kind of ear usually goes hand-in-hand with a larger, heavier dog. It seems to be a tie-in factor with most very heavily boned dogs. This ear tends to break too low or sidewise, and it will require some extensive attention.

Now to the most important portion of the Collie—the *head.* On a young Collie, it does not much resemble the long, lean, elegant head that one sees on the adult. Actually, at birth a good Collie head looks almost

An exceptionally lovely litter by Glen Hill Spring Table Talk. Litter bred by Diana Stearns. (Photo by Diana Stearns)

square, perhaps oblong would be a better description. There should be no pinching in of the muzzle nor flaring of the skull.

As the puppy reaches about eight weeks, the head is starting to lengthen. However, the same oblong appearance should remain. The muzzle will be full and round and blunt at the end. The sides of the head should go back from muzzle to ears, with little or no perceptible widening or flaring. The bones on the side of the head, running horizontally from eye to ear, should be flat and smooth, not protruding.

Now viewed from the side, or profile, the puppy's head will show more stop than you would wish at maturity. There should be a straight line from the end of the nose back to a position at the corner of the eye. There should be a slight rise at that point. Then the head flattens out and goes back to a point behind the ears called the occipital bone. This bone is rather pointed but should not be very prominent. On a good head the occipital bone almost disappears, as the dog matures, and flesh fills in the sides.

If there is little or no stop, the head will probably be Borzoi-like, or even Roman-nosed at adulthood. A Roman head is an abomination in the breed. It looks somewhat like a parrot's beak. The muzzle will rise from front to back in an arch, or curve, showing none of the desired stop. This is foreign to the Collie, but occurs occasionally. At one time it was fairly common, but now rarely appears.

Another extremely important part of the Collie is the eye. Some even think it to be all and end all. That of course cannot be right. No matter what anyone says, remember the Collie, like any other dog, runs from nose tip to tail tip.

The best way to describe the proper Collie eye is to quote the standard: "They are necessarily placed obliquely to give the required forward look. Except for the blue merles, they are required to be matched in color. They are almond shaped, of medium size, and never properly appear to be large or prominent. The color is dark, and the eye does not show a yellow ring or a sufficiently prominent haw to affect the dog's expression."

I have mentioned *expression* twice so far, and it deserves to be stressed. To quote the standard again, "The eyes have a clear bright appearance, expressing intelligent, inquisitiveness, particularly when the ears are drawn up and the dog is on the alert."

And more from the Collie Standard: "the large, round, full eye seriously detracts from the desired 'sweet' expression." As I mentioned earlier, this has somehow been misinterpreted by some to mean the eye should be tiny.

There is almost no way the expression can be emphasized too much. In some ways, it is the essence of the Collie. The sweet look reflects the gentle Collie heart within.

The eye, as pointed out in the standard, should be dark brown, unless in a merle. The eyes also, as directed by the Standard, should be obliquely placed; they are described as almond shaped. However, there are many breeds that have eyes described as almond shaped including the Boxer. So

Four-month-old pup by Glen Hill Top of the Line (cover dog). Note the smooth muzzle, nicely tipped ears, good bone and alert expression.

A tri-colored bitch. The litter sister to Ch. Bellvue Spring Lady and Ch. Bellvue Spring Sir Lance. Note the proper stop for 8½ weeks.

"Solo" at three months. By Ch. Glen Hill Knight O'Round Table. Note the nice eye, good bone and sweet expression.

Talk about expression! Here it is in a Clarion puppy. (Photo courtesy of Clarion Collies)

you can see there is a great leeway in the interpretation of an almond eye. I personally prefer to describe the proper eye as looking triangular as it looks forward over the well-rounded muzzle.

The Collie expression has been called "sweet." It also is called alert and intelligent in the Standard. In my experience, Collie expression can range from sweet and melting to exciting, vibrant and thrilling. When the dog within has a wonderful diamond-edge personality, this shows in those beautiful eyes. The dog with personality bubbling over is going to be the best dog as a family companion, as well as the best dog in the show ring. Personality shows up in the puppy at an early stage. Best to choose the one that is curious, mischievous, and tail-wagging happy

If a Collie puppy can look at you in a certain way—if his expression makes your heart stop, then some other things can be forgiven. After all nobody's perfect, not even a Collie!

The following is a quotation regarding show training from Frank Sabella's book (written with Shirlee Kalstone), *The Art of Handling Show Dogs*, published by B & E Publications:.

Introduction

Show training is so important that it becomes a part of the puppy's life. Training for the show ring should begin as soon as you purchase your puppy or from the time it is weaned, if you were its breeder. Especially with a baby puppy, your main objective is to begin establishing a pleasant, loving relationship which will become the basis of more formal training in the future.

Dogs are required to do two things in the conformation ring: to be set up or posed (and to hold that pose for an indefinite length of time during the judge's examination) and to gait (individually and in a group). While show training is not difficult, it does require time, patience, sensitivity and consistency on the part of the trainer.

Many people make the mistake of waiting for a puppy to grow up and then begin to train it. We don't mean to imply that some successful dogs did not start this way but, without a doubt, dogs that have the right kind of basic training as puppies are always the ones that stand in the ring with head...up, full of assurance. Just the repetition of correctly posing and leading the puppy will teach it to walk confidently on lead and to feel comfortable while being handled—and that's really what early training is for— to ensure that your puppy will grow into an adult that is confident and self assured in the show ring!

At what age should you begin training your puppy? Each dog is an individual and should be treated as such, so there are no "set" age limits as to when to begin basic or advanced training.

Generally, when you start basic training depends not only on your patience, sensitivity and consistency, but also on the puppy's capabilities and desire to accept being posed and lead trained.

Very young puppies are highly motivated by and responsive to their owners but, like babies, they have short concentration periods. Even though intelligence develops rapidly in a puppy, early training should always be started on a "fun" basis. Don't be in a hurry to start formal training too early; the first part of a puppy's life should be fun time and every dog should be allowed to enjoy its puppyhood.

Early Socialization Important

As the owner or breeder of a young puppy, you alone are responsible for its early socialization and training. Socialization can be described as the way in which a dog develops a relationship with its dam, littermates, other animals and man. Just as a youngster must receive a formal education and also learn to become a responsible member of society, so must you provide the best environment for you dog's potential to be brought out and developed completely. A young puppy is very impressionable and the socialization and training it receives at an early age sets the tone for its lifetime characteristics. If a puppy receives the proper socialization, is treated with sensitivity, patience and consistency, if it learns to be loved and respected, then it will always be happiest when pleasing you.

Earlier we mentioned that with a young puppy you want to begin basic training by establishing a happy and loving rapport between you and the dog. Pat and handle the puppy frequently,

speaking reassuringly and using praise often. Let the puppy become accustomed to being petted and handled by strangers. A well-socialized puppy loves to make new friends and this kind of interaction between puppy and humans or other animals will be a prerequisite for the basic show training to follow.

Ch. Glen Hill American Hero. Some terrific front! Believe it or not, this shows a very promising smooth puppy at five weeks.

Hopefully, by the time the puppy is about 7 to 8 weeks old, it has learned a little about life. If it has been properly socialized, it is light-hearted and untroubled, because it has learned that it is loved and respected. Now it must be taught certain basics which lead eventually to more formal training for the show ring.

Here are some suggestions to consider before you begin basic training:

1. First training sessions should be given in familiar surroundings, preferably at home, and without noises or other distractions.

2. Make the first training periods short, not more than 10 minutes in length. As the sessions progress successfully, gradually lengthen each training period, but never more than 30 minutes in any single session.

3. If the puppy is restless or won't concentrate, postpone the lesson and try again the following day. Be sure, too, that you are not tired or impatient for the training sessions should always be relaxed and enjoyable for both of you.

4. Be consistent during the lessons. Use a firm tone of voice when giving commands. Some of the first words you puppy will learn in posing and lead training are "Come," "Stand," "Stay," and "No." Be sure you use the same word for the same command each time.

5. Remember that a young puppy is inexperienced, so be gentle and patient. Don't rush your puppy; give it time to understand what you expect and to learn how to respond.

6. Don't be too insistent at first. Puppies learn by repetition, correction and praise. Don't punish a puppy if it seems confused; instead, correct it until it does what you want, then offer plenty of praise. It is important that your puppy understand each training step thoroughly before going to the next.

7. Always end each training session on a pleasant note and once again, give plenty of praise and perhaps reward the puppy with its favorite treat. A puppy can learn almost anything if given love and understanding.

Table Training

...The majority of coated breeds require some type of regular grooming in addition to preparation at the show before going into the ring. Even smooth-coated breeds need regular care. Early grooming training on the table will teach the dog to learn to relax. Later on, when the coat grows longer or the dog needs special attention, it will not object if it has to spend longer periods on the table and will rest and feel totally secure while being worked

Ch. Bellvue Spring Lady Ann at six months, by Ch. Glen Hill Knight O'Round Table ex Bellvue Spring Lilac. In the Top Ten for three years.

A puppy at the so-called "uglies" between pup and adult. He is Glen Hill Spring Table Talk.

Here is the same dog at 18 months with a different look at maturity.

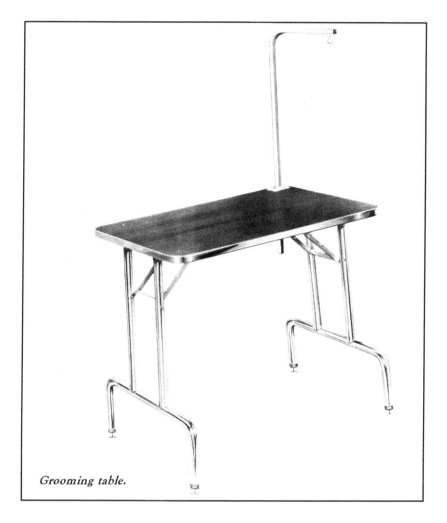

Grooming table.

on. As a part of the training you should practice posing the dog at the end of each grooming session.

The table you select should be sturdy and covered with a non-slip rubber top. There are many different types of grooming tables: portable (which fold up and are easy to carry along to matches and shows), adjustable (which move up or down) or a combination crate with grooming table top (these often have drawers between the crate and top to hold equipment). Some tables are equipped with a post and loop collar, which can be slipped around a dog's neck to hold the head up and keep it from moving or jumping off the table. If you do use a loop to give the puppy more confidence, never use one with any type of choking action. Never leave a young puppy alone with its head in a loop or standing by itself on a table unless you are sure it will stay.

Posing

You can start posing your puppy on a table as early as 6 weeks. In the beginning just stand the puppy on the table and get it used to being off the ground. Once this has been accomplished, then start positioning the legs in a show pose. Next, begin training it to be handled—feel its body, look at its teeth and let other people do the same. Experiencing all this at an early age will give the puppy confidence and make it used to being handled by strangers, which will be invaluable later on for the puppy's show career. If you persevere in the beginning you will discover that your puppy will never forget this basic training and later it will be much easier to work with.

When lifting the puppy for the first time, care should be taken not to frighten it. Don't come down too quickly on the puppy or attempt to lift it by grasping the back of the neck or picking it up by the front legs. Instead, kneel down to the puppy's level and let it come to you. Speak assuringly and pat the puppy ... Then using both hands t lift the puppy's front and rear, pick it up and place it on the table. Do be aware that a puppy might try to wiggle out of your arms so make sure you have a secure grip on the dog as you lift it and after you set it down on the table.

...

After your puppy learns how to stand properly, start posing it for longer periods of time. When the puppy can pose without fussing, the next step is to enlist the help of friends by having them go through the motions of lightly examining the dog—checking its bite and feeling the body—doing the things a judge will do in the ring. If you are training a male, in the ring the judge will check to see if both testicles are in place, so do remember to train your puppy to accept this procedure at an early age.

As the posing sessions progress, you can begin practicing the more subtle aspects of show posing, *i.e.*, setting up the puppy in a variety of situations and on different ground surfaces, especially grass.

Lead Training

Of all the steps necessary to prepare a puppy for the show ring, probably lead training is the most important because there have been many potentially fine show dogs ruined by improper lead training. So many exhibitors wait until the last minute to lead break a dog then expect it all to happen in one try. Then they become impatient and treat the dog roughly and the puppy's reaction to all this is fear. Do remember that extreme patience is necessary because introduction to a collar and a lead can be a frightening experience for a young puppy.

Most canine behavior experts agree that at 6 weeks, a dog can have a small soft collar put around its neck. The younger the puppy becomes accustomed to wearing a collar around its neck, the easier it will be to lead train it later on. Begin by placing the collar around the puppy's neck for short periods of time and only while someone is in attendance. The first few times the puppy wears the collar, it may roll on the ground or try several other things to get the collar off, so never allow a baby puppy to be unsupervised. Make the first lesson short, not more than 5 to 10 minutes, then remove the collar, play with the puppy and praise it for being such a good dog.

After a period of about a week (or when the puppy is relaxed about wearing the collar) snap a lightweight lead onto the collar and let the puppy drag the lead freely about the floor. Allow the puppy to walk wherever it wants to go. If it starts to follow you, fine; but the first time the lead is attached, don't pick it up and jerk and pull the puppy in any way. After a few times of allowing the puppy to drag the lead around the floor, pick up the lead in your hand and let the puppy take you for a walk. Speak gently and walk wherever the puppy wants to go. Once again, don't pull or tug on the lead in an attempt to make the puppy follow you until it is completely accustomed to wearing the collar and lead.

A puppy of about four months trained to a perfect show pose.

When this has been accomplished, the next lesson is to try to walk the puppy on lead. The first time you try this, don't be surprised if your puppy pulls back or rolls over on the floor. Don't panic, just learn to be patient and speak gently. Put the snap adjustment under the puppy's neck at first so it won't be tempted to look over its shoulder or try to bite the lead. Squat down and call the puppy's name and the word "come" in your most inviting voice, to get the dog to move forward to you. If it balks or sits, try coaxing it to come forward for its favorite tidbit. You may have to give a slight forward pull to the lead to start the puppy toward you but remember, a slight pull does not mean a neck-breaking jolt for you can injure the neck and the puppy will associate the resulting pain with an unpleasant experience. If this is done several times without thinking, it can develop into a deep seated fear of the lead.

When the puppy comes to you, pat and praise it; then walk ahead with the lead in your hand and repeat this action to make the puppy move forward again. It should only take a short while until the puppy follows you. Eventually, the puppy will learn that if it obeys and follows you, there will be no pulling or jerking of the lead and that it will receive plenty of praise.

Once again, we caution that because a puppy's attention span is short, try to make each session brief, 10 minutes at most, then remove the lead, praise and play with the puppy. The main idea at this stage of training is to make the first lessons a "train and play" time that the puppy looks forward to and not something it dreads. After a few lessons, you'll find your puppy can be lead trained rather quickly and what is more important, that it enjoys the experience.

At this point, we want to offer some advice about early training. Always try to train the puppy to move on a loose lead to help develop its natural carriage. In the show ring you will be asked by many judges to move your dog on a loose lead and you will be prepared if you accustom your puppy to do it at an early age. When a puppy is taught to gait only on a tight lead, it gets used to leaning into the lead and without that pressure, feels completely lost. There is nothing harder to break than a dog that is used to leaning into the lead for support. Dogs that are trained on a tight lead also lose their natural head carriage and they often learn many other bad habits including sidewinding. In the ring, it is not uncommon to see exhibitors string up their dogs so tightly that the front feet hardly touch the ground. There is a trend to show certain breeds on a tight lead to make a more positive topline.

However, if a knowledgeable judge wants to discover whether the dog's topline is natural or man-made, he will ask that the dog be moved on a loose lead and, if that fault is present, it will be exposed.

...

As the gaiting sessions progress, teach the puppy to move on your left side (eventually the dog should learn to move on your right side as well as your left). Encourage the puppy to stand naturally at the end of the lead each time it stops. To help get the puppy to stand alert, try attracting its attention with a squeaky toy, a ball or by offering its favorite tidbit. Doing this will start to teach the puppy the fundamentals of baiting.

After a while you will be ready to begin more advanced training. Replace the training collar with a one-piece show lead or, on large breeds, switch from the training collar to a choke chain or a more substantial type of collar for better control. (As the dog grows older, remember that any collar or chain should be worn only during practice sessions and then removed to prevent the hair from wearing away around the neck.) Before starting advanced training, be sure that the lead is correctly positioned around the dog's neck. It should be high under the chin and behind the ears to keep the dog under control at all times. This position will also help to train the puppy to keep its head up because for the first few weeks, a puppy may need a gentle reminder under its chin to learn to keep its head up.

Next you should begin advanced training by teaching the dog to move down and back in a straight line. Once the dog does this well, then try moving it in a circle. As a prerequisite to executing the individual patterns, practice doing figure-eights because this will teach the dog how to turn smoothly. Then you can begin the other movement patterns that will be used in the show ring—the "L," the "T," and the "Triangle." Vary the movement patterns in each session and remember not to overtrain. Always end each session on pleasant note and give the dog lots of praise.

As your puppy matures, it should learn to gait on grass, concrete floors and other surfaces including rubber mats (these are used at indoor shows). Once the lessons go well at home, take the puppy out and get it used to walking on a lead and being posed in new and different surroundings. Parking lots of supermarkets and department stores are excellent for this as there are usually lots of people and all kinds of distractions. For the first few outings, be patient and give the puppy plenty of time to adjust and respond to strange surroundings. Occasionally, because of a pup's insecurities, it may revert back to not being well trained for the first few outings.

The greatest pitfall for most young dogs seems to be going to indoor shows because the lighting is strange and the echoes inside a building can sometimes distract a young dog. The inside of a department store or shopping mall can help you to overcome this problem. Always try to anticipate experiences that might distract and frighten a puppy at a show and try to solve them while the

puppy is young. If you live in a rural area and none of these suggestions apply to you, take the puppy to matches as often as you
can for this is the best place to gain experience with the least
amount of tension.

You must work with your dog to determine its best speed in
gaiting. Each dog is an individual and looks best when moving at
a certain speed and if you want to show your dog to its best advantage, you should determine that correct speed. Have a friend
move your dog at varying speeds in front of a knowledgeable person to learn the right speed for your puppy. Then practice the
movement patterns at that speed until the dog can do them
smoothly. No dog can move at its best speed if the handler moves
improperly, so you should take long strides when gaiting the dog.
A common error of the novice is to move the dog too slowly.
Short, stilted steps look clumsy and prevent the dog from moving
smoothly. If you do not move fast enough yourself or with free and
easy strides, you will prevent your dog from executing its most efficient movement... For the medium or large breeds move at a fast
walk or run.

We should end the puppy lead training section with some advice about two common problems: sitting and sidling.

Sitting

When stopping, if you find that your puppy constantly sits,
keep moving forward a few steps while attracting its attention at
the same time with a piece of food or a toy, until the puppy understands that it must stand when it stops. If that does not work,
bring the puppy forward a few steps, stop, then put your toe under its stomach to prevent it from sitting.

Another solution is to ask a friend to stand holding a long
piece of rope or a show lead which encircles the dog's stomach.
When you bring your puppy forward and it starts to sit, have your
friend brace up its rear, but do not make this correction with a
jerking motion...

Sidewinding

A common characteristic during lead training is when a dog
has a tendency to sidle. This can be caused by:

A. *The dog pulling away from you.* Solution: When the dog
starts this habit on the lead or shows indications of doing so when
moving individually, train the dog to move on your opposite side.
In other words, if you are going away or coming back with the dog
on your left side and it sidles, switch to going and coming with the
dog on your right.

B. *A dog that has a tendency to look up at its handler while be-*

ing gaited. Solution: Never show a dog a toy or food while you are gaiting it as this can cause the dog to look up which may cause sidling. You can also try the alternate side method mentioned in (A) above.

C. *A dog is too short in back.* Solution: If you move at a faster speed, it will go sideways to be able to move at a faster speed. The best way to deal with this problem is to get someone to move the dog at different speeds so you are able to decide at what speed the dog levels off. Another solution to sidling is to put two show leads on a dog and have a person walk on either side of the puppy so that the puppy walks straight in the center. If after a few tries you feel this method is working, the best way to keep the problem from recurring is by constantly alternating the sides each time you take the dog up and back. Gaiting next to a fence or a wall so that the dog can only move straight ahead is another solution to sidling.

Temperament

Temperament plays a major role in puppy training. While most dogs need consistent training to learn what is required of them in the show ring, some dogs are "naturals" at showing. They are outgoing and love being the center of attention and always seem to show themselves off to the best advantage. While these extroverted dogs are exceptions, they always train quickly and easily.

If you experience a temperament problem ("sound" shyness or hand shyness for instance), try to determine what is causing the problem and especially whether you might be the cause of it, as poor temperament can be the result of environment as well as from breeding. In the event you have purchased an older puppy that exhibits temperament problems, consider obedience training for that is a good way for an animal to learn regimentation and to get out among people. Obedience training has been used successfully on dogs that were kennel raised without adequate human socialization at the proper time.

Another part of training your puppy for the show ring has nothing to do with the ring itself, but a means of making going to the show a lot easier on you and the dog. This part of the training has to do with getting the puppy "crate trained." At an early age the puppy should be introduced to the crate that will be his home away from home. One of the best approaches is to put the crate down on the floor near where the puppy has his water bowl. Leave the door open. Put a favorite tidbit inside and let the puppy size it up. Most puppies will be somewhat leery of this new object. However, the puppy—by its very nature—is a curious animal and so will begin to approach it, at first giving it a wide berth. Now this process may take hours as the puppy, often unsure of what this thing is will leave the room for awhile before screwing up its courage and coming back. Gradually, it will approach closer and closer until finally it will be within inches of the crate. Typically, this is when the puppy stops short and reaches out its neck and head while keeping the body ready for flight if this "thing" should prove to be unfriendly. If nothing jumps out of the crate the puppy will feel safe to try to go further and eventually get the tidbit. However, staying inside, oh no, not me!

With this first success you know you have him hooked. Leave the crate down and pay no attention to it or the puppy. A couple of times during the day, place a tidbit in the crate. You will find it gone sometime later. After a few days of this game and you are sure the puppy(and not the cat!) is eating the tidbits, place a favorite toy in the crate. Let this game go on for a couple of days as well. Your next step is to gently pick up the puppy and place it in the crate with a tidbit inside and gently close the door. Be sure the puppy can see you as you go about your daily chores. He will most likely fuss about being confined. Talk to him, tell him what a great fellow he is and—if necessary—give him another tidbit. He should be confined for only about 10 minutes the first time. When you let him out, praise him lavishly for being a good dog. Over the next weeks you can extend the time slowly until the puppy comes to accept a few hours confinement as natural.

Once you have gotten to this point you can begin to let him sleep in the crate. Be sure you get up early enough so he will be let out of the crate before he soils himself. It's a good idea to put in some rough toweling or carpeting. Later on you might want to use a wire bottom or papering.

Next, you want to take him for a car/van ride to accustom him to motion. One of the trips to a shopping center referred to above would be ideal. Don't make his first voyage out into the world too long, however. Many puppies get car sick rather easily so keep the trip short and talk reassuringly to the puppy the whole time you are on the road. If people pull up along side of you at stop lights and see you talking to yourself, don't be worried, just put your hand up to your ear and they will think you have a car phone.

CHOOSING AN ADULT COLLIE

There are many looks, many types out there. When you start to look for an adult Collie, you must first decide the purpose of the dog. If he is to be a pet, looks will not matter very much. The important thing will be temperament. You will want a friendly, outgoing yet not rowdy animal. This is a fairly large dog, and should be sweet, loving, easy to handle, and responsive to commands. It is not important that the dog have obedience training. If he does—fine—if not, the best course all round is for you to take the dog to classes yourself. That way you and the dog learn together and anything you learn you can use on other dogs in the future. I suggest that all pet owners and all breeders and fanciers take a course in obedience training at least one dog. The techniques learned will make your life and your dog's much happier.

Health is the most important factor in choosing any dog. A Collie should have bright, clear eyes. He should be upbeat and vigorous, never lethargic. The coat should be in good condition, shiny not matted. It does not matter whether the coat is shedding—all Collies shed at one time or another. But the coat that is shedding should be combed out. There should be strong healthy hair covering the body, with no sores or crusted areas.

The body should be solid, with well-developed loin, which does not fall in, giving a wispy appearance. The ribs should be well covered with flesh, and the hip bones should not protrude. If they do, the dog is underweight.

If you watch the dog in motion, the gait should be strong and firm, with no "hitch" or limp. Fortunately hip dysplasia is extremely rare in the Collie breed. If you do not see any limp, it is probably safe to assume the hips are all right.

You would be wise to ask the breeder if the dog is a good eater, although that would show if he were not. Find out if the dog has any particularities in his eating habits.

SELECTING A SHOW COLLIE

If you are considering a dog for show purposes, there are almost innumerable characteristics to keep in mind. First, I would hope that you have attended dog shows and visited leading kennels. This must be done to select the look you like. Some lines are very elegant, with high heads,

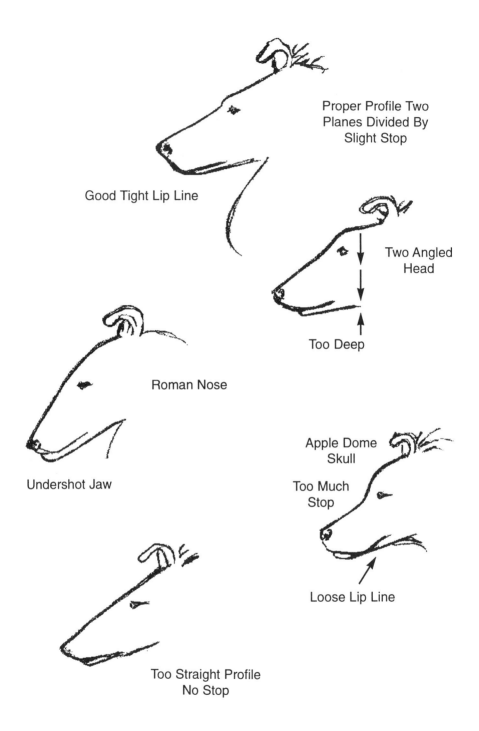

Proper Profile Two
Planes Divided By
Slight Stop

Good Tight Lip Line

Two Angled
Head

Too Deep

Roman Nose

Apple Dome
Skull

Too Much
Stop

Undershot Jaw

Loose Lip Line

Too Straight Profile
No Stop

Drawings by the author.

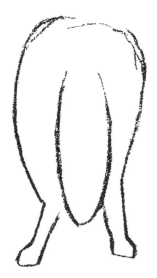

Cow Hocked Rear

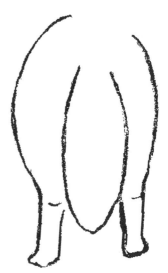

Good Straight Rear

Too Close Front

Fiddle Front

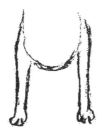

Too Wide Front

Good Front

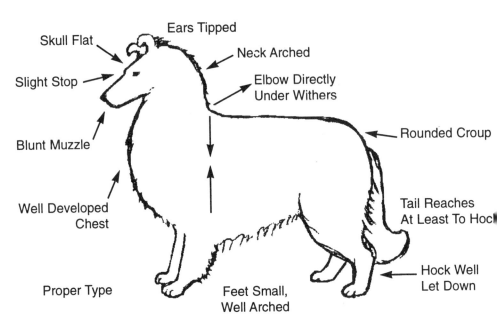

Skull Flat

Ears Tipped

Slight Stop

Neck Arched

Elbow Directly
Under Withers

Blunt Muzzle

Rounded Croup

Well Developed
Chest

Tail Reaches
At Least To Hock

Proper Type

Feet Small,
Well Arched

Hock Well
Let Down

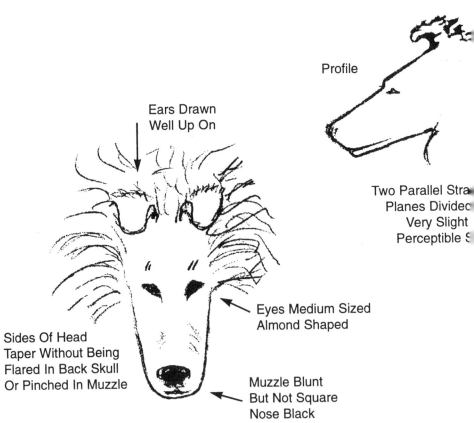

Profile

Ears Drawn
Well Up On

Two Parallel Stra
Planes Divided
Very Slight
Perceptible S

Eyes Medium Sized
Almond Shaped

Sides Of Head
Taper Without Being
Flared In Back Skull
Or Pinched In Muzzle

Muzzle Blunt
But Not Square
Nose Black

Head Resembles Well Blunted Lean Wedge

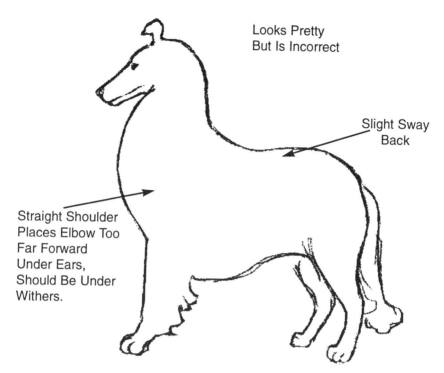

Looks Pretty
But Is Incorrect

Slight Sway
Back

Straight Shoulder
Places Elbow Too
Far Forward
Under Ears,
Should Be Under
Withers.

This Front Could
Not Reach As Desired

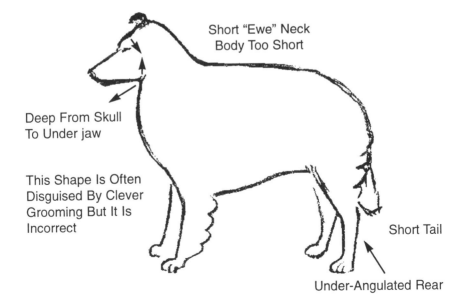

Short "Ewe" Neck
Body Too Short

Deep From Skull
To Under jaw

This Shape Is Often
Disguised By Clever
Grooming But It Is
Incorrect

Short Tail

Under-Angulated Rear

arched necks, glamorous looks. Some are sturdy, strong-looking dogs with bushy coats and heavy bones. Some are racy and high stationed, perhaps with more of a long hanging coat than with a standoff coat. Some are brilliantly colored, some are more dependent on qualities of head and eye. All these things make up a look that you may or may not be drawn to. If you select a "look," that may be a good start toward creating a line in the future, a look of your own.

The first thing to look for in any dog is the overall look. Does he look like a Collie? Does he have any "foreign" look like any other breed? Is he within the loose size limits that appear in the standard, 22 to 24 inches at the shoulder for a female, 24 to 26 inches for a male. Does he fall within the right, general weight limits: the male: 60 to 75 pounds; the female, 50 to 65 pounds. Remember that the standard says: "An oversize or undersize Collie is penalized to the extent to which the dog appears to be undersized or oversized." I have had prospective buyers tell me they had a 100-pound Collie and they want another. I am sure they must have either misjudged the weight of their dogs or have seriously overfed them.

After the over-all look, you must study the head. The Collie is a "Head Breed," and no Collie can be a good, show-type Collie without a good head. The head must appear light in proportion to the overall dog. The heavy-headed dog lacks Collie type.

The head viewed from the top should go back smoothly from the nose to the ears without flaring or widening. The sides should be smooth and flat without bony ridges or protruding along the cheeks. The nose must be black, and it should be blunt and well rounded. The muzzle should be smooth, not veiny, and should not show bulges or boniness before the eyes. There should be a slight rise (stop) at the corner of the eye, then the skull should go back completely flat to the occipital bone between the ears. That bone should not be prominent at all.

Viewed from the side, the line of the muzzle will go back in a straight line from nose end to the eye. At the eye there should be a slight rise of the eyebrow. Then from that area, the skull goes back straight and flat to the ears. The flatness of the skull is a very important facet of the proper head. A receding skull is a severe fault in the Collie. It should not recede either front to back, nor side to side.

The profile of the Collie head must appear lean with no "depth" or widening from top of head to throat. Excessive depth of head is an undesirable feature. It is best to keep in mind that the Collie head should always appear light from all angles. The standard says: "The head is inclined to lightness and never appears massive. A heavy headed dog lacks the bright, alert, full of sense, look that contributes so greatly to expression."

The bite, or occlusion, of the Collie must always be a scissors bite. That is where the upper jaw fits snugly against the lower jaw, with the upper jaw slightly forward but touching. Any deviation from the scissors bite is a fault. The other bites, overshot and undershot, are faulted, with undershot the more severely penalized.

Perhaps the next thing to look for is a good, strong back. Many Collies fail in this department. The back should be level from the withers back to the end of the croup. There will be some dogs that appear to be high in the rear. However, in some cases that is due to a huge growth of hair, particularly evident in "coaty" puppies of 8 to 10 months of age. If you see this effect, check it out to see if the rise is structural or just excess hair.

The chest of a Collie is supposed to reach to the elbow. Some may not fill out in forchest until they are mature, a year of more of age. The chest should fill the area between the forelegs, but should not be excessively wide. If the elbows stick out beyond the shoulder line, that is excessive. The elbows should fit compactly right beneath the shoulders. A weak or narrow chest may fill out with maturity.

A nice well-rounded croup is necessary to complete the picture. A too-short croup will throw the dog out of balance. A too-sharp croup will make the dog resemble a German Shepherd. A rounded croup will fill out the desired picture. It also ensures proper tail carriage. A tail set too high will be carried too gaily.

The tail, while it is the end of the dog, is not the least important feature. The tail should be long and bushy. It must reach at least to the hock. The standard says the tail may be carried gaily when excited, but must be carried low when at rest. The expression "gaily" may be too extreme. The tail must always be carried below the level of the back. In extreme excitement the tail tip may ride above the backline, but below that is always preferred. There may be a slight swirl at the tip of the tail but this should be moderate.

The legs are immensely important. There must be sufficient angulation both front and rear to allow for freedom of movement.

In the front there should be a long shoulder blade, reaching forward to the forechest. Then the upper arm reaches back to connect with the foreleg. The forelegs should be placed directly under the wither. If there is insufficient angle from blade to upper arm, and back to foreleg, the dog's gait will be stilted.

The hindlegs are to be moderately well boned. The thigh bone will bend forward (at rest) and join the stifle. The stifle then bends backward to join the hock. From the hock joint, the leg runs straight to the ground. All of these angles are necessary to the appearance of good angulation. If the joinings are too straight, the dog will appear stilted and too straight in stifle. The hind feet are slightly longer than the front feet, but still well arched and tight.

The coat on a rough Collie is to be a double coat. There is the long standoff outer coat and the deep furry undercoat. If a dog is shedding or has shed, the greater part of the undercoat will be missing. The coat always comes back, though some individuals carry far more undercoat than others. The outer coat is to be straight and harsh. The function of that coat is to form a thatch in the warm weather. In cold weather it tends to shed rain, snow and sleet. There is plenty of cold, wet weather in the Scottish highlands where the Collies originated. The furry undercoat helps keep in the dog's body warmth. As said before, the color of the coat is immaterial from a show point of view. All colors are equal in the judge's eyes.

The dog should have a firm, solid loin—slightly arched but definitely not roached. The whole body should feel solid and well muscled.

When the dog gaits he should move with strong reach and drive when viewed from the side. When viewed from the front, the forelegs will single track, each foot landing directly ahead of the last one. There should be no crossing over, or paddling.

Viewed from the rear, the hindlegs will be straight and parallel, with the toes pointing straight forward. There must be no tendency toward "cowhocks" or "barrel" hocks. In motion, the hindlegs move straight and parallel, comparatively close together.

I still have not described that which makes one dog a show dog and another one not. There may be two dogs that pretty well have all the attributes we have described. Yet one may consistently beat the other in the ring. There is a certain *je ne sais qua* that the winning dog has. It may be a slightly better all-over balance, it may be a truly superior head, it may be just an attitude. Whatever it is, some dogs have "it" some dogs do not. As an old time judge often said: "A show dog is like a Follies girl. She has to have it, and know how to show it!"

To learn to recognize those qualities that make up a winner is to start to develop that priceless quality called: "AN EYE FOR A DOG."

Perhaps the quality that most sets the winner apart is *expression.* How to describe expression? It has defied writers as long as writers have tried to describe the qualities of the Collie. There is no question that the size, shape and color of the eye are of great importance—perhaps I should say prime importance. When a good-looking Collie gives you that *look,* that loving mischievous look, your heart must melt. And it takes the eye, plus the muzzle, plus the ears to form that lovely triangle known as Collie expression. If you want a top winner, and his expression does not make your heart stop, look further.

The ears and the whole form of the head go into the desired look. The ears have to be well up on the head, softly bent, and carried at attention.

Attitude is as important as any other part of the Collie. The dog should shine with the joy of life. He must move happily and as if he owns the world. He must strut his stuff in a way that says "Hey, look at me! I'm gorgeous!" And, if the dog thinks so, chances are the world will think so as well. Judges and all.

THE SMOOTH COLLIE

The smooth variety of Collie is probably a later off-shoot of the original Collie breed. Legend has it that the "drover's dog" of England was bred in with the Collie and produced the smooth variety. The drover's dog is still to be seen in the countryside of the British Isles, and I have also spotted dogs of a similar look in France. The breed in question is often, in fact generally, blue merle in color, and of a short coat. The coat is either single or double. In the case of the Smooth Collie, which has probably resulted from this cross, the coat is double. There is a harsh, flat, short top coat and a softer dense undercoat. The top coat is not quite as long or as abundant as the coat of a German Shepherd. It is not as short and slick as that of a Boxer or Greyhound.

It does seem logical that the blood of the Collie and the drover's dog would mingle. Proximity leads to commingling and these two breeds would often occupy the same farm. The Collie was there to herd the stock and the Drover's dog was there to escort the stock to market.

It quite astounded me to see many dogs of doubtful pedigree wandering the streets of Europe in definite blue merle color. The surprise to me was that I had thought the blue merle color was a property of certain herding breeds, and theirs alone. The smooth Collie comes in all the same colors as the rough Collie. There have been champions in each of the colors. It is impossible to say which of the Collie colors is the most beautiful. That, like beauty itself, is in the eye of the beholder.

It is a rather widely held opinion that there is a definite difference in temperament between the rough and the smooth Collie. The smooth is thought to be stronger, healthier, and more aggressive. The Collie at birth is prone to low-birth weight, and is generally a fragile being. In litters of rough and smooth individuals, the smooths may tend to be larger and hardier. This has been the case in the few mixed litters of rough and smooth that I have raised. It is not possible to document these differences without wider studies than have been done.

To me it seems hard to believe that differences in temperament could exist after so many years (a century or so) of mixing dogs of the two coats.

Most breeders of smooth Collies tend to breed their smooths to roughs. In this way the near equality of quality between the breeds has been attained. In the past, perhaps as recently as 20 years ago, this was not the case. The smooth variety was inferior in type and quality; there were a few examples of equal and superior quality in the smooths. However, until the advent of such a dog as Ch. Black Hawk of Kasan, there was a great gap between the dogs of the two varieties.

The smooth breeders of today deserve a round of applause for the *excellence* of today's smooth Collie. The flaws that had plagued the variety were such things as weak muscle tone, lack of bone and substance, receding skulls, slack feet, prick ears, and weak backlines. Today's best smooths represent a vast improvement in those features. In fact, they present an admirable picture of the Collie.

Fortunately the popularity of the smooth Collie as a show dog has increased by leaps and bounds. When I judged intersex at the CCA in 1991, there were an equal number of rough and smooth champions shown under me (99 of each variety). In my critique, I said that I felt possibly the smooths showed a greater degree of quality than the roughs in an over all comparison. This trend has continued and the roughs better look to their laurels.

Smooth Collies have been advertised as "wash and wear" Collies. Their smooth coat is definitely easier to maintain than the rough coat. The smooth takes about one tenth the grooming of a rough. A smooth will usually follow the same shedding pattern as the rough. That is the male will usually shed as hot weather comes, but the bitch will shed after her seasons. The smooth Collie sheds the undercoat as does the rough. The outer coat remains. Fortunately, many smooths will look presentable enough after or during a shed to appear in the show ring. Not true of many roughs.

The smooth so far has not attained the general popularity of the rough Collie and I do find that to be unfortunate. The smooth has all the wonderful endearing qualities of the rough in his heart and soul. And the smooth has a beauty of his own—plus an appealing lack of combing and brushing time.

One endeavor in which the smooth Collie outshines the rough is as a leader of the blind. The coat is the factor that makes the difference. With a long-coated Collie, the blind person would not be able to keep the coat cared for. With the very practical coat that the smooth sports, there is an absolute minimum of care.

The Collie temperament, with his eagerness to please, his sweet affectionate disposition, and his unquestioning loyalty has proven ideal for a leader dog. There is a constant demand for these lovely dogs to perform this wonderful work.

I personally feel that maintaining a smooth or two along with a breeding kennel of roughs provides an excellent yardstick. It is easy, when dealing only with roughs, to get carried away with head, expression, coat, and to forget structure. When looking at a smooth, the eye is immediately drawn to the over-all balance, the top line, the legs, everything is of equal importance. This well-balanced sound dog that makes up the ideal smooth Collie must also have the head, eye, ear and the expression demanded of every top-quality Collie. Overall soundness has improved in both varieties of Collie. I feel some of the improvement can be attributed to the fact that people are seeing good smooths. They are learning what good structure looks like, and increasingly to value it. In the past, I urged people to observe smooth-coated dogs like Pointers, Boxers, Great Danes, and Doberman Pinschers to teach themselves about structure and movement. Now, I can suggest the novice breeder of rough Collies would do well to watch the best Smooth Collies.

Yarrow, a smooth-coated Sheepdog on the left and Hornpipe, a rough-coated Sheepdog on the right, from Cassell's Illustrated Book of the Dog.

THE SMOOTH-COLLIE

By Doris Werdermann
Dorelaine Collies

That beautiful, elegant, sleek Collie unadorned with the fuller, longer coat of his rough counterpart, possessing high intelligence and ingenuity has increased in popularity and success in the United States show world. Adaptable as a companion dog and extremely tractable for obedience work, and with many possessing instinctive herding abilities—this is the American Smooth-Coated Collie.

Although the origin of the smooth, like that of the rough, is inextricably merged with the development of the early British sheep- and cattle-herding dogs, we have some clues concerning their more immediate ancestors. While the general name "sheepdog" or shepherd's dog was still being employed for the dogs used for these purposes, both smooth- and rough-coated types had already made their appearance. The roughs, generally developed and used in Scotland, were relatively short legged and long bodied by today's standards and substantially smaller than their smooth counterparts. The smooths, on the other hand, were fancied by cattle men in Northern England where some of the dogs were used for herding, some for driving the stock to market and often the same dog for both purposes. They were in general balance and conformation close to today's type of Collie rather than the early rough-coated dogs. Though the days of the purebred fancy had not yet arrived, these dogs were thoughtfully bred, and crosses of Shepherd's Dog, Cur-Dog, Ban Dog and the Drover's type were consciously made to improve the dog's performance. Thus, the two varieties may have developed simultaneously and share a common ancestry. Rough/smooth crosses were common in these early days and continue today in the United States though prohibited in England.

The following Smooth Collie FIRSTS have been compiled by Claudia Schroeder Allen for Volume I of *The Smooth Collie* (10/83), Charlotte Coviak, Editor, The American Smooth Collie Association:

•The *first* dog show class for Sheepdogs (including rough and smooth Collies, Old English sheepdogs, (etc.) was held at the third organized show in England, at Birmingham, December 3 and 4, 1860.

•The *first* divided classes were held in 1870 at the Crystal Palace show: "Sheepdogs Rough and Sheepdogs Smooth). Unfortunately there were only two smooths entered and the following notation tells their story: "Dogs: Prize not awarded, want of merit."

•The *first* smooth to win in a separate class for smooths was Mr. W.R. Daybell's NETT (sex unknown), at the Nottingham show in October, 1872.

•The *first* separate listing of roughs and smooths in the *English Kennel Club Stud Book* appeared in Volume II (1875) under the headings: "Sheepdogs and Colleys, Rough Coated" and Sheepdogs and Colleys, Smooth-Coated."

•The *first* mention of a rough-to-smooth mating came in Volume III (1876) of the *Kennel Club Stud Book*, in the entry of TRIAD (EKSB no. 5441), owned by Mr. S.E. Shirley, M.P. Mr. Shirley founded The Kennel Club in 1872. It was the first national organization having jurisdiction over the showing and registration of purebred dogs; Mr. Shirley remained actively involved with The Kennel Club until his death in 1904. He is perhaps better known among Collie fanciers as the breeder/owner of Trefoil, from whom all registered Collies, rough and smooth, descend in direct tail-male line.

•The *first* smooth Collie to win the fabled Collie Club's Challenge Trophy for Best Collie over rough and smooths was Miss P.M. Deveson Jones's **Ch. Babette of Moreton,** at the Collie Club's 17th show in 1902. Ch. Ormskirk Venice, owned by T.H. Stretch, repeated this feat in 1906; R.G. Howson's Ch. Eastwood Eminent (later imported to the United States by Winthrop Rutherfurd of Warren Kennels in New Jersey) did it in 1907, and Howson's CH. Eastwood Extra twice defeated roughs (in 1912 and 1913) to win the coveted trophy.

On this side of the Atlantic:

•The *first* AKC-registered smooths appeared in Volume IV of *The American Kennel Club Stud Book Register* (1887). There were three of them, one dog and two bitches, all imported.

TOSS (smooth-coated dog)-6505. Corwin Importing Co, Waynesville, Ohio, breeder William Hendry, Scotland. Whelped August 1885, Black, tan, and white, by Charlie VIII x The Smith bitch, by Bob x Jennie, by Duke X Hattie; Charlie VIII by Peter IIIx Meg, by Peter II x Tam & Betty.

FANNIE MCSHEE (smooth-coated bitch)-6514. Corwin Importing Co., Waynesville, Ohio. Breeder George McSeee. Scotland. Whelped March 1885, black and tan; by Jimmie x4 Jennie.

LADYBIRD (smooth-coated bitch) -E. 19306, AKC 6518. Chesnut Hill Kennels, Philadelphia, Pennsylvania, breeder Mr. Britton, England. Whelped January 25, 1885. Black and Tan with a little white on breast; by Shila x Lady.

•The *first* smooths entered at Westminster were at the February 1891 Madison Square Garden show, under Judge A.D. Lewis. Winner was TAFFY, owned by J. Van Schaick, first CCA president (1886-1899—he died in office).

The first smooth to go over roughs was WELLESBOURNE VETO owned by Henry Jarrett. Veto defeated roughs in 1898 at Westminster and again at Chicago in 1900.

In the first decade of the new century, four smooth champions were recorded in the United States. The first American-bred smooth (blue merle) bred by C. Frankland, Ch. Clayton Countess finished in 1906. Next came the sable, Ch. Ormskirk Mabel in 1907 and her daughter, Ch. Ormskirk Lucy (blue merle) the following year. In 1909, Ch. Warren Patience (blue merle, owned by Winthrope Rutherford of Allanuchy, New Jersey, exhibiting under his Warren prefix, gained her title. The first president of the CCA, Mr. Jenkins Van Schaick, was a well-known smooth enthusiast. Smooth entries declined with a brief flurry of interest lasting through 1923, principally in the Northeast, but no champions. There is no record of the variety being shown at all from 1923 to 1940. Because of the lack of competition, there were no opportunities to make up smooth champions during this period. However, Hewmark Hallmark, an imported tricolor bitch, won Best of Breed over roughs for three points and went on to place second in the Working Group at the Hampton Roads Kennel Club show in Norfolk, Virginia, in 1941.

Due to the lack of smooths in this country, a syndicate was formed in 1939 with the specific purpose of importing smooths from the Laund Kennels in England. The syndicate consisted of the following respected rough fanciers: H.R. Lounsbury of Halmaric Kennels, Mrs. Clara M. Lunt of Alstead, Robert G. Wills of Alloway, Arthur Foff of Tamalgate and Mrs. Genevieve Torrey Eames of Torreya. Laund Blue Peter, a blue smooth male and Laund Loftygirl, a smooth tricolor bitch, were purchased and bred twice with syndicate members drawing lots for the puppies. It was known that Mr. Arthur Foff of San Francisco acquired a tri bitch and a blue male as his share. And, that Mr. Hal Lounsbury received a blue male who became Halmaric Baronet, an influential sire in midwestern smooths. Unfortunately, the syndicate disbanded after a few years due to lack of interest and the remaining progeny scattered.

No chapter on the Smooth Collie would be complete without including the stories of two kennels: Pebble Ledge and Glengyle, who through dedication and determination assured the American Smooth Collie its current secure place in history. Oddly enough, I met both Margaret Haserot of Pebble Ledge and Lucienne and Omer Rees of Glengyle at the American Smooth Collie Convention in the 1970s held at the home of Lucienne and Omer in Danville, California. It was through the gesture of generosity of one and hospitality of the other that I was there—traits that were shared by the three along with a strong partisanship for the Smooth Collie.

Margaret Haserot, Pebble Ledge Collies

Born shortly before the turn of the century to a prominent family in Cleveland, Ohio, Margaret was never without a horse and several dogs (of different breeds) to love. In 1919, *National Geographic Magazine* published an issue focusing on dogs, with pictures and descriptions of the various breeds and varieties, including the Smooth Collie. Margaret's favorite breed was the Collie and she quickly adopted the Smooth Variety. She wrote the AKC for names of kennels that raised Collies, but none raised the smooth variety. Several years later, she initiated her importations.

Disappointed in early imports, she finally was successful through purchases from Laund Kennels in England resulting in a tri bitch, Pebble Ledge Duchess (Laund Larchfield, 6/39) and finally, a quality blue male, Laund Laventer, (1/390. Bred together several good litters were produced. A lovely tri bitch was retained from the first litter, **Pebble Ledge Little Dorrit**, who in turn was bred to Mr. Lounsbury's blue smooth from the syndicate, Halmaric Baronet.

The resulting tri color smooth, Halmeric Trilby, who when bred to the rough, Ch. Halmaric Scarletson, produced the first smooth champion since 1909—a span of 38 years. This sable smooth became the truly outstanding **Ch. Pebble Ledge Bambi**. Bambi bred to the sable rough, Ch. Harlines Son of Cainbrooke, produced Ch. Christopher of Pebble Ledge (1946) and littermate, Ch. Pebble Ledge Inca, C.D. A grand-daughter of Ch. Pebble Ledge Bambi, **Ch. Belle Mount Bambi**, owned by Tom Kilcullen won the *Dog World Award of Canine Distinction for Obedience* in 1956 and had completed her title with four Group placements, a record for the variety at that time. It has been stated that both Ch. Christopher of Pebble Ledge and Ch. Pebble Ledge Bambi were undeniably smooths who approached perfection and that these along with other Pebble Ledge smooths contributed to the development of the American Smooth Collie as we know it today.

Though Margaret Haserot was not the first to import the smooth Collie to this country, the credit for reviving interest in the variety, developing stock of show quality, inspiring others to breed and show smooths, and nurturing the American Smooth Collie Association, must go completely to Margaret Haserot.

Margaret Haserot passed away on February 24, 1980, and was inducted into the prestigious Quarter Century Group *Hall of Fame* in 1986.

Omer and Lucienne Ress, Glengyle Collies

It has been stated that "Lucienne can do more things successfully at one time than most people can do one at a time." In order to appreciate that statement one would have to visit Glengyle where it would quickly be noted that this is the hub for house guests, guest dogs, boards, their own stock, including sheep, with probably a Sheltie Specialty show at one end of the week and two Collie Specialties sandwiched between. Yet, excellent meals would be served, agendas followed and tours of the San Francisco area organized and chauffeured by Lucienne. Incredibly committed members of all-breed, specialty clubs and the advocates of the smooth Collie.

This dedication to the smooth Collie began in 1953, while on a trip to England, with the purchase of a two-month-old smooth sable bitch from Miss Margaret Osborne of the famous Shiel Kennels. This puppy became the beautiful **Ch. Scio from Shiel** (1953) and was the ancestor of nearly all the western smooths. "Solo produced four champions and several point winners and held her fine quality until she died in 1965. Her bloodlines included the Beulah and Grangetown lines. For a decade her son, **Ch. Glengyle Smooth Sailing**, was the leading smooth sire with nine champions out of four litters. Of the champions he sired, many became influential producers and top winners in their own right, including the beginning of the well-known Paladin Collies.

"The Sailor," however, will be probably best known for siring Ch. Paladin's Blue Sapphire who would, in turn, produce Ch. Kasan's Fine and Fancy, the dam of the world-renowned **Ch. Black Hawk of Kasan**. This elegant tricolor also has the distinction of being the first ever to defeat roughs when awarded Best of Breed at the Collie Club of Northern California Specialty Show in 1958. "Sailor" was sired by the rough, Ch. Hertzvill Hightop, who descended from Ch. Hertzville Headstone and Ch. Hertzville However. Smooth Sailing and his dam, Solo and their offspring are indisputably responsible for the high quality and great popularity of smooths in Northern California.

What is interesting to consider is the breeding patterns that have been responsible for some of the most important smooths. Going back to Pebble Ledge, it is noted that both

Laund Laventer by Black Donovan ex Merrion Blue Dorrit. Foundation sire of Margaret Haserot's Pebble Ledge smooths. Imported from Laund Kennels in England. Laventer was a brother to Laund Blue Peter, imported by the 1939 syndicate. (Photo courtesy of Gayle Kaye)

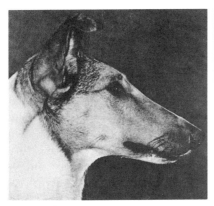 

Left: Ch. Pebble Ledge Bambi, 1944, by Ch. Halmaric Scarletson, rough, ex Halmaric Trilby. Bambi was the first smooth champion in 38 years. Right: Ch. Belle Mount Bambi, C.D. (1953). By Luke of Pebble Ledge, a son of Ch. Pebble Ledge Bambi, ex Belle Mount Rosey Future, rough. She and her sister Lulabelle of Belle Mount were influential in the development of modern smooths. (Photos courtesy of Gayle Kaye)

Scarletson and son of Cainbrook trace in tail male to Lodestone Landmark, one of the foundation American-bred rough sires. Of the smooths featured, namely Smooth Sailing and both Bambis, all trace in tail male to Landmark and some are also linebred to him. These patterns of breeding leading smooths indicate a strong rough influence that somehow fits into the entire Collie picture.

Champion Black Hawk of Kasan

Since the championships of Ch. Solo From Shiel and Ch. Glengyle Smooth Sailing, top smooths were being exhibited in higher quantity and quality across the United States with a particular depth of both in Northern California. In 1966, a smooth, tricolor, male puppy entered our world to be owned, loved and revered by Sandra Tuttle of Kasan and the Collie clan. Sired by the sable rough, Ch. High Man of Arrowhill, out of Ch. Kasan's Fine and Fancy, a granddaughter of Ch. Glengyle Smooth Sailing, he was to become the world celebrated Collie, Ch. Black Hawk of Kasan, whose astounding sire and show record has yet, after 20 years to be surpassed or equaled! It reads as follows:

- Completed US Championship undefeated in 1967
- The first smooth in history to win an all-breed Best in Show
- The first and only smooth, to date, to win BOV six times at the National

•The first smooth to be awarded Best of Breed at the National
•In 1971, he became the Top Working Group Sire and missed becoming Top Sire all-Breeds by three champion progeny
•He leads the All-Time Top Smooth Sire list with 78 champions
•His daughter, Jancada Tender O'King's Valley, leads the All-Time Top Smooth Dam list with 14 champions

A legend in his time, "Hawk" has become a legend for all time. Smooth history was irrevocably altered by this big-bodied, sound-moving tricolor from California who revolutionized the quality of smooth Collies in this country and made competition keener within the variety and the inter-variety. In 1959, at the Collie Club of Maryland Specialty Show, Mrs. Ada Bishop, daughter of the famous W.W. Stanfield of Laund Collies in England, judged both the rough and smooth entries and remarked that the smooths were the largest collection of quality she had ever seen. The majority of the entry were Hawk sons and daughters.

Since about 1940, smooth champions have steadily increased in numbers. No chapter can do justice to the many breeders, exhibitors and fanciers who have successfully developed and shown this variety, whether in conformation, obedience or herding trials. Photos of early smooths in England and the US, along with those from succeeding periods, have been collected for an over-all composite of smooth type progression. These are only some of the representatives of the variety.

The smooth has greatly improved his aesthetic image, particularly head qualities; however, his strong versatility talent has remained secure. This versatility, coupled with physical and mental soundness, stamina, vigor and a maintenance-free coat, renders the smooth Collie ideal, whether as companion, for obedience, in herding, or as therapy and guide dog for the blind.

Credit should be given to the American Smooth Collie Association and the American Working Collie Association for the promotion of the variety and the preservation of the strong working capabilities of the American Smooth Collie.

More Smooth Firsts:

•First smooth bitch to go Best in Show, **Ch. Mel-Bar's Brandwyne Bobbi, C.D.,** owned by Diane Washburn
•First smooth Champion U.D.T., **Ch. Holyjan's Hawkeye of Markay, U.D.T.,** owned by Janet Holland
•First Smooth champion U.D., **Am. and Can Ch. Shamrock Smooth Rocket, U.D.,** (first of either variety) owned by Gail Thompson
•First U.D. smooth, **Ebonwood Escapade, U.D.,** owned by Mary Groh

•First American Smooth Champion, **Ch. Clayton Countess,** 1906

Although the Collie Standard is the same for both varieties, with the exception of coat type, there are some subtle and obvious differences that are noted when raising both varieties. A litter of combined varieties will show a stronger and quicker growth rate in the smooth pups. Upon maturity and, often earlier, their ingenious mind and fortitude is revealed. This stamina and acuity probably comes from their original function as a drover and general stock dog, when only those sheep or cattle dogs who possessed these traits were bred. The smooth was particularly suited because of his short, harsh, double coat that protected him from the harsh weather and terrain and was maintenance free.

The correct smooth coat is important to the over-all quality of the smooth as the full coat is to the rough. The smooth is a double-coated dog with a short, soft, dense undercoat required for insulation—as in the rough. The outercoat should be straight, harsh and close to the body and of sufficient length to cover the undercoat. The head and ears are smooth as are the forelegs and the hind legs below the hock joint. The neck is furnished with slightly longer, thicker hair forming a slight ruff. The forming the "pants" or "skirts" is also slightly longer and more abundant than the body coat.

A correct short coat should never require scissoring or, worse, shaving. A hard, dense, flat coat does not mean soft, loose, open and wavy—a loss of purpose and outline. As in the rough Collie, the well-fitting and properly textured coat contributes to the distinctive smooth type.

In Sunbright, Tennessee, a partially disabled and nearly deaf widow had rescued a smooth, two-year old, tricolor female from the local shelter she named her Molly. One morning, two months later, at 2:00 A.M., the smooth came in the room, pulled back the covers and licked her owner's face until she got up to discover a terrible brightness in the living room from the blazing porch. They both managed to escape before the house burned down.

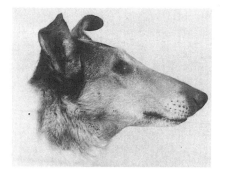

Ch. Solo From Shiel, 1953. Imported from England by Mr. and Mrs. Omer Rees of California, Solo was bred by Miss Margaret Osbourne and is the foundation for most western smooths.

Ch. Black Hawk of Kasan (1966) winning Best in Show under Judge William Kendrick, handled by Leslie Canavan, at the York Kennel Club, 1970. (Photo by Evelyn M. Shafer)

Ch. Glocamora Morning Mist (1963) with owner/breeder Isabel Chamberlain and Judge Ada Shirley. Sired by Coronation The Blue Saint ex Shamrock Smoothie O'Shadalon. (Photo by Morry Twomey)

Ch. Dorelaine Smooth Domino (1968) winner of the CCA Junior Sweepstakes in 1970. Sired by Ch. Black Hawk of Kasan ex Dorelaine Star Miss, owned and bred by Doris Werdermann.

Ch. Pinewynd's Sparkling Brut (1993). Bred by Frank and Sara Novachek and owned by Dan and Bonnie Begle and handled by Donna Williams. (Photo courtesy of Bo-Dandy Collies and Shelties)

Below: Ch. Row-Bar's Southern Exposure, C.D., (1990) winning a Group placement at the Brevard Kennel Club, 1994, handled by Diane Steele for owners Robette and Stephen Johns. (Photo by Earl Graham Studios)

Ch. Sage Brush Mardi Gras (1988), bred by Kimberley Dorris and Lloyd Dorris. Owned by Jerry and Pattie Fitzgerald and M. Dorris. (Photo courtesy of Shamrock Collies)

Ch. Storm's TNT (1983), bred by P. Lessard and S. Keehn, owned by Jan Wollett.

Ch. Foxbride's McLaughlan (1987) winning the Award of Merit, CCA, 1995, owned by Dee and Debbie Batchelor. Bred by Lynne Fox and Barbara Kilbride. (Photo by Kohler)

Am. and Can. Ch. Lisara's Morning After (1981) with handler Brian Phillips and Judge Robert Slay. She set records as a great producer and show winner. (Callea Photo)

Ch. Cherrison Dreams of Kings (1981) winning a BIS with Bertha Garrison and daughter Sara in 1983. Bred by Elizabeth Burton and Sondra Calhoun, owned by Betty Johnson, Robert and Ellen Fetter and Sondra Calhoun. (Photo by Martin Booth)

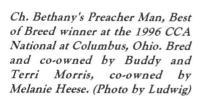

Ch. Oakhill Kismet Anticipation (1986) at Westminster Kennel Club in 1988. Linda Burns handling, the author judging. Owned by Nancy Greenwood, bred by O. Curry and M. Gallagher. (Photo by Charles Tatham)

Ch. Bethany's Preacher Man, Best of Breed winner at the 1996 CCA National at Columbus, Ohio. Bred and co-owned by Buddy and Terri Morris, co-owned by Melanie Heese. (Photo by Ludwig)

Molly's heroism resulted in statewide honors and she was given a medal and plaque during the Tennessee Veterinary Medical Association's fourth annual Animal Hall of Fame induction ceremony in Nashville. The award is given to "animals who have saved or preserved human life." The widow believes Molly's act was in repayment for her adopting the dog.

I would like to extend appreciation to Gayle Kaye, CCA Archivist, for her assistance in records and photos. And, to Bob Hawkins for his "Hawkins System" records. Also, to Virginia Holtz whose prior assistance and information has contributed to this section.

EARS

The Collie ear is the product of two mutually incompatible forms. The original Collie ear was much like the Border Collie ear of today. It was rather large, of soft leather, and lay somewhat flat on the head. It either pointed to the side or lay on the forehead.

As the Collie became a more elegant animal, with longer, leaner head, breeders wanted a higher earset. That type of earset would give the dog a more alert and stylish look. In order to breed in the new look, dogs with high-set and probably prick ears were brought into the breeding programs. Dog genes appear to be almost infinitely mutable. Since in nature nearly all dogs have stand up or pricked ears, that upright tendency became evident all through the breed.

I mentioned earlier on, that few Collies of the present day are born with what fanciers call "natural" ears. The tendency now is toward the too-straight ear, and most breeders fight a lifelong battle to keep the ears down where they belong (or where they want them to be). This is a seldom-discussed matter. The fancy pretends that the ears are largely inherited in the desired state.

However, there has been a growing tendency to outflank nature by taping ears from about six to eight weeks onward. Some show dogs, especially in California, wear braces on their ears all of their lives. That is, except when they are in the ring. I have always referred to the striking earset of certain dogs as having "California ears." The fanciers out there have devised an especially effective method of taping.

I shall list for you some various ways of bringing the ears to the desired "up and over" position. Though it would certainly be preferable to have all Collies born with the desired ears, it does not happen. So we do the best we can in this not-the-best-of-all-possible-worlds. Fortunately, the

Am. and Can. Ch. Natural Explosion (Boomer) winning Best of Variety at the Palisades Kennel Club in 1993. Breeders/owners/handlers Sharon and Thomas Frampton. (JC Photo)

work we do on Collie ears is not invasive or painful in any way. Compare that with the ear mutilation done on Boxers, Great Danes, and others

While I mentioned that too high, or pricked, ears are the more usual problem, there are also some specimens with low or side-breaking ears. These will be taped in the same way as high ears, as the end result will be the same.

My first preference is what I call the "telephone." This refers to the shape of the piece of tape that will join the ears together. A friend of mine guessed that the telephone referred to "ear-to-ear," a good guess, but wrong. The tape is cut to resemble a hand-held telephone.

Before this work is done on the ears, they must be cleaned of all the dirt and oil. This can be done with alcohol, but I prefer to use ether for more complete job. Because ether is a controlled substance in many places, I get around that by using engine starting fluid, which is, guess what, ether.

I clean the inside of the ears with the fluid, getting them shiny pink clean. If there is an excessive amount of hair on the inside of the ear, it may be gently cut away.

I take a piece of *Dr. Scholl's Moleskin* and cut out a circle about the size of a 50-cent piece. Spray the circle with the fluid. Let it dry for a few seconds, and then apply it to the inside of the ear (one ear at a time). Then the ear must be held for a minute or two to let the moleskin adhere.

Next, comes the aforementioned telephone. In order to assure the wonderful up-and-over look, I recommend that the ears be brought together on top of the skull. Attach the wide part of the moleskin to the circle inside one ear, then while holding that one down, attach the other side of the telephone to the circle in the other ear. Hold each for a minute

"Graham" at six weeks. A lovely Foxbride puppy with ears tied up on head.

or two. At this point you should be looking at the dog with ears well up on the skull, and bent about in half. It is important to remember to bend the ear lower than you will want it to be when free. They always pop up some when the contraption is removed.

Now, take a strip of moleskin about five inches long and roll it inside out. Spray it with the fluid. Apply the sticky side of the rolled moleskin to the inside tip of the ear. Then bend the ear over upon itself and attach the top to the lower portion of the moleskin. Thus, you will have ears that are tipped correctly and held there by the tape.

This type of taping is widely used and very effective. However, the California method is a bit different. You clean the ears as before. Cut a piece of moleskin for each ear slightly smaller than the lower half of the ear. Then you put a hole at the inside base of each piece of moleskin. Through this hole insert a piece of yarn about four inches long. Bring the yarn through until each end is about two inches long. Make such a contraption for each ear. Then spray the moleskin, and attach one piece to each ear. Tie the two ends together on the top of the head. Thus the ears are held in proper position. I suggest that the ears be rolled over and attached down as suggested in the last method.

Still another way to bring the ears into position is to take leather repair glue called VAL-A (see Glossary) and stick the long hairs between the ears together. This will bring the ears up. Then glue them forward by the inside tip, attaching tip to hair at the base of the ear.

Each of these methods has many vocal adherents. It is certainly best if you have some knowledgeable fancier show you the method. But if that isn't possible, try each of these methods and see how it works.

For pure simplicity, the oldest method on the books is sometimes used. There are times when it is the best. This is for pricked ears only. You get *Antiphlogistine* (available at drugstores) and apply it to the inside tip of the ear. Apply at the tip. Then take some clean dirt (that is not oxymoron) and apply it over the *Antiphlogistine*, a heavy paste made for chest colds. I am not sure whether the company knows how much of it is used for Collie ears. The application of dirt over the paste is to make the whole thing heavier. Also, it will keep the *Antiphlogistine* from getting all over everything, including you and the dog. One great advantage is that this paste is completely water soluble. The dog can wear it right to the dog show, if necessary. Just be sure to take a jar of warm water along to clean off the mess, and a towel to dry. No longer than a half an hour before judging will be required for a nice, clean, dry, tipped pair of ears to appear.

Regarding the other methods, a good solvent will be required. Probably the best known on is Unisolve. This may be available from a drugstore, hospital supplier, or veterinarians. It is important not to use any solvent that will burn or irritate the tender skin of the ear.

While I have talked of all methods of improving the ears on a Collie, let's face it, The ears should take the proper position by themselves. That would be the ideal. The only way that will hap-

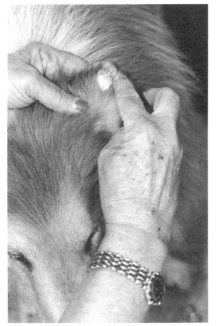

Left: Applying Val-A-Glue to inside tip of ear. Right: Ear folded over to hairs at front of ear and glued with Val-A-Glue.

pen is if breeders start selecting dogs with a natural-eared tendency. There are such creatures I know, for I have some in my own kennel. My strong suggestion is that we do the right thing and let the moleskin people and the *Antiphlogistine* people do without our business. If we bred as carefully for ears as we do for flat skull, dark eyes, beautiful expression, we would be way ahead. How about it? Let's try.

Let me warn that if the dog or puppy is allowed to carry his ears upright too long, it may be a lost cause. I suggest you NEVER LET THE EARS STAND STRAIGHT A SINGLE DAY. That sounds very stringent, but when you consider that a prick-eared dog useless in the ring, then the discipline needed may come to you. Remember, not a single day.

Even if you do not plan to show, your Collie will be much more attractive looking, if his ears are bent over.

EYES

There is a world of misinformation circulating about Collie eyes. This confusion is understandable because certain conditions have several different names. I will attempt to clear up some of the mysteries regarding the Collie eye.

The gradations of the Collie eye syndrome, according to veterinarian ophthalmologists are as follows:

Normal
Collie Eye Anomaly
    Choroidal Hypoplasia   Grade II
    Chorioretinal Change   Grade II
  Staphloma/ Coloboma, Ectasia
  Retinal Detachment
  PRA

Grade I is no longer considered significant.

Normal is the most desirable of these eye checks. However, some of the others are quite acceptable to the pet owner and the breeder. These dogs will not go blind.

The condition that I have listed as Collie Eye Anomaly (CEA) is also known under the names of Chorodial Hypoplasia, Chorioretinal change, sometimes simply as "Collie eye." The important fact about this condition is that it does not affect vision. Somehow the idea has gotten about that any of these eye checks other than normal will cause blindness. This is simply not true. Choriretinal change /Choroidal Hypoplasia will not cause blindness. This is called Grade II.

The syndromes that will probably lead to blindness or impaired vision are retinal detachment and PRA. Very few specimens will exhibit these problems.

From the breeder's point of view, it is recommended not to breed Collies that have an eye rating worse than Grade II or CEA. Most breeders will not breed a dog with coloboma /staphloma for fear of a worse rating developing later. No reputable breeder will breed a Collie with a detached retina. No one should ever breed a dog that has PRA or that has parents with PRA. The one exception is test breeding. This is not for beginners.

PRA, which stands for Progressive Retinal Atrophy, is a terrible disease. It cannot always be detected in a young puppy. As the name implies, this is a progressive disease that becomes worse with passing time. The dogs actually become blind.

In cases in which certain great dogs have been found to have produced this disease breeders have found a way around it—cases wherein PRA-blind Collies have been bred as a test. In these instances, a dog is "proven" to be, or not to be, a PRA carrier. If the progeny in the entire litter (a good-sized litter) does not show PRA, then the tested parent is deemed to be clear of the genes for the disease. Through this method, and by careful culling, certain suspect lines have been cleared. There is far less PRA in the breed than was evident many years ago. Breeders who are serious always consider the eye checks of the parents when planning a breeding. It is a healthy development that good eyes have become an important component of the breeder's thinking. Remember, Grade II does not affect vision!

COLLIE COLOR

The Collie has several colors that are recognized by the American Kennel Club. The most prevalent is the sable and white or "Lassie" color. This was earlier described as "gold, red, mahogany" and shades in between. This color has enjoyed wide popularity partly due to the book and movie, "Lassie Come Home," and the television series derived from that book and movie. Lassie became the ideal companion in the dreams of American children. This dog was a broadly marked sable.

Another widely admired color is the blue merle. This is a silver-gray color with black patches throughout the gray, and with the white trim usually associated with the breed. Also, the blue merle will carry tan mark-

SABLE: Ch. Future of Arken, bred by Charles A. Wernsman, owned by Mr. and Mrs. Charles A. Wernsman

BLUE MERLE: Ch. Clarion's Light Up The Sky, owned by Judie Evans. (Photo by Krook)

TRICOLOR: Ch. Glen Hill Star Ridge Star Dust, owned by the author and Marilyn Marcantonio.

WHITE: Am. and Can. Ch. Marlena's Sudden Sunburst, owned and bred by Mary M. Wells and Helena J. Adcock.

Color Genetics of the Collie

I	PS	Pure For Sable
II	TRI	Tricolor
III	TS	Tri-Factored Sable
IV	BM	Blue Merle
IX	TSM	Tri-Factored Sable Merle
XI	WM	White Merle
XV	PSM	Pure for Sable, Sable Merle
XVII	Wf	White Factored
XVIII	WfBM	White Factored Blue Merle
XIX	Non	Non White Factored

PARENT + PARENT = PROGENY

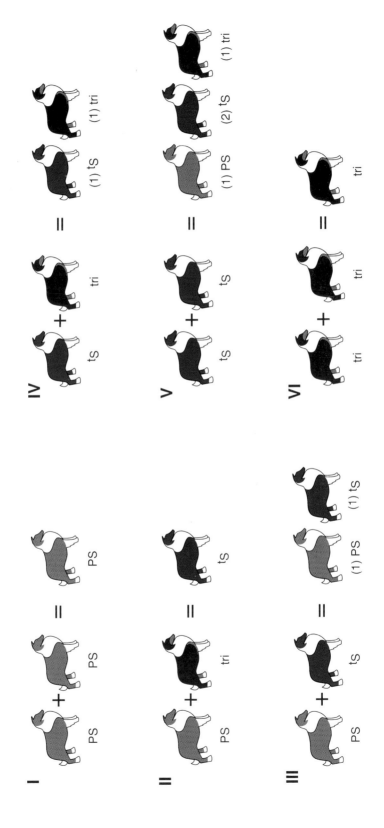

PARENT + PARENT = PROGENY

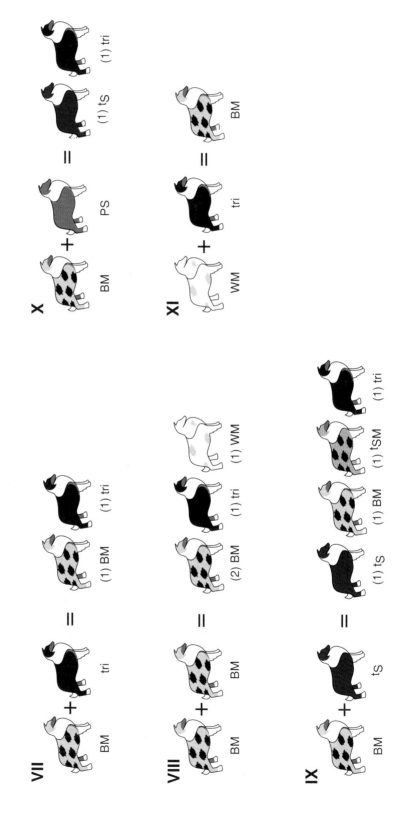

PARENT + PARENT = PROGENY

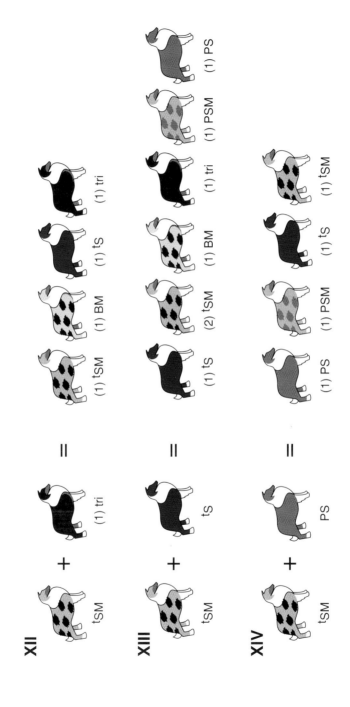

PARENT + PARENT = PROGENY

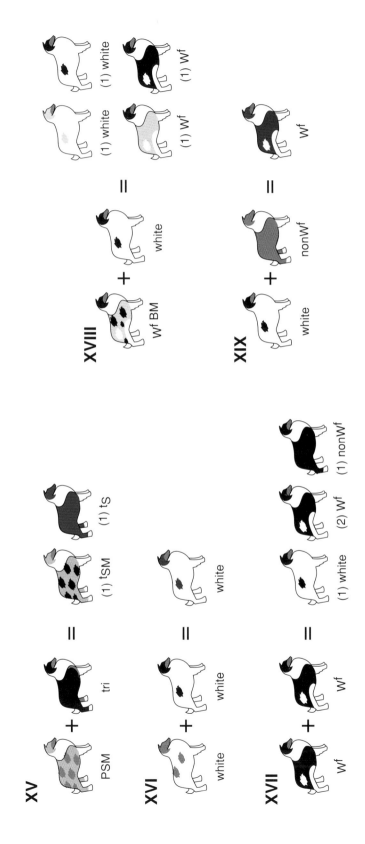

XV   PSM + tri = (1) tSM (1) tS

XVI   white + white = white

XVII   Wf + Wf = (1) white (2) Wf (1) nonWf

XVIII   Wf BM + white = (1) white (1) white (1) Wf (1) Wf

XIX   nonWf + white = Wf

ing on the muzzle and eyebrows and sometimes on the legs. This very striking color is highly prized among many exhibitors and has great success in the show ring. A blue merle is usually produced from the mating of a blue merle to a tricolor. The result is about half of the pups being each color in the litter.

My own favorite color is the tricolor. This dog is mostly black with black body and head. White is an essential for this dog, as it presents a glorious contrast to the black base coat. The white is usually around the neck, down the front and on the legs. In addition, the dog will have the same tan markings as a blue merle, that is on the muzzle eyebrow and legs. A well-groomed Tri looks dressed for a night on the town.

Another color exists, which is somewhat controversial. This color is the sable merle. The color occurs when a blue merle is bred to a sable. Many colors may result. If the sable carries a tricolor factor, the puppies may be sable, tricolor, blue merle and/or sable merle. The sable merle is born a light brownish color, with grayish or brown spots. As the puppy matures most of the spots will disappear, and the dog usually becomes a light tan, nearly indistinguishable from a sable. Since the blue merle may or may not have blue eyes, the sable merle may also turn up with one or two blue eyes. While the blue eye is acceptable in the blue merle, it is not acceptable in the ring in the case of a sable merle. Some judges seem to be prejudiced against the sable merle, others recognize it as a naturally occurring color in the breed. At maturity, often the only way to tell a sable merle from a sable is to check the ear tips. Most sable merles will retain a silvery and sometimes spotted color on the tips of the ear.

Left: Am. and Can. Ch. Marlena's Arctic Commander, owned and bred by Mary M. Wells and Helena J. Adcock. (Vincent Smith Photo) Right: Ch. Tesoro Incandescent Imp, owned and bred by Janine Walker-Keith and Carol Shahan.

There is another beautiful color in the Collie spectrum. This is the white Collie. In this color variety, the dog is almost entirely white with no more than 20 percent foreign color. It is preferable that the white Collie carry some other accepted color. This usually is found on the head and ears, and often on the upper part of the body. Since color is such a spectacular part of this dog, it is important. The foreign color may be sable, tricolor, blue merle, or sable merle. There is no preference between the colors. All-white Collies are not desired.

No preference between the colors also holds true in the judging or assessment of the value of individual dogs. Color and marking are not to be considered in evaluating quality.

It is rather traditional that the Collie will have a white ruff around his neck and white frill around the front of the chest, pure white legs and white tip on tail. While this is a rather ideal distribution of white, the actual placement of the white color is unimportant when compared to the true quality of the animal. There have been great champions with almost no white trim and others with huge white collars. There is an ancient saying, "no good dog is a bad color," meaning that type, soundness, all over quality, outweigh color and marking, to a good judge.

There is an old opinion that a Collie that does not have a white tip on his tail is not all Collie. I have seen literally thousands of them and every one has had at least a couple of white hairs at the very tip. Perhaps the reason we are seeing less white at the tail tip is that tails are getting shorter. The tail is supposed to come at least to the hock, but many do not these days.

GROOMING

Grooming the Rough Collie

Naturally, there is a great difference in grooming time and trouble between the rough coat and the smooth coat. Later, I will describe the grooming of the smooth for a show.

With the rough, the grooming has to begin long before the show. The coat must be kept brushed out and any mats that form should be removed as soon as they are detected. Mats that are left in will tend to grow and become more and more entangled. Start with an unmatted coat in good condition.

These are the implements that you should have to do a proper job: a pin brush with rather long needles to brush through the coat; a spray bottle for dampening the coat; good, sharp scissors; a good quality pair of thinning scissors; a nail clipper; and, a blow dryer. In addition, you will want a some kind of white chalk material to whiten certain areas. There is a product called *Chalk Mate.* Or, you may use corn starch. There are several good products that can be sprayed on the coat to enhance the appearance of volume. These must be of a soft nature as it is not permitted in the ring to have the coat feel lacquered. The nails should have been kept short as part of general care. However, it is a good idea to trim them back again specifically for the show..

Start by giving the dog a thorough bath using any good shampoo. It is really not necessary to invest in expensive shampoo, especially for dogs. This is one of the minor economies that can be achieved by using products designed for humans.

Following the bath, towel dry the dog for a few minutes. Then start to blow dry the coat, blowing against the grain of the hair. After the coat starts to dry a bit, take the pin brush and brush the hair forward as you are blow drying it. This will give the coat a good lift and add to the sheen. Be sure to get at all the hard to reach parts, such as under the arms and under the tail and under the belly. If you have trained your Collie to lie still on a crate or grooming table, it will be far easier to get to the chest hair. This is an area that tends to get tangled and needs to be thoroughly brushed out. This should also be a part of general maintenance of the coat. When the coat on the chest and under body has been thoroughly brushed, the entire coat looks fuller and longer.

Now, I suggest you sit the dog on the grooming table and cut off the whiskers. This will make the head look much smoother. It is also good practice to trim the excess small hairs around the mouth. This vastly improves the lip line. You will see that there are wild straggly hairs around the ears. These may be trimmed to a neater look by using your thinning shears. It must be done by small snips, getting only a few hairs at a time. Always remember when trimming a Collie that the trimming should never appear obvious. You are after the natural look. So, if you are using scissors anywhere around the head and ears, take it easy.

There is a great deal of head trimming that can be done to enhance the head of each dog. Most of it should be done by a professional; otherwise, it can look "hacked up." If the dog appears high over the eye, you can take your thinning shears and laying them flat on the eyebrow, gently trim off the highest part. Just take a tiny bit at a time checking to see that you do not overdo it.

If the dog is heavy in the skull, or "cheeky," you may trim the area down a bit. You must pull the outer hair forward and use the thinning shears on the undercoat, which will be a softer hair than the outer. There is not much of it and it should be trimmed very sparingly. You must be sure to get the outer hair out of the way and trim only underneath. If the outer hair is cut, it leaves an ugly, chopped-up appearance. After each small cut, brush the outer hair back to be sure you work has left a natural appearance. If this has been done incorrectly, the damage will take months to grow out. So, heed my warning and handle with care.

If the dog is throaty, that is too deep in the throat latch, this can be handled. Take your sharp scissors and trim the excess hair off the lower jaw to make it parallel with the line of the top of the muzzle. You will be surprised at how much excess hair exists in this area. It may be trimmed all the way back to the area where the jaw meets the throat. Never trim at finish (end) of the underjaw.

Now, you are really getting to the ticklish part. You must always keep in mind that after you finish trimming, you should not be able to see where the work was done. It should have a natural but improved look. That is not an oxymoron—after you have done this several times you will get the idea. I suggest you do your first trimming on a dog who will not be shown. Just trim up your, or someone else's, pet. That way, it won't matter if it is a hacked-up job. And the first few usually are.

If there is someone in your area who is an expert in head trimming, take advantage. Some breeders and handlers are only too happy to show off their skills. Some may show you the tricks of the trade just for fun. Others may charge for the lesson. If a slight payment is necessary, it will be well worth it. Make sure that the person who is to teach the lesson is a real expert. One thing I will say many times is: Be sure your expert is an expert! There are many phonies in this field, as in most others. If you are going to learn from someone or take someone's advice, check his or her credentials. I would want to be sure that mentors involved have had success in the show ring with their dogs. Just having been in the breed for many years does not make an expert. Or, having had one champion that someone else bred does not qualify one for the status of expert. Seek a breeder or handler who has a solid record of success. This is important in seeking any type of advice about your dogs.

Now, we come to my favorite part—trimming the feet is something I love to do. Probably because it is the part I do best. This part will be much easier if you have trained the dog to sit on a grooming table and allow his feet to be handled. That part of the training should have started at about eight weeks of age. While the dog is sitting, or standing, take a very sharp pair of scissors and trim around the outside edge of each pad. Do not trim between the toes as that will make the foot look splayed.

The look you are after is to have the foot at completion look like a nice, round, white marshmallow. I used that metaphor to describe the correct foot in my first book on Collies. I was quite surprised later to hear that expression used country-wide as the look of a proper foot. It has become part of the lingua franca of Collies. I am proud to claim credit.

There will be straggly hairs on the bottom of the foot and they should be removed. But do not cut between the toes. The same method of trimming applies to both the front and the rear feet. If there are wild hairs sticking up above the toes, they may be carefully removed. But, keep that high, white marshmallow in mind.

It is a good idea to do one foot as well as you can and then compare it with the other foot. You will see how vastly improved the look is.

Forelegs: There will be longish hair hanging from the back of the foot and up to the pad which is behind the pastern. It used to be that the hair was cut up to the pastern, but that is no longer done. Now the hair is only cut to about three fourths of an inch above the last pad of the foot itself. There is an additional pad above that does not touch the ground. Leave that covered by hair. The long coat on the backs of the legs, incidentally, is called feathering.

If you check old pictures of early Collies, you will see that the feathering was trimmed all the way to the pastern. It made the legs look longer and lighter in bone. The present style of trimming gives a more compact look which is more in balance with the dog.

Hind feet: The pads will be outlined by sharp scissors as in the front. In a mature dog, there are profuse feathers from foot to hock. This is an area of grooming that probably takes an expert demonstration before you can master it. I will do my best verbally.

Take a slicker brush and brush and brush until each hair is standing out straight. You may want to use a very fine comb, in addition, to get the hair fully separated. When it is all well combed and brushed you will find it is very long on a well-coated adult dog. Take thinning scissors and trim back the longest part of the feathering. Trim it to a well-rounded look. Do not trim down to the leg itself. It is far more attractive to leave, if possible, a half inch to an inch of deep coat over the area. The hair should be shaped so it appears vertical from foot to hock joint.

There are certain ways to shape the hair to make an appearance of more angulation than the dog really has. In my opinion, this should be left to experts who have learned from other experts. I am describing the grooming that the beginner can learn to do easily.

Legs: The hair on the legs will probably still be damp. Take a rough towel and rub it nearly dry. Take the aforementioned *Chalk Mate* and with a tooth brush apply it to the legs—the white part. The idea here is to get the gooey *Chalk Mate* down through the hair to the skin. It should be evenly distributed over the legs. Now take your white powder (powdered chalk or corn starch) and brush it into the hair of the legs. Remem-

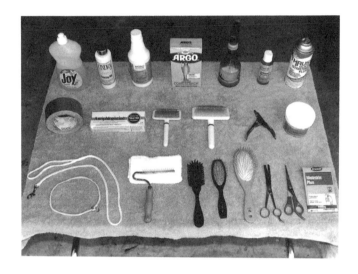

Items needed for proper grooming of the Collie for the ring. Top row: Joy *detergent for bathing;* Cindra *texturizing spray for giving coat volume; flea repellant to keep fleas off do at show;* Argo *starch to whiten white parts of dog; solvent for* Val-A *glue (for ears);* Val-A *glue; starter fluid for cleaning ears (ether) Middle row: Duct tape for taping ears over;* Antiphlogistine *for training ears over; slicker brushes for coat; toenail trimmer;* Chalk Mate *Bottom row: white nylon collar and lead; steel tooth comb; nylon hair brush (for applying starch or chalk); small pin brush for the ring; large pinbrush for general grooming; thinning shears; sharp scissors for whiskers, feet, etc.;* Moleskin Plus *used to roll the ears over if necessary.*

ber, you are not only getting the leg hair white, you are building up the look of bone. If you are doing it right, the legs will look far bigger, rounder and fuller when you are finished. You want the look of lots of bone. This helps to balance the sturdy body and voluminous coat of the true show Collie.

Coat: You have washed and blow-dried the hair. It should be standing out attractively by now. I suggest line brushing the entire coat. You may use a spray bottle to dampen the undercoat as it becomes open between the lines of brushing. It is always wise to dampen a coat before brushing as this will help prevent coat breakage. In line brushing, always brush forward.

You may use plain water in the spray bottle or one of a number of different products. There are sprays available for rough coats that are called bodifiers or texturizers. These are available at dog shows and show-dog equipment catalogues. You had better follow the directions on the bottle so the spray, mixed with water, will not be too thin or too sticky.

The idea is to make the coat look as voluminous as possible. The brush must reach down to the skin and the hair must be brushed forward and upward to make it stand out away from the body. A friend of mine who is a grand groomer says that if you are grooming and your arm is not ready to fall off you have not groomed enough. That is my witty Collie friend, Dory Samuels (Royal Guard Collies).

A son of Ch. Glen Hill Top of the Line showing voluminous coat grown in Florida and beautifully groomed.

At this point, the white areas around the neck and chest should be rather dry. Take your *Chalk Mate* and work it in to the long hair of those areas. Work it well down into the undercoat. Take a brush (preferably a woman's nylon hairbrush) and apply your white chalk to the area. Get the chalk deep into the chest and apply it evenly all over the neck and chest and finally the underbelly. You may leave a good amount in as the dog will shake out most of it. However, it must be well-brushed out before you go into the ring. In the ring, a cloud of white dust is a definite No! No!

Now you will shape the dog. Get the neck and chest hair to stand up and form a halo around the dog's head. Then take a pin brush and straighten out the back line so the neck rises from a level plane. Take your brush and round off the crop as a finishing touch.

Stand back and look at your Collie. He should be a shining thing of beauty.

Now, catch your breath. I must tell you that all I have written must be done the day of or the night before the show. Well, not of bathing or the scissoring, but all the rest.

Do it all again and go in there and win!

Grooming the Smooth Collie

When grooming the smooth Collie, the first part of the procedure for the rough, will be followed. The dog should be bathed with a good shampoo. The coat will preferably be blow dried to assist in its appearance of depth. The smooth Collie is a double-coated dog, even though the coat is short instead of long. If he is losing undercoat it must be combed out, in order to give a smooth, sleek appearance.

The feet will be trimmed in the same way as the feet of the rough. However there is no feathering to be trimmed and shaped. The legs will be brushed in an upward direction, and *Chalk Mate* will be applied. It should be worked down to the skin. The legs are then covered with either white chalk or corn starch. The white substance should be brushed firmly into the leg coat and down to the skin. The purpose again is to maximize the impression of bone size and substance.

The chalk will be brushed into the white parts of the neck, chest and underbelly. The rest of the coat will be brushed down to enhance the sleek look of the dog. Some handlers will brush the hair of the back and sides of the neck forward to make the neck appear more arched. And there you have it! With the smooth Collie, what you see is what you get!

Ch. Glen Hill The All American showing glorious grooming of neck and chest. (Ashbey Photography)

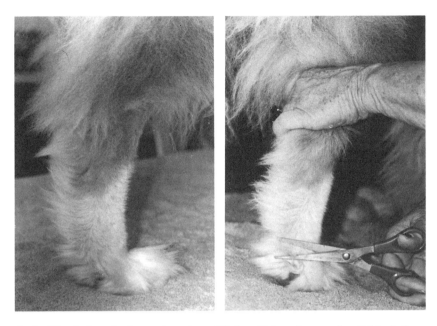

Left: Hind foot before trimming. Right: Trimming arch of hind foot.
(Photos by Libby Lewitt)

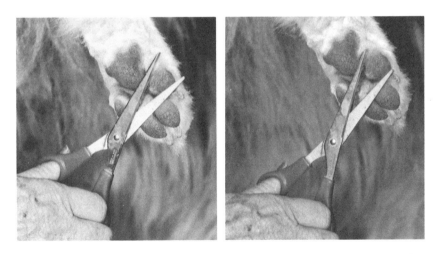

Left: Trim excess hair on bottom of all four feet. Right: Trimming under feet.
(Photos by Libby Lewitt)

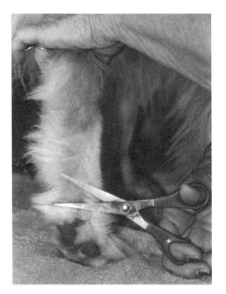 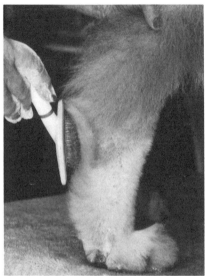

Left: Trimming the hind foot. Right: Using slicker brush to finish off the hock. (Photos by Libby Lewitt)

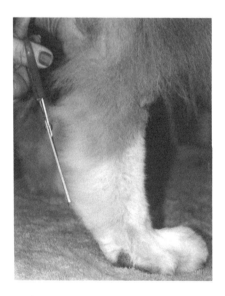 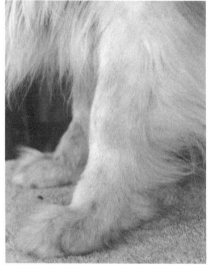

Left: Well-trimmed hind foot and hock. Right: Front foot before trim and finishing touches. (Photos by Libby Lewitt)

Trimming edges of front foot. (Photo by Libby Lewitt)

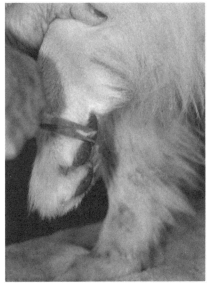

Trimming front foot with sharp scissors. (Photo by Libby Lewitt)

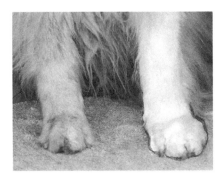

The nicely washed and chalked foot, as compared to the merely washed foot. The trimming of the foot shows up the nice, round, white marshmallow look. The very strong arched foot is a desirable look in the Collie. It takes proper trimming to show it off. (Photo by Libby Lewitt)

 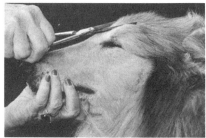

Left: Profile before trimming. Right: Trimming down hair over eyebrow to flatten skull. (Photos by Libby Lewitt)

Profile after trimming. (Photo by Libby Lewitt)

Above: Trimming under lower portion of head back to throat latch. Left: Lower jaw after trimming. (Photos by Libby Lewitt)

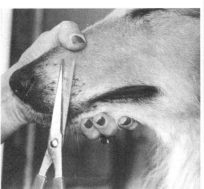

Trimming along lip line. (Photo by Libby Lewitt)

Trimming whiskers. (Photo by Libby Lewitt)

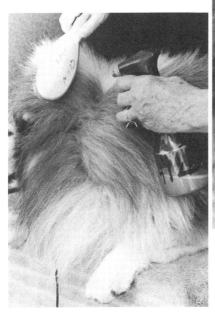

Apply starch to white parts of coat (neck, chest, legs and underbody. (Photo by Libby Lewitt)

Line brushing, shown here, starting at head and spraying water or texturizing mist. Divide the hair in lines about two inches apart and spray the whole length of the body. Use pin brush. (Photo by Libby Lewitt)

COLLIE CLUBS

Collie Club of America

Collie fanciers are fortunate to have a national organization that is devoted to the welfare of the Collie breed. This is the Collie Club of America (CCA), a group that has many subdivisions, each involved in the promotion of the health, comfort and popularity of the Collie.

There are many fanciers who devote a great portion of their time and energy, year after year, to supporting and guiding the aforementioned groups. Some of the committees: Archives; Collie Welfare/Rescue; Ethics; Health Policy; Judges; Library, including video library with Interviews with Leading Collie Figures, The Versatile Collie and Video Collection of Collie Champions, both rough and smooth. (These films may be rented.); National Show Rules; Versatility and Herding Instinct; Working Collie; CCA Foundation Inc.

In addition, the CCA stages a national Specialty show annually. This show is held in a different part of the country each year, giving fanciers from various areas a chance to exhibit there.

To contact the CCA for information, write to Carmen Leonard, secretary, 1119 S. Fleming Road, Woodstock IL 60098.

President of the Quarter Century Club Chip Atkins and Secretary Pat Atkins.

There are many pamphlets of interest that may be sent to you. The club also puts out a fine yearbook, as well as a magazine called the *Bulletin*. These items come free with a membership in the club.

The Quarter Century Collie Group

The Quarter Century Collie Group is an organization that honors outstanding individuals who have contributed much to the Collie breed.

PART II
PROMINENT BREEDERS
AND KENNELS

Famous breeder Steve Field with Ch. Parader's Country Squire and Judge Ralph Morrison. (Photo courtesy of John Buddie)

Ch. Hazeljane's Bright Future handled by Hazel Youngjohns, bred and owned by Hazel and Jane Youngjohns, at the 1949 St. Louis Collie Club Show. (Photo by Ralph E. Morrison)

DOMINATING THE DECADES
A look at the rough Collie families that dominated the last five decades
by John Buddie

Influence of Collie lines and strains is what contributes to the overall look of the Collie at a given time. This look is created using the national gene pool contributed by the successful dogs from a variety of kennels. By mid-20th Century, the American Collie kennels had taken a firm foothold in the overall picture. Often times, these were large operations necessary to achieve the homozygosity within the strains, and these gene pools were shared by new up-and-coming breeders to help create new Collie families. By the 1950s, the sport of purebred dogs was changing for the better. Inoculations against diseases that once wiped out whole kennels were introduced. The war years were over, and the ability to breed dogs became easier as methods of transportation and shipping improved. It was during the 1950s and 1960s that one was able to see more of a melting pot of Collie families, as people were able to make use of dogs in different parts of the county that had been out of reach. A look at the general picture and scheme of things helps put into perspective the continuation of improvement within the breed.

The 1950s
By 1950, the picture of the Collie seemed intact. The 1949 CCA Best Of Breed winner created a record still unbroken by any other Collie by scoring four Best of Breed wins at this prestigious event—these were in 1949, 1950, 1951 and 1952. The record might have continued had this outstanding show dog not died in an auto accident. This dog was the incomparable **Ch. Hazel Janes Bright Future**, bred and owned by Hazel and Jane Youngjohns.

While some of the pillar lines, Bellhaven, Arken, Sterling, Hertzville and Tokalon were moving along putting out good ones, the newer American-blended families were gaining momentum. Throughout this decade, Steve Field and his Parader Kennels would begin having an impact on the Collie picture. The phenomenal success of **Ch. Silver Ho Parader** as a sire would carry down generations: through **Ch. Paraders Golden Image** to a grandson, who would lead the field for the Paraders during the 1950s, **Ch. Paraders Bold Venture**, along with his litter sister, **Ch. Paraders Dancing Girl**, who finished in 1951. Bold Venture would make headlines as both a sire and a show dog, taking the most prestigious of wins—the CCA's Best of Breed wins in 1955 and 1956. One of the strongest direct sire lines would be noted with the Parader family.

The 1950s also saw one of the favorites of the Tokalon family carrying the banner of this elegant line. His name was **Ch. Tokalon Golden Ruler**, and he typified the balance, outline, style and coat that were synonymous with the Tokalon name. This family of dogs was extremely dominant for these traits. At the end of this decade, Mrs. Browning, the lady of the great Tokalon Kennel, announced her retirement from the show ring. Two important champions were then shipped off to Glen Twiford, whose Wind Call Collies in the West were having quite a bit of success on their own. The Wind Calls were noted for their beautiful blues, with graceful outlines and profuse coats. These two dogs were **Ch. Tokalon Harvest Weather** and **Ch. Tokalon Blue Banner**. The latter, would later be sold to the Bannerblu Kennels (named in honor of Blue Banner) of Mrs. R.L. Rickenbaugh of Denver, where Blue Banner would go on to become a notable sire in his own right.

When Mrs. Elisabeth Browning's daughter, Mary, married Lloyd Beresford, they set up a kennel across the river from Tokalon and established the Poplar Kennels in 1948. By the 1950s, they were putting out a string of winners, including the CCA winner of 1954, **Poplar Pencil Stripe**, who was BW that year. One of the non champions at Poplar was **Poplar By Storm**, who in turn sired five champions, and who was a dog with great impact on the breed. One of his sons, **Ch. Gaylords Mr. Scalawag**, would carry influence forward through continuing generations through his siring ability.

The first champion to carry the Glen Hill prefix was awarded her title in 1953 as **Ch. Glen Hill Dainty Miss**. Following a spectacular win at Westminster, she opened the gates for a number of new champion bitches to follow—all carrying the Glen Hill prefix. These would include **Exquisite, Excellence, Gwenivere, September Song** and **College Try**. But it was in the middle of this decade that Pat Starkweather would purchase Ch. Paraders Typesetter and combine his blood with that of Dreamers Glen Hill Black Tea, a bitch of mostly Lodestone breeding, to produce the spearhead of another tail male line that would carry itself down through several decades beginning with **Ch. Glen Hill Dreamers Nobleman**.

The Gaylord/Brandwyne dogs were coming on during the 1950s as well, the most notable being the tricolor, Ch. Gaylord's Mr. Scalawag, who as mentioned earlier was sired by Poplar By Storm, his dam, Ch. Gaylord's Gay Glory, being a Sterling/Tokalon cross. He topped the breed at the 1953 National Specialty and sired some really good ones for his family. Among his most prominent offspring were two additional winners **Ch. Cyn Sans Black Lancer** (WD in 1958) and **Ch. Cherrivale Darn Minute**. Another tricolor from this family, **Ch. Gaylord's Flyer**, was the top-win-

Ch. Brandwyne Destiny's Echo in 1963. (Photo courtesy of John Buddie)

ning Collie in 1957. **Brandwyne Tom Foolery** began a spectacular siring career during this decade as well, and among his earliest winners were **Ch. Brandwyne No Foolin'** and **Ch. Brandwyne Needless to Say,** the CCA Winners Dog in 1957. Tom Foolery was considered to be the pillar of the family, and his linebred and inbred descendants were still winning up through the '70s.

In the East, Long Island was home to newcomers who were quickly staking their claims in the Collie world. In the eastern corner of Southampton lived a congenial Irishman by the name of Brian Carabine. During the late '50s, he had a string of dogs who quickly created a look of their own. **Ch. Erin's Own Professor** and **Ch. Erin's Own Professor's Touch** left their marks on several generations to follow. One daughter of Professor's Touch served as a solid base for the Glen Knolls Kennels of Mrs. Daniel Levine. While breeding on a small and limited scale, the impact of Glen Knolls would carry forward through kennels in the '60s and '70s while it increased its own record of winners.

Two Midwestern kennels gained prominence during the 1950s as well. Mr. and Mrs. Leonard Jabaay in Illinois were having great luck with the Vi-Lee Collies, finishing **Ch. Dutch Master** in '58 and **Royal Rocket** and **Starring Jovi** in '59.

Cherrivale, owned by Mrs. and Mrs. Gus Segritz, became another great contender and dominating influence during this decade. Cherrivale purchased **Parader's Portrait** from Steve Field. A daughter of Ch. Parader's Golden Image, she was out of Parader's Pamela, by Ch. Silver Ho Parader. Gus bred her back to her grandsire to get **Ch. Cherrivale Checkmate,** a dog known for his superb expression. At the beginning of this decade, Portrait herself would score a great win as Best of Opposite Sex to Ch. Hazeljane's Bright Future. But the dog who would dominate the field of the '50s would have to be **Ch. Cherrivale Darn Minute,** the outstanding tricolor son of Ch. Gaylord's Mr. Scalawag. This dog took the breed honors at the National in '58 and '59. Another important dog to finish in this time frame was **Ch. Cherrivale Mainspring** (owned by Mrs. Leo A. Sturm) who served as one of the foundation bitches for the Lick

Creek family of Collies. She was sired by the outstanding show dog and CCA winner of 1967, Ch. Jorie's Mr. G.

On the West Coast, breeders were also active. From an early purchase from Nancy Caldwell of Silver Ho fame, Lois Hillman was to acquire two Collies who would make the Roneill Collies well known in Collie circles throughout the country. **Ch. Silver Ho Scheherazade** and **Silver Ho Tall Dark N' Handsome** were offspring of Ch. Silver Ho Shining Arrow, sire of Ch. Silver Ho Parader. Tall Dark N' Handsome would be quite an influential sire although a serious illness cut his life short at just two years, but not before he sired **Ch. Dark Town Strutter of Roneill**. Dark Town Strutter helped the success of two new upcoming families on the West Coast. For Milt and Laverne Walker of San Lori, he would sire the three-champion litter of **Citation, Bewitch** and **Enchant**. For Louis and Helene Carpenter, he would sire **Ch. Lewellen Summer Escapade,** who would in turn sire one of the most prepotent sires of the West during this period—**Ch. Lewellen Call Collaire,** sire of 15 champions.

From Arrowhill Skysail, purchased from the Arrowhill Kennels of Mrs. Louis Cummings, Mary Kittredge made a series of breedings that created a family of individuals of superior type. From one of the earliest litters came the beautiful **Ch. Kittredge Adventuress,** sired by Ch. Paraders Bold Venture. She was a Group winning bitch who gained national prominence when she was Best of Opposite Sex to her sire (Venture) at the 1955 National. Another Kittredge homebred, owned by Gladys Reardon, would take top honors by going Winners Bitch and Best of Winners in 1959. Her name was **Ch. Kittredge Jeannie**.

Another special litter was born on the West Coast during this decade. Mr. and Mrs. Euril F. Wharton bred their Barkalow's Autumn Mist to Dorellaine's Crusader. A sable bitch from this litter became an outstanding winner, finishing with a Group first while still a puppy. Some astute forethought was used in breeding her, and the use of **Ch. Kinmont Sheyne** made a mark in the history of Collies. There resulted a multiple champion litter containing **Ch. Country Lane M'liss, Ch. Country Lane Afterglow** and **Ch. Country Lane Renegade**. M'liss would take her place in Collie history at the turn of the decade when she took the coveted Best of Breed win in the 1960 National Specialty.

In the Northwest, Billy Aschenbrener and his Pleasant Hill Collies were making great strides. After finishing the exciting tricolor **Ch. Pleasant Hill Torch Song** with a National Specialty win (Winners Bitch, Best of Winners), he brought out another outstanding tricolor bitch in 1950 by the name of **Ch. Pleasant Hill Enchantress,** sired by the East-Coast bred Blackout of Tokalon. Another CCA win would be scored by **Pleasant Hill Audacity** when she was Best of Opposite Sex at the CCA in 1952.

The 1960s

The opening of this decade brought forth a beautiful bitch as the breed winner of the National Specialty, as Ch. Country Lane M'liss topped the breed at the CCA National Specialty Show. This outstanding bitch was bred by Mr. and Mrs. Euril Wharton and owned by Mr. and Mrs. Richard Hillman. Best of Opposite Sex to her was the previous two-time Best of Breed winner, **Ch. Cherrivale Darn Minute,** owned by the Segritzs. Cherrivale, Country Lane and the Hillmans would continue to play major roles throughout the 1960s, amassing new champions for each, but also serving as foundation stock for new and upcoming kennels as well.

Ch. Merrie Oaks Manzanita was Best of Winners at the 1960 CCA event and brought prominent attention to the Merrie Oaks Kennel of Mrs. Judy Mansure. Merrie Oaks established an enviable record throughout this decade. **Ch. Merrie Oaks Humdinger** won some of the toughest shows from coast to coast and would eventually sire 15 champions. Several of the Merrie Oaks bitches produced multiple champion offspring, among these being **Ch. Merrie Oaks Sweet and Lovely** and **Ch. Merrie Oaks Treasure.** An impressive list of champions and champion producers followed. A tricolor male champion born in 1961 would eventually relocate to Lt. Col. and Mrs. George H. Roos' Wichmere Kennel where he would play a major role. He also sired extremely well for the Alteza family of dogs for the Beverly Dampfs and the Celestrial family of Mr. and Mrs. Bill Crawford. **Ch. Celestrial Thor Thunderbolt,** a heavily coated tricolor, made quite a name for future generations. **Ch. Alteza the Silver Lining** produced a record during this period that would remain unparalleled for nearly 20 years—that of being the top-producing bitch in the history of the breed to that time.

A great number of Wind Call champions received their titles during this time for breeder Glen Twiford. **Grey Knight, Woodsprite, Cheyenne,** and **Ballerina** were among these ranks. Some of these dogs would be owned by the Bannerblu Kennels of Mrs. R.L. Rickenbaugh.

The Gaylord Brandwyne dogs of Jim and Trudy Mangels were among the greatest contenders during this decade. More than 100 champions were produced using this family of dogs, and their propotency set a record. They won the coveted Breeder of the Year award on several occasions. The efforts of this kennel, though begun years earlier, were particularly felt during the 60s. Closely linebred on the blood of Brandwyne Tomfoolery, line descendants became some of the most noteworthy winners. **Ch. Brandwyne Pandora,** the puppy "flyer," who created quite a name for herself by going BW at the '64 CCA Specialty Show, broke records with her impressive finishing. **Ch. Brandwyne Destiny's Echo** became one of the top-producing sires in breed history—siring 22 champions. The offspring of **Ch. Brandwyne The Grey Ghost** would also serve as foundation stock for new up and coming families. From this time period, the names of Destiny's Echo, Royal Gold, Tom Foolery and Grey Ghost would be firmly entrenched in Collie history, as they set the standard for many champions to come.

The phenomenal success of the top-winning **Ch. Stoneykirk Reflection,** owned by John and Evelyn Honig would earmark a place for their Accalia Collies. Topping the breed at the National Specialty in '62 and '63, Reflection would score several Group and Best in Show wins as well. Reflection's daughter, **Ch. Welcome Mayoline Reflection,** also owned by the Honigs, established her own place in history by going Best of Opposite Sex to her sire at the 1962 CCA event.

The Marnus Kennels of Ron and Marcia Keller was a prominent name during this period. **Ch. Marnus Evening Breeze,** a heavily coated, light sable bitch, spearheaded her own family and was Best of Opposite Sex at the '68 and '70 National Specialties. She set the stage for Marnus champions to take top honors at this event for decades to come.

Mrs. William H. Long and her Noranda Kennels of Long Island, New York, seemed to rise to the top generation after generation from the 1930s and the decade of the '60s was no exception. In typical Noranda style, some of the best in bitches finished their titles—**Ch. Noranda Whistlestopper**. A dream came true for Mrs. Long in 1968 when her dark-mahogany sable male **Ch. Noranda's Daily Double** took Best of Breed at the prestigious Westminster Kennel Club show under Judge Patricia Starkweather (then Shryock) and took the Best of Breed honors at the CCA National Specialty Show. This dog was a Group and Best in Show winner as well. Always working on a small scale and always giving back to the breed, Mrs. Long was one of those special people to whom Collie people owe a great deal.

The sire of Daily Double was from another Long Island kennel, that of Leslie Canavan and Verna Allen, whose Royal Rock Kennels were finding great success during this 10-year span. The sire of Daily Double was **Ch. Royal Rock Gamblin' Man** and his list of champion offspring was most impressive. One of his earliest champions was another National Specialty winner, **Ch. Cyn San's Signet,** owned and bred by Alexander Fraser Draper. Gamblin' Man was Best of Winners at the 1962 National Specialty show. From Royal Rock would also come some outstanding winners during this period: **Ch. Royal Rock The Whistler** and **Ch. Royal Rock Daddy's Girl**. Leslie Canavan was also a professional handler during this period and she piloted Daily Double to his prestigious wins.

Long Island sported a few other prominent breeders whose success seemed to continue to produce champions. The Carabine's Erin's own

Above: Ch. Parader's Typesetter shown with the author at a large eastern Specialty show. In the picture are some of the greats of the Collie world: in corner, Trudy Mangels; with tricolor, Brian Carrabine; moving, Sally Barbaresi (now Futh). Left: Ch. Glen Hill Emperor Jones, sire of the great foundation dog, Ch. Glen Hill Full Dress. Both owned by the author.

Right: Ch. Parader's Typesetter, owned by the author and bred by Stephen Field (Ch. Parader's Bold Venture ex Parader's Royal Countess). He is behind all Glen Hill Collies. (Photo by Hector Smith)

Collies continued to win. One of the best known was the sable bitch sold to Lorraine Perry, called **Ch. Erin's Own Gold Rush.** Other descendants of this family were found in another beautiful bitch, **Ch. Valley View Satin Slippers,** Best of Opposite Sex in two National Specialties.

The effect of the Glen Knolls Kennels of Edith Levine was particularly strong here as well. **Ch. Glen Knolls Spun Gold** took Winners Bitch at the National Specialty and Best of Opposite Sex 1964. A white son of hers not only finished his title, but became a real fountainhead in his own right as a sire. This dog was **Ch. Glen Knoll's Flash Lightning,** whose impact would be felt at the end of this period. In one of his early litters, he produced the first of the champions for Barbara Schwartz' Impromptu Kennels. This was **Ch. Impromptu Repartee,** Winners Bitch at the '67 National and Best Opposite in '69. The breeding that produced Repartee also produced the Best in Show winner, **Ch. Impromptu Burnt Norton,** and a handful of other champions.

In Pennsylvania, the Glen Hill Collies continued to put out a string of champions. It was in this period that the strength of the sire line of Glen Hill was most noticed. Prior to the exportation of **Ch. Glen Hill Dreamer's Nobleman,** he had sired **Ch. Glen Hill Emperor Jones,** a notable winner and sire in his own right. Emperor was also exported but not before siring the important **Ch. Glen Hill Full Dress.** All three of these individuals were champion producers, but the strength of Full Dress was as a pivotal sire. He had a widespread effect on the breed from coast to coast. His daughters were sought for their producing ability. Many kennels infused his blood through the use of his daughters, intensifying his prepotent characteristics of elegance and type. At the end of this decade, the Full Dress son, **Ch. Glen Hill Star Ridge Stardust** completed his title and took his place as the torchbearer for the next generations. His influence was felt the strongest through the 1970s and the generations of Glen Hill stars continued through him.

Across the water in New Jersey, George Horn was establishing quite a name for his GinGeor Collies. **Ch. GinGeor Bellbrook's Choice,** bred by John Guiliano, served as an outstanding foundation sire for his family. He sired, in one of his early litters, the standout winner, **Ch. Jadene's Breeze Along.** Campaigned by George, he was bred and owned by Barbara Woodmancy but was eventually purchased by the Horns. An outstanding Group-winning Collie, he would take the Best of Breed honors at the 1967 National and was the sire of the aforementioned Ch. Marnus Evening Breeze. Another GinGeor sire of note during this period was **Ch. GinGeor's Indelible Choice,** whose influence would continue to be felt through the 1970s.

To the south in the Maryland-Virginia area, the beginnings of several new families were already stirring. Bill and Mary Hutchinson of HiVu were busy finishing **Ch. HiVu Ravette Mist,** who lead the family to prominence in the 1970s. Ravette Mist, along with **Ch. HiVu the Invader,** Winners Dog at the '68 National, were both acquired from Joyce Avery. Her Ravette family had tremendous impact on the overall picture of the breed in later years. Although shown sparingly, the Ravette dogs were used to great advantage by other breeders.

Up the road, one would have found the Wayside family of Rose and George Soellner, a family with solid Parader base stemming down through the Bellbrooke and GinGeor dogs. Marion Durholz, from the same area, was making quite a name in both rough and smooth Collies under the Jancada prefix. Farther south, Joyce Dowling was finishing the foundation bitch for Shenstone in **Ch. Shenstone's Diamond Tiara.**

In the Chicago area, the Vikingsholm Kennels of Drs. Ted and Betsy Kjellstrom made quite a name for themselves. **Ch. Vikingsholm Vagabond** and **Ch. Vikingsholm Josefina, Ch. Vikingsholm Ulrika** had a definite look with family appeal. Offshoots of this look veered into several new families in later generations. The Patrician family of Jim and Sue Crotteau were another force to be reckoned with from this area.

The Parader family continued to show strength and vigor, and the sire line remained constant. Along with the Gaylord/Brandwyne line during that period, Parader was most decidedly one of the most dominant sources. The strength of this family, which started during the 1940s, seemed to gain strength and momentum with each succeeding generation. By the end of this decade and well into the next, many a successful kennel had a firm foundation with a dog from Steve Field's vigorous line. The offshoot families of the Paraders were found from coast to coast. During the 1960s, **Ch. Parader's County Squire** probably had the most impact, and he too eventually made the top sire's list. A son, **Ch. Parader's Reflection** continued still another generation, siring champions for several kennels across the country. Steve Field continued to be an influence on the breed, sharing his knowledge in articles and symposia.

While champions continued to finish for the Pleasant Hill prefix for Billy Aschenbrener and Dennis Day, an addition by the name of **Ch. Lunett Blue Print** became the star of the Abbehurst Kennel during this period. This striking blue merle with outstanding coat and soundness became one of the top winners of the decade, consistently placing in the Group and was a Best in Show winner.

The Chapman family of Hanover dogs would be based on a combination of Ch. CulMor's Conspirator daughters crossed with Ch. Parader's County Squire. These bitches produced some standouts: **Chs. Hanover's Star Fall, Victory Song, Agena,** and **Star Trek.** From these combinations came a sable male who became the foundation sire for another famous family of dogs—**Ch. Two Jay's Hanover Enterprise** owned by Jim Fredrickson and Jim Noe. Finishing in 1969, this dog had great importance during the 1970s. The Hanover's bred out to Glen Hill Wheeler Dealer, producing top bitch **Hanover's Love Song**. She became the foundation dam for Bobbie Fairbanks' winning Azalea Hill Collies.

The Vi-Lee family of the JaBaay's continued to finish a string of winners. Though bred on a small scale, the bloodlines were beginning to be used as complementary outcrosses and for early foundation stock. **Ch. Vi-Lee's Jubilent Jonathon** and **Ch. Vi-Lee's Classic Contender** played major roles in these families.

Hanovers Love Song (Bonnie), 1969-1982. Dam of Ch. Azalea Hills Mr. Christopher, Ch. Azalea Hills Rosemarie, Ch. Azalea Hills Marianne, Ch. Azalea Hills Touch of Magic, Ch. Hanover's Love for Sale and Ch. Azalea Hills Dear Playboy. She was sired by Glen Hill Wheeler Dealer. (Photo courtesy of Richmond J. Fairbanks)

Sara Barbaresi and her Starberry Collies triumphed during this period with offspring of Starberry Lalla Rookh and Starberry Kittredge Kilt. Lalla Rookh bred to Glen Knolls Knightswood Sky produced **Ch. Starberry Caliph** and **Yankee Sabra**. Kilt's litter by Ch. Stoneykirk Sir Echo produced **Ch. Stoneykirk Starberry**.

In Indiana, the Lick Creek family of Mrs. Leo Sturm was gaining momentum. Early bitches like **Ch. Lick Creeks Almost Angel** and **Ch. Lick Creek's Debonette** set the stage for generations to come. In 1969, **Ch. Lick Creek's Trademark** nabbed the Winners Dog placement at the CCA National.

Arrowhill continued to be a dominant source. Mrs. Cummings achieved a dream in 1966 when **Ch. Arowhill Oklahoma Tornado** took Winners Dog and Best of Winners at the CCA Specialty. As was typical of her nature, Mrs. Cummings continued to teach and nurture all comers who sought her out.

The following six pictures of Collie greats are from a collection owned by Robert Hawkins, author of the Hawkins Rating System.

Ch. Two Jay's Coming Attraction.

Ch. Black Hawk of Kasan.

Ch. Silver Ho Parader.

Ch. Glen Hill Full Dress.

Ch. Gingeor Bellbrooke's Choice.

Ch. Tartanside the Gladiator.

George Dahl, whose Floravae prefix dated back a few decades made headlines with two influential litter brothers during the 1960s: **Ch. Floravale Perfect Gentleman** and **Ch. The Clown Prince of Floravale**, later sold to George Shroeder. The Clown Prince would later best the competition at the National in '64 and '66.

The Midwest saw some of the early title holders bearing the Twin Creeks prefix during this period as well with **Ch. Twin Creeks Golden Boy.**

Several new and prominent families evolved during the '60s. The era of the big kennels had ended and the smaller hobby breeders were dominating the show scene. It was an age of transition when few families seemed to dominate the shows, but when the wealth seemed to be spread about. New breeders from coast to coast were creative and challenging, using the best of what was available. They began to build new dynasties, but along with those came truly dedicated breeders who were well into their second decade of breeding and whose names would continue to be prominent in the next decade.

The 1970s

It is interesting to study the progression of the Collie families by decade. Using this 10-year span as a measure, one is able to see not only how families evolved and gained strength, but how the approach to breeding Collies underwent transition: from the earliest periods of history of the American Collie when the importing by early kennels was a sport for the affluent, to the hard work of the pillar lines that created the true American Collie picture in the 40s and 50s, to the large kennels that used blended families to create new foundations of the 60s, to the smaller, but quite successful kennels of the 70s.

The decade of the 1970s saw patterns of siring in which certain individuals seemed to monopolize the siring charts, thereby creating great recognition for the kennels whose banner they bore. At the turn of the decade, the influence of the Ch. GinGeor Bellbrooke's Choice was still going strong, while Choice himself took the honors of top sire. During the rest of this decade, it is interesting to note that two dogs vied as top sire. As a result, the impact of these two individuals was conspicuous in the show ring as well.

Ch. Two Jay's Hanover Enterprise was top sire in '71, '73 and '75. In 1971, one of his finest sons, **Ch. Baymar's Coming Attraction**, took the Best of Breed rosette at the National. Jim Fredrickson and Jim Noe had quite an impressive record during this decade by using the blood of Enterprise carefully and creating a family of dogs based on him. He consistently produced deep-chested dogs with well let-down hocks and set low to the ground with pleasing outlines. These were timely and desirable virtues. By the end of the decade, the Two Jay's predominately sable and tricolor line added blues with the beautiful **Ch. Two Jay's Silverfire** and **Ch. Two Jay's Free Spirit**. Enterprise sons and daughters played important roles in the success of other families as well.

Ch. Tartanside The Gladiator was top sire in '74, '76, '77 and '78. Equally as impressive as his siring ability, this dog gained great acclaim by taking Best of Breed at the National Specialty in both 1973 and 1974 and then returning to the ring as a veteran in 1978 and making breed history by being the first Collie to take breed honors from the Veterans Class. He spearheaded a family of Collies for John Buddie that were distinctive for their overall balance and expression, and the Tartanside family became a major contender during this period.

The fact that both Enterprise and Gladiator were direct Parader descendants, demonstrated the strength and power of the Parader family, as both of them traced directly back to the strong tail male Parader line. Though campaigning on a most modest level during this decade, Steve Field continued to breed and sell good ones to others, and the number of Parader champions continued to grow.

While known for a kennel of quality bitches in the 60s, the stud force at the Hanover Kennels during the 1970s brought a new dimension to its breeding program. **Ch. Hanover's I Am Legend** and his son, **Ch. Hanover's Flaming Legend**, joined **Ch. Hanover's Follow the Sun** at stud, and the offspring of these dogs was duly noted in many of the winners throughout the decade. Flaming Legend sired 15 champions.

Ch. Tartanside The Gladiator. (Photo by Krook)

The Wickmere Collies of Lt. Col. and Mrs. George Roos (Bobbee) hit the peak during this period as well. Although quite well established by 1970, the tricolor son of Ch. Wickmere War Dance, by the name of **Ch. Wickmere Chimney Sweep** took on all comers at the 1972 National, and topped a large array of top winners, while a daughter, **Ch. Wickmere Golden Chimes**, topped the futurity at the same event. Throughout the 70s, the Wickmere Collies with their huge, profuse coats and pleasing heads were often in the limelight winning at some of the finest shows in the country. Another War Dance son, **Ch. Wickmere Battle Chief**, sired another top producer in his blue merle son, **Ch. Wickmere Silver Bullet**.

Another kennel that reached its peak during this time was the Impromptu Kennels of Barbara Schwartz. In 1970, Impromptu received the Breeder of the Year award. From the great winning Ch. Impromptu Repartee came a substantial number of outstanding champions. The breeding of Repartee to Brandwyne New Legacy brought gratifying results, particularly in the tricolor sire **Ch. Impromptu Ricochet**, another who became one of the top sires in the breed. He helped perpetuate the Brandwyne and Glen Knolls influence into future generations, particularly since New Legacy was the sire from six successive generations of Gaylord/Brandwyne-bred individuals, inbreeding closely on Brandwyne Tomfoolery. Though he was well into old age at this point, this kept the important gene pool of Tomfoolery alive and well. Coupling this gene pool with the strong qualities coming through the "typey" Repartee, there was no doubt that Richochet would become an important sire in this family.

Ch. Glen Knoll's Knightswood Sky, another Tomfoolery son, continued to sire well for Edith Levine's Glen Knoll's Kennel, and a duet of white champions made quite a hit during the 1970s. Glen Knoll's Knightswood Sky's influence would continue to be felt through the siring ability of his son, **Ch. Valley View's Whirlaway**, a top sire in the breed, bred from Cebobs Black Diamond, a daughter of Ch. Brandwyne the Grey Ghost.

By the 1970s, we once again see some dominating forces in the field, whose ultimate success, caused them to stand out from the crowd. Texas gained great strength during this period, and two kennels continuously produced outstanding individuals. These were the Celestial Collies of Bill and Bettie Crawford and the Alteza dogs of Beverly Dampfs. Celestial created a discernible type through a carefully planned breeding program, and several very strong sires emerged from this who continued the line and added to a quality gene pool in the area.

Alteza Aureate, who finished back in the 1960s, was heard from often during this time by several champions who moved him into fame as a sire.

During the 1960s, a tri bitch named **Antrum Glen Hill Empress** arrived in California from Glen Hill. From a litter sired by Ch. Glen Hill Sayonnara came a Group winning daughter, **Ch. Antrums All Alone**. Bred to the champion-producing Ch. Paraders Reflection, a dog emerged from this combination who would have phenomenal impact on the picture of the Collie in California, and whose influence would spread

Ch. Antrum's All Alone, handled by Frank Ashbey for owners Mr. & Mrs. W.H.D. Hornaday, winning Best of Winners under Judge Donna Hausman in 1965. (Photo by William Brown)

throughout the country. The dog was **Ch. Antrum's Alltheway II**. He first attracted notice when he took WD at the 1970s National, but it would be in the stud that he would really shine, and his breeder-owner, Louise Hornaday was rewarded for her ingenuity in breeding him.

The handler of Alltheway, Terri Parker, had been successful in creating her own line of Cinderella Collies and now introduced the blood of Alltheway into some of her original stock with rewarding results. Continuing efforts at Cinderella produced several champions, including the CCA RD and Best Puppy **Ch. Cinderellas Thrill Seeker**, sired by the top winning Alltheway II son, **Ch. San Lori MacD**, a dog much admired during this decade.

Another kennel using Ch. Antrum Alltheway II to advantage was the Kanebriar Kennels of Peter and Helga Kane, who had begun producing a string of champions with firm foundations in **Ch. Kanebriar Briquette** and **Ch. Kanebriar Holbrook Halloo**. The Group-winning **Ch. Kanebriar Keynote** and **Ch. Kanebriar Countdown** were names to be reckoned with during this time.

Soreham, the kennel name of Al and Helena Forthal was often in the limelight, particularly with the glamorous sable bitch **Ch. Shoreham Desdemona**.

The Arrowhill dogs during the 1970s were being managed by Sandra Tuttle along with her own Kasan smooths, and the success of both of these families during this period was most impressive. At the 1970 National Specialty, history was made when **Ch. Black Hawk of Kasan** beat out the rough competition for the Best of Breed spot. The impact of this dog both as a winner (multiple Group and Best in Show winner, often Best in Specialty winner) and as a sire (top-producing smooth sire of all time) is legendary even to this day. But the influence of Hawk and Kasan dogs did not overshadow some outstanding roughs through this period, particularly some excellent sires such as **Ch. Arrowhill Oklahoma Tribute, Ch. Jude of Arrowhill, Ch. Advantage of Arrowhill**.

Making good use of some of these individuals and combining them with crosses to the GinGeor family, Gayle Kaye created a strong family with her Chelsea Collies in California, a family duly noted for some outstanding bitches.

GinGeor continued putting out some of the best ones, and several lines were making good use of these bloodlines to help create new families. The important offspring of Ch. GinGeor Bellbrookes Choice and Ch. Jadenes Breeze Along, were now with the blue and tri champions being produced by **Ch. GinGeors Indelible Choice** and **Ch. GinGeors Indelibly Blue**, the heavily coated blue merle who topped the breed at the 1976 National.

The Country Lane Kennels of Buck and Alice Wharton made use of some of the GinGeor dogs at this point adding **Ch. Country Lane GinGeor Sequel** and **Ch. Country Lane GinGeor Patrice** to their growing list of Country Lane champions.

Mrs. Richmond (Bobbee) Fairbanks in South Carolina founded a line of successful individuals during the 1970s carrying the Azalea Hill prefix, crossing offspring of two of the leading sires of the day, Ch. Tartanside The Gladiator and Ch. Two Jays Hanover Enterprise. **Ch. Azalea Hill Top Man**, who finished during the 1970 topped the breed at the 1980 National, and a great number of the Azalea Hills would be Group and Best in Show winners.

The Bandor Kennels in Indiana found a magic formula that worked well during this period. One of the strongest producers was **Ch. GinGeors Waiting Choice**, bred by the Horns, who, when bred to the strong sire Ch. Two Jays Hanover Enterprise produced an abundance of champions to keep the name Bandor in the limelight. They combined the best virtues of both of these families, creating typey individuals with pleasing outlines and expression.

Ch. Azalea Hill's Magnum Force, handled by Wade Burns, winning BIS under Judge Richard Greathouse. Presenting the trophy is M.V. Wendell. Owned by Mrs. Richmond Fairbanks (breeder) and Mr. & Mrs. Charles Rhoad. (Photo by Kathleen Kidd)

Ch. Azalea Hills Mr. Christopher winning BIS under Judge Roy Ayres with handler George Schlinker. (Photo by Morry Twomey)

The Briarhill dogs of Judy Klosterman quickly gained recognition as a family of individuals with outstanding style and showmanship. The good producing **Ch. Briarhill Quicksilver** (by Lick Creeks Pizazz) would produce some outstanding winners by Ch. Tartanside the Gladiator and Ch. Ravetts The Silver Meteor and move her into the realm of a top-producing bitch. A tricolor from this combination, **Ch. Briarhill Solo,** became the top-winning bitch in the country in 1976. **Ch. Briarhill High Voltage** was a multiple Group winning blue merle who made quite a name for himself as an outstanding showdog, while **Ch. Briarhill Glen Hill Sky High**, co-owned with Glen Hill became one of the outstanding sires for the family.

In upper New York State, the Clarion Kennels of Judie Evans was gaining strength. The 1969 winner, **Ch. Kemricks Silver Satin** served as a solid foundation bitch. **Ch. Clarions Midnight Sky** was RD at the '73 National, and the list of champions with the Clarion prefix continued to grow. **Ch. Valley Views Whirlaway** and **Ch. Clarions Nightrider** (by

Ch. Briarhill Glen Hill Sky High owned by Judy Klosterman, bred by her and the author. He is grandsire to top-producing stud of all time, Ch. Tartanside Th'Critics Choice. This blue merle had a great record as a show dog and stud.

Impromptu Ricochet) headed the stud force during these years with each of them adding a goodly number of new champions, specializing in blue merle and tricolors. The style and elegance of the Clarions dogs seemed to emerge from the combination of these two sires and made them a most distinctive and discernible family.

Still farther north in New York State, not far from Niagara Falls, the Marnus Kennels continued in their pursuit of excellence, and the 1970s proved rewarding to them as several new Marnus champions completed their titles. **Ch. Marnus Kelly's Blues,** bred by them and owned by Shirley Dowski Meger, was WB at the '71 National, while **Marnus Night Traces** took WB at the '74 event.

Ch. Valley Views Whirlaway taken in 1972 at the age of 7½. (Photo courtesy of Clarion Collies)

The impact of Ch. HiVu the Invader was still prevalent at the HiVu Kennels where sons and grandsons continued to keep his name in the forefront. The continuation of his offspring, combined often with the blood of Ch. Glen Hill Full Dress served as a very workable cross complement. The tricolor **Ch. HiVu Valiant** became a noteworthy sire for them along with **Ch. HiVu the Intruder.**

The sire of Ch. HiVu the Invader, Ravettes Wayside Traveler, who was bred by Rose and George Soellner, was found in many pedigrees, and the Soellners used him as successfully as anyone for the continuation of their Wayside Collies. **Ch. Wayside Windjammer, Ch. Wayside Star Spangled** and **Ch. Wayside Southern Man** kept Waysides name at the fore.

From the original triumvirate of the Glen Hill sire line came the fourth in the line in **Ch. Glen Hill Star Ride Stardust** and during the 1970s, Glen Hill took a turn. Having successfully produced a great number of champions in sable and tricolor, a blue daughter of Ch. Glen Hill Full Dress, by the name of **Ch. Glen Hill Blue Dress,** created a new branch to this family in the blue merle color. New champions were now sprouting up in all colors and the strength of the line continued on strongly.

The use of Ch. Glen Hill Full Dress by the Ravette Kennels of Joyce Avery, scored another plus as two important individuals emerged in **Ch. Ravettes The Silver Meteor** and his sister **Ravettes Midnight Image.** Silver Meteor became a Best in Show winner and sired the aforementioned Ch. Briarhill High Voltage, as well as two 1980 CCA winners, **Ch. Carnwaths Evergreen** (BB 1981 CCA) and **Ch. Carnwaths The Great Pretender** (BOB CCA 1982). Ravettes Midnight Image, when bred to Ch. Tartanside the Gladiator produced **Ch. Glen Hill Ravette Review,** the sire of the impressive West Coast sire **Ch. Asil Who's Who** and **Ravettes Tar N' Feather,** dam of the champion producing **Ch. Tartanside Heir Apparent** and **Ch. Pattimacs Lion in Winter.**

A tail male line of champions beginning from Ch. Royal Rock

Gamblin Man right on down through Ch. Royal Rock Brass Tacks, gained great momentum for Royal Rock and Janet Leek, as successful decade for them. **Ch. Royal Rock Touch of Brass** was RB at the 1976 CCA .

The purchase of **Ch. Gerthstrone Parader Encore** from Steve Field was a wise move on the part of Dot Gerth, who used this dog and combined him with the bloodlines of the early Gerthstones tracing back to Ch. Socrates. Champion after champion seemed to evolve from this combination.

The merging of Starberry and Bobbi Jeans kennels with the marriage of Sally Barbaresi and Robert Futh brought gratifying results during the 1970s, with dogs like **Ch. Starberry St. Patrick**, WD and the 1971 CCA, and the Shenanigan's daughter **Ch. Starberry String of Pearls** later in the decade.

Ch. Lick Creeks Drummer Boy scored a BOV at the 1970 CCA in Massachusetts, keeping the Lick Creek name up in lights, but he would be hard pressed for the spotlight by his kennelmate **Ch. Lick Creeks Pizazz**, a dog much in demand as a sire. Profuse coats and great substance could always be found in this family, and these virtues were there for the taking.

When Ch. Shenstones Touch of Gold was bred back to her sire Ch. Tartanside the Gladiator, the Shenstone Kennels of Ted and Joyce Dowling hit a nick that seem to work. The best bitch in this litter, **Ch. Shenstones Gold Nugget**, steered the direction of the Shenstone dogs to a family known for their overall type and expression.

The Shadaglen Kennels of Joyce Berk and Bonnie Young in Washington were well established by the 1970s and Dick Moffat's Glenecho dogs, linebred on these and crossed with Ch. Tartanside the Gladiator were also gaining momentum. **Ch. Glenecho Set The Style**, by Gladiator became an important sire in the Pacific Northwest.

With the purchase of **Ch. Wickmere Cotillion** by Linda Sanders, the Shamont Kennels began. Cotillion bred to Ch. Wickmere Battle Chief gave Linda the good producing **Ch. Shamont Sabrina**. Sabrina was bred to Ch. Baymars Coming Attraction and **Ch. Berridale Macdega Mediator**, and while these two breedings produced a multitude of champions, three of the most noteworthy individuals were the Best in Show winning **Ch. Shamont Top Billing**, the CCA WB in 1976 **Shamont Sand Castles** and the CCA Winners Dog of 1978 **Ch. Shamont Stormalong**.

Working quietly on a small scale but having great success down in Texas during this time was LuAnn Young, whose Younghaven dogs were proving quite consistent in type. From a foundation in the Gerthstone family, crosses to Ch. Two Jays Hanover Enterprise and others proved most successful for this family.

Twin Creeks was a kennel name that seemed to attach itself to more and more champions each year. The first Best in Show white carried Twin Creeks in **Ch. Twin Creeks First Frost**. Two top-winning bitches during the decade also came from this kennel in **Ch. Twin Creeks Scrube Duba Do** and **Ch. Twin Creeks Scrumptious**. At the end of the decade, **Ch. Twin Creeks True Grit** appeared on the scene, but his impact would hit during the 1980s.

The 1980s
In studying the history of and influence of kennels during this time period, it is always helpful to look at the results of the Hawkins system. This is a method of determining or rating the top-winning Collies. It was developed by lifelong Collie enthusiast and breeder-judge Robert Hawkins. His rating method is used, among others, to determine the top 10 winning Collies each year.

In looking at the 1980s, one cannot help but be impressed by the impact of the Twin Creeks Collies. At the 1980 CCA Specialty Show, a lovely tri bitch with the appropriate name of **Ch. Lee Aire's Amazing Grace** took the Best of Opposite Sex award. Prior to this win, she had produced a litter sired by Ch. Lochloman Interlock, a son of Ch. ViLee's Myster Mac. From the litter, a sable male was named **Twin Creeks True Grit**. He finished quickly and, by 1980, took the award for top sire in the country. He maintained this position for four consecutive years, giving up this position to his inbred son **Ch. Twin Creeks Postscript** who held the position for two years. This no doubt fostered the Housers ability to retain the Breeder of the Year award for eight of the ten years in this decade. Champions came in a variety of colors and in both varieties and the phenomenal success of this kennel was dramatic.

Another strong siring force during this period was from the Tartanside family, with **Am. and Can. Ch. Tartanside Heir Apparent** garnering the top spot as a sire in 1986 and his son, **Am. and Can. Ch. Tartanside Apparently,** taking it in 1987 and 1989. Ch. Apparently, like his grandsire Ch. Tartanside the Gladiator had influence both as sire and show dog. He took the coveted Best of Breed honors at the 1985 National Specialty, while his younger full brother **Ch. Tartanside Presentation** took the Winners Dog honors at the same event. While the strength of the sire line remained constant during this period, the success of the bitches was also strong. **Ch. Tartanside Fairwind Fantasy** would wind up with nine champions, eight of them sired by Heir Apparent. Her offspring would continue to make significant contributions to the gene pool. While greatly interested in breeding to Ch. Heir Apparent and Appar-

Am. & Can. Ch. Tartanside Heir Apparent. (Photo by Krook)

Ch. Tartanside Th' Critics Choice, owned and bred by John Buddie, is the Top Producing Sire of All Time as of 1996. (Photo by Krook)

ently, the siring abilities of **Ch. Tartanside Spellbound** and **Ch. Tartanside Th' Critics Choice** were also quite noteworthy, as the champion lists continued to grow.

Often sitting in runner-up position for breeder of the year during this 10-year span, we find Rita Stanzik. Her Executive prefix was founded strongly on blood of **Braedoon Halleulejah** a daughter of Ch. Roni-Lee's Bold Adventure. This bitch would quickly move into position as one of the all-time top-producing bitches in breed history. Successive crosses to the Twin Creeks family and others gave Executive a number of champions including the CCA 1989 winner, **Executive Halo of Hearts**.

A blue bitch by the name of **Ch. Starr's Blue Jeans** brought great recognition to the Starr Kennels of Pam and Lou Durazzano. This exciting blue bitch came out at the 1986 National Specialty Show to take her Best of Breed placement, following up with a Best of Opposite Sex in 1984, and returning one more time to win Best of Breed at the 100th Anniversary show of the CCA. Her daughter, sired by Ch. Tartanside Heir Apparent, **Ch. Starr's Uptown Girl** was Winners Bitch at the same event. As a producer, Blue Jeans was equally impressive and was the top producing dam in 1987. The Starr Collies cultivated a strong foundation from her champion sons and daughters by both Heir Apparent and Ch. City View's Advantage.

The sire of Blue Jeans, Karavel Sudden Wyndfall was owned by Marrianne McDonough, Libby Lewitt, and Dory Samuels. His sire, **Lick Creeks Hellzapoppin'**, was owned by Dory Samuels, whose Royal Guard Collies in Florida had quietly been guarding some of the best of the Lick Creek line. Dory's management of these lines, and her own ingenuity in breeding her Royal Guard dogs, kept a quality source open to the South.

Blue bitches seemed to be popular during the 1980s. **Ch. Barksdale Early Light** from Nancy McDonald's Barksdale Collies was Best of Opposite Sex at the '81 National, and though shown sparingly through the period she made quite a name for herself. Sired by Ch. Wickmere Silver Bullet, **Ch. Barksdale Bullseye, Ch. Highfield Whispering Hope** and **Barksdale Best Dressed** were her littermates.

The year 1984 was a great one for **Ch. Twin Creeks Beanies Best** as he became the #1 Collie in the nation. This handsome male was bred by Carol and Sue Fabeck, who earned the title of Breeder of the Year during that period. Myriah and Westwend were kennel names to notice.

Also gaining fast recognition was a dog named **Twin Oaks Joker's Wild**, bred and owned by Mary Benjamin. Sired by Rita Stanzik's **Ch. Executive Table Stakes**, this youngster doubled the blood of Ch. Twin Creeks Post Script, and like his double grandsire held the position for top sire in 1988. Twin Oaks Collies founded a strong family on this dog.

The Highcroft Collies were also making quite a name for themselves in this decade, and seemed to hit a number of "nicks" that made it work well for them. **Ch. Highcroft Double Dare**, a son of Ch. Twin Creeks Postscript sired well for them, and **Highcroft Quintessence** eventually took honors as top-producing bitch.

Early crosses of the HiVu and Two Jay's families resulted in the production of **Ch. Candray Concord** for the George Wanamakers. This dog set the stage and direction for generations of Candray champions to follow. **Ch. Candray Mardi Gras**, Winners Bitch at the 1985 CCA Specialty, 1988, showed the strength of this family.

The Pebblebrook Kennels of Peter and Marian Liebsh were constantly in the winners circle during the 1980s. **Ch. Twin Creeks Damn Yankee** sired well for them, and several champions boasted the Pebblebrook prefix. In 1987, **Ch. Pebblebrook Twin Creeks Affair** was Best of Opposite Sex at the National Specialty. This elegant sable was owned by Maret Halinen, and through her, generations of Collies under the Napier prefix would continue to appear. In 1987, the Winners Dog at the National Specialty was **Napier's Foolish Affair**, while **Napier's Bejeweled** was Reserve Winners Bitch at the '88 event.

Val Nessetta and her Paradice Kennel, though not new to Collies, seemed to hit a peak in the 1980s. A series of blue winners, such as **Paradice's Macho Man, Ch. Paradice's Moonlight Lady, Ch. Paradice's Lady O**, and **Ch. Paradice's It's my Party**, but it was the sable male **Ch. Paradice's Along Came Jones**, who seemed to be the most influential on a long-term basis. Although he met an untimely death at a young age, this dog sired extremely well for Paradice and other kennels as well.

Ch. Glen Hill Flashback (so named for his resemblance to his illustrious ancestor Ch. Glen Hill Full Dress) was one of the leading sires for Glen Hill, a successful kennel now into its fourth decade of breeding—and still going strong. Few kennels can claim this distinction as often times the breeding well seems to run dry, but this family, still holding to the original tail male line, continued to prosper. During these four decades, Pat Starkweather not only had time to judge both in the United States and abroad, but also to carry on the Glen Hill line of Collies, write three editions of her book *All About Collies*, and to speak at seminars.

When the beautiful **Ch. Glen Hill Blue Lace** was bred to her full brother **Ch. Glen Hill Prototype**, the exquisite **Glen Hill Dorian Gray** was the result. This breeding intensified the gene pool back to all of the earlier Glen Hill greats: Nobleman, Emperor Jones, Full Dress, Star Ridge Stardust, and it is no wonder that Dorian would prove to be a cue to that treasure. He in turn would produce Ch. Glen Hill Flashback, a major contributor to the family as well. His daughter, **Ch. Glen Hill Campus Cutie**, would continue the line for future generations.

Ch. Clarions Light Up The Sky, a son of **Ch. Clarions Nightrider** quickly made a place for himself as the top blue merle sire in the breed for several years. The CCA Best Puppy Winner **Ch. Clarion the Platinum Minx** and **Ch. Clarions Too Much Heaven** were two of his influential daughters at Clarion. Clarion continued to lead the field of blues through this decade with several new champions wearing the Clarion colors. The impact of both Ch. Clarions Nightrider and Ch. Light Up The Sky helped to hold the *look* that was working its way into its third decade.

A son of Ch. Clarions Light Up The Sky, **Ch. Impromptu Banner Still Waves**, did indeed carry the banner of Impromptu as he took Winners Dog honors at the 1984 National. The blue **Ch. Impromptu the Silver Bullet** also finished during this period for the Schwartzs.

Another family was quickly gaining recognition as a source of winning blue merle Collies and that was the Donnybrooke family of Collies owned by Barbara Linder and Linda Simmons. Begun in the 1960s, and producing the 1976 RD at the National Specialty in **Donnybrooke Lucky Lindy**, this team continued on an even keel of producing good ones, but the 1980s seem to be their pinnacle years if numbers are used as measurement. Two blue bitches made a great impact, consistently sharing Breed wins at the specialties: **Ch. Donnybrook Silverjeans** and **Ch. Donnybrook Afterhours Silk**, who was BOS at the CCA in 1989. This, in addition to a host of other champions bearing their prefix.

The 1980s started off with a bang for the Royal Rock Kennels as **Royal Rock Minstrel Boy** took WD honors at the National Specialty that year. In the mid 1980s, the handsome **Ch. Royal Rock Keyman** would make quite an impression and sire well.

Marion Durholz was having a heyday in the eighties. From her early, rough bitch lines came a dog called **Jancada North Country Flash**, and using him with the sable **Ch. Pattimacs Lion in Winter**, whom Marion purchased, proved a noteworthy cross for her. **Ch. Jancada Fairwind Martini Blue, Ch. Jancada Blue Skies, Ch. Jancada Autumn Haze, Ch. Jancada Whispering Wind**, were just a handful of the many Jancada bitches who finished their titles at this time.

Ch. Two Jay's First Sensation brought a resurgence to the Two Jays family of dogs, as this dog drew much attention at the '86 National. **Ch. Two Jays Silver Frost, Ch. Two Jays Mountain Man** and **Ch. Two Jays Second Chance** would finish and join the stud force for the forthcoming generations of champions.

When **Ch. Jil Chris Liberty Legend** took WD at the National in

Left: Ch. Incandescent Blackgold, owned and bred by Janine Walker-Keith.

Right: Ch. Incandescent Limited Edition, owned by Janine Walker-Keith. Bred by Janine Walker-Keith and Monica Stinson.

1981, Joe Koehler hit a stride which piloted his dogs in the right direction, and several Jil-Chris winners would follow. Legend returned to the National in 1989 to take Breed honors at the prestigious event.

The Incandescent Collies of Janine Walker-Keith were having a good time in the 1980s. Early winners included **Ch. Incandescent Gold Rush, Ch. Incandescent Black Gold** and **Ch. Incandescent Intrepid Image,** but it would be **Ch. Incandescent Limited Edition** who would be the shining star, creating a most enviable record as one of the top winners of the breed.

The Collies in Arizona were well represented by the hard work of John Kavanaugh throughout this period. He finished many champions under the Kingsmark prefix, several of them making quite a splash in the Group rings. Also in Arizona, Lynn Davis and her Asil dogs were attracting much attention and interest.

Having had great success in the '60s and '70s, it is no surprise to see the Marnus prefix still finding its way to the winners circle during the 1980s. The end of the 1980s brought forth a really special dog for them in **Ch. Marnus Gold Medalist,** who, though finishing during this period, would take top honors at the National in 1990 and go on to become a Best In Show winner as well.

The Future

From the early breed history of the Collie coming to America to this look at the Collie through the last four decades, one is able to view a pattern of transition that leads to the constant pursuit of excellence. The transition that any breed undergoes is often a result of the strength of various families and prominent sires. As the new blood of these individuals or lines is introduced, we change.

As the '90s commenced, carryover of prior breed strength continued. In 1990, **Ch. Twin Oak Jokers Wild** held the top sire position, while his son **Ch. Marnus Gold Medalist** topped the Nation's Specialty. The top winning Collie that year was **Ch. Grandhill Heirloom**, a daughter of Ch. Tartanside Apparently, one of the top sires during the late 1980s. She was BOS at the National the same year. With Joker at the helm, Mary Benjamin and her Twin Oaks Collies also received the coveted Breeder of the Year award.

Many of the prominent names of the past continued moving forward with new dogs taking over the eminent positions. At Glen Hill, a new star was on the rise with **Ch. Glen Hill The All American**, who became the #1 dog in the country for 1991. **Ch. Glen Hill Knight O' Round Table** is quickly making a name for himself as sire of note, with some top-winning offspring to his credit.

In the top producing categories, the stud force at Tartanside continues to be prolific, as **Ch. Tartanside Th' Critics Choice** moves into position as top sire for several years at the beginning of the decade and eventually breaks all records as the Top Producing Rough sire of all time. **Ch. Tartanside Animation** vies the kennel record of **Ch. Tartanside Fairwind Fantasy** by producing seven champions, with several others well on the way. A daughter, by Critics Choice, **Ch. Tartanside Imagination** takes BOW and Best Puppy at the '91 National.

Ch. Executive's The Equalizer, who had produced well for Executive during the '80s, produces an impressive sire in **Ch. Fury's the Spirit of Legends**, and Executive introduces **Ch. Executive Gemstone Tycoon** into the family, which appears to be a most successful *nick.*

The Pebblebrook family of Pete and Marian Liebsch have phenomenal success with three National winners, **Ch. Pebblebrook Show Biz**, **Ch. Pebblebrook Intrigue**, and **Ch. Pebblebrook Show Bits.**

Clarion continues to grow in strength with **Ch. Clarions's Color My World**, a son of Ch. Paradice's Along Came Jones producing elegant youngsters and holding the type.

Though champions were not new to the Overland family of Collies, Mike and Marcie Fine seemed to strike gold in the '90s, adding the illustrious Ch. to a multitude of exciting youngsters.

Ch. Executive's Ride the High Wind, top-winning and top-producing stud, owned by Ria Stanzik. (Photo by K. Booth)

Joyce Weinman also found great success at the turn of this decade and her kennel name was soon a common prefix found in the winners circles. **Ch. Venessee Sculptured in Blue** and **Ch. Venessee Midnite Express** were making their way to the top sires list.

The Starr and Countryview Collies of the Durazzanos and Danny Cardoza were also attracting national attention, **Ch. Sealore Grand Applause,** owned by Judy and Annette Stringer topped the 1992 National Specialty. The Starr-owned and Candray-bred **Ch. Candray Brilliance** was Winners Bitch at the same show. Pam and Lou Durazzano along with Dan Cardoza shared the Breeder of the Year award with Joyce Weinman of Venessee.

Deborah Falk and her Aurealis Collies in the Pacific Northwest had a heyday as well. **Ch. Aurealis Silver Screen** topped the breed at the 1991 National Specialty, under Judge Pat Starkweather. In the mid-nineties, Debbie Falk and Marian Stempler were having a great winning streak with their **Ch. Aurealis Charidan Regina.** The beautiful tricolor daughter of Ch. Aurealis Silver Screen was knocking them dead, with breed and Group wins. Also from the Pacific Northwest came the 1994 Breeder of the Year, Marie Markovitch and her Markos family of Collies.

Highcroft Quintessence broke all records as the top-producing bitch of all time with 14 champions to keep the Highcroft name forever etched in Collie history.

While the name Lisara has always been associated with some of the finest smooths bred during the last 25 years, the rough counterparts have been in the winners circle as well. During the 1990s, a cluster of outstanding individuals, such as **Ch. Lisara Chasing Rainbows, Ch. Lisara's Love Dove,** and **Lisara Love Hugg** came to mind.

California homebreds from the kennel of Linda Robbins and Barbara O'Keefe were gaining titles regularly, but among the most impressive would have to be the blue **Ch. Gambits Freeze Frame,** Best of Opposite Sex at the '92 National, Best of Breed at the 1995 National Specialty show.

Nancy McDonald and the Barksdales seemed to have come up with a formula for producing Group winning bitches. From her first champion in the '70s, **Ch. HiVu Winover Glitter,** to her '90s Group winners, **Ch. Barksdale Busybody** and **Barksdale Blush,** typey Collies were becoming synonymous with the kennel name.

Debbie Holland, taking time between handling assignments was able to develop the kennel name Fantasy into a kennel to be reckoned with. The Fantasy champion list continues to grow.

When **Ch. HiCrest Knock On Wood** took Winners Dog honors at the '82 National, it was obvious that Joe Reno would continue to knock on the door with some good ones. The early '90s brought about a bevy of blue and tri bitches carrying the HiCrest prefix which would gain great attention from fellow breeders. Elegant and heavy coated, these girls were followed by some impressive male champions as well.

And the beat goes on. As we approach the 21st Century it seems that the breed is in good hands.

Ch. Barksdale Blush, winner of the 1996 Pedigree Award as # 1 Collie in the nation, owned by Nancy McDonald. (Photo by Millknock Images.)

The Parader Story
By Gayle Kaye

During the war years, a kennel was started by an eager young man just out of college. He not only wanted to create a line of Collies, but he wanted to make a difference. Ultimately, his contributions were of such significance, that the breed would never again be the same. Not only are the effects still with us 55 years later, but it is safe to say that as long as there are Collies, this man's name will always be known for his great accomplishments and major influence.

On January 15, 1943, an event occurred in Council Bluffs, Iowa, that would forever alter the history of the Collie. On a cold wintry night, a tawny ball of fur was born, along with seven other puppies. They were a blend of the day's top Collie families. A large, dark male puppy, with a huge shawl collar, stood out from the very beginning. Even the rankest amateur would not have missed "Lad."

So began the story of **Ch. Silver Ho Parader**—a dog who would go on to set Collie records never before dreamed of by a young, unknown Collie fancier named Steve Field. Every decade or so, there are certain predestined dogs who, because of their genetic dominance of desirable characteristics, exert a tremendous and lasting influence on the breed. Silver Ho Parader was one of those dogs. Remarkably, not only did he spearhead the Parader family of dogs, but he set into motion one of the most dominant sire lines in existence. He would begin a series of consecutive generations of studs unlike anything ever seen in the history of the breed. This was the beginning of Parader Collies; a kennel that would become synonymous for more than 50 years for great siring ability, endurance, strength and temperament. However, the story actually began some years prior to Lad's birth.

Ch. Silver Ho Parader, owned and bred by Steve Field. (Photo courtesy of John Buddie)

Steve Field was raised on a small farm, the youngest of nine children. He was no stranger to dogs, as there was always the typical farm Collie wandering about.

He was influenced early on by two things: a neighbor's purebred Collie who frequently sought his company, and his reading of the Albert Payson Terhune stories. He considered Mr. Terhune his guru. After graduating from college, he decided to embark on a career of raising and showing Collies. His first quest was to find a good bitch. He read every piece of Collie literature he could find and frequently attended dog shows as a spectator. Shortly after beginning his search, a Collie bitch became available in Omaha, Nebraska. She was owned by a couple who had just had an accidental litter from her. On the advice of the noted all-breed handler, Sadie Edminston, Steve decided to purchase her. Sadie had seen the bitch and thought she was a really good one.

Upon the payment of $5, "Lady" became Parader's first official brood bitch named **Lodestone Bandolier II** in honor of her Lodestone ancestors, whom Steve had long admired through kennel brochures. He had been fortunate enough to see both of her parents. Heatherton Pal, her sire, was a heavily coated, white-factored male of Tazewell and Bellefontaine breeding. He traced in tail male to one of the all-time great sires in the breed, **Ch. Future Of Arken**. Her dam, Landmark Lady, was a

One of the breed's foundation sires, Lodestone Landmark, 1929. (Photo courtesy of Gayle Kaye)

quality bitch of Lodestone breeding. She traced in tail male to Future's much underrated full brother, Ch. Cock Robin Of Arken. Steve felt Lady would be a valuable asset not only because of her excellent breeding, but because of her many good qualities. She was a dark, heavily coated sable, with a huge shawl collar—it would turn out that she was white-factored. Her chief attributes were a sound body combined with a long, flat head. She excelled in temperament. Her one noticeable failing was a very high set of ears. All in all, Lady was exactly what he wanted.

Lady was bred two different times prior to the litter that contained Lad. One litter was by Ch. Honeybrook Big Parade, the leading sire of the day. For years, Steve had been following his career and admiring his puppies, who were winning futurities and points at some of the largest shows in the country. This litter produced Steve's first show dog, **Honeybrook's**

Golden Boy. Though he did not finish his championship due to an injury in a dog fight, he would play a key role in future Parader breedings through several of his daughters. Steve realized early in his breeding program that whatever success he would have with Collies, Big Parade would play a significant role. Upon the advice of Ed Pickhardt of Sterling Collies, Lady was bred for her third litter to Ch. Silver Ho Shining Arrow. Shining Arrow was a beautiful sable son of Ch. Honeybrook Big Parade, while his dam, Silhouette of Silver Ho was a lovely tri bitch of Noranda breeding. This breeding culminated in the birth of Lad on that stormy January night.

Ch. Silver Ho Shining Arrow. (Photo courtesy of Gayle Kaye.

Lad was a big upstanding dog with many of the good points of both parents. From his dam he inherited a sturdy body coupled with soundness, and from his sire he inherited a nicely detailed head with beautiful muzzle and expression. Lad excelled in attitude and showmanship. He finished his championship at one year of age and became the first champion bred at Parader. In a 1948 magazine ad, Steve described him as a "dark, reddish sable, mask, shawl collar, heavy year-round coat, exquisite dark eyes with dark haws, clean-cut flat head—a great showman with superlative style and bold affectionate temperament."

It is almost impossible to understand fully or properly evaluate all that Silver Ho Parader has meant to Collie bloodlines for the last 55 years. The majority of today's Collies trace in tail male to Silver Ho Parader through several of his high-quality sons. His influence was equally important on the distaff side of pedigrees. Early in his stud career, it became apparent that he would click with a variety of bitches from diverse bloodlines and that he was going to be dominant for his excellent qualities, of which he had many. It would also appear early on, that he was going to break some records.

Often, in successful breeding, timing is everything. Lad came along at a time when Collie temperaments left much to be desired. His greatest claim to fame was that he consistently improved temperaments throughout his career at stud, as did many of his descendants. Indeed, it is something for which the Parader dogs became famous. He went on to sire 37 champions—a record held for close to 30 years.

Throughout the years, Steve acknowledged that Lad's greatness came from his superior ancestors. He was a descendant of one of the most prolific sire lines of all time, **Ch. El Troubadour Of Arken,** through his two sons **Ch. Future Of Arken** and **Ch. Cock Robin Of Arken** (full brothers). He felt the key to Lad's excellent producing record was his dominance for passing on three particular qualities: temperament (attributed to Ch. Honeybrook Big Parade), expression (attributed to his Arken background) and soundness (attributed to his dam). A bonus was that he could be inbred upon without running the risk of physical weakness or too many faults cropping up.

The next important step in the Parader family was **Ch. Parader's Golden Image,** sired by Silver Ho Parader out of a solid Sterling bitch, Sterling Starsweet. After him, came the impressive winner and top sire, **Ch. Parader's Bold Venture.** He was by Golden Image out of the Silver Ho Parader daughter, Paraders Cinderella. His four-generation pedigree was heavily linebred in all directions to Silver Ho Parader. He was born and bred to produce and produce he did. He came very close to breaking

Ch. Parader's Golden Image.
(Photo courtesy of Gayle Kaye)

his famous grandsire's all-time siring record. From Venture, we come to **Ch. Parader's Country Squire,** whose pedigree was intensively linebred on Silver Ho Parader, with a Saint Adrian cross.

The next great Parader stud, in direct line, was the Squire son **Ch. Paraders Reflection.** Again, he was almost solid Parader breeding, with a cross to Ch. Arrowhill Oklahoma Redman. Redman himself traced many times to Silver Ho Parader. The Reflection son, **Ch. Parader's Kingsmark** was hoped to be next in a long line of productivity. Unfortunately, around

Ch. Parader's Bold Venture, owned and bred by Steve Field. (Photo courtesy of John Buddie)

this time, breeding activities at Parader began to slow down, so Kingsmark's full potential never came to pass. Altogether this unparalleled record, represents five generations of champion, mahogany sable males, all producing 17 or more champions: from Ch. Paraders Reflection (17) to Ch. Parader's Country Squire (24) to Ch. Paraders Bold Venture (35) to Ch. Paraders Golden Image (24), and finally back to Silver Ho Parader (37). When put into proper perspective, the record becomes even more significant. Out of the top 10 Rough Collie sires of all time, *all* trace to Ch. Silver Ho Parader in tail male. Out of the top 10 Collie sires, four were Parader-owned and bred. Parader influence was equally remarkable in the smooth Collie. Ch. Black Hawk Of Kasan, the all-time top sire with 78 smooth champions, traced in direct male line to Silver Ho Parader, via Arrowhill Ace High.

While Parader was a kennel that concentrated heavily on the males, the bitches were not ignored. Though none came close to the producing records of the Parader males, several, such as **Parader's Cinderella, Parading Lady, Ch. Parader's Pamela, Parader's Royal Countess, Paraders Starlite** and **Parader's Golden Baby Doll**, produced multiple champion litters. Because the Parader studs produced so spectacularly, nobody seemed to notice Steve's good producing bitches. However, this did not prevent many new breeders from purchasing Parader bitches with which to start their kennels.

Although this kennel was known mostly for its studs and their breeding records, Parader was also known for some very impressive winning at the dog shows. This kennel truly did it all. The show record began in 1944 with the championship of Ch. Silver Ho Parader and culminated in 1979 when the last champion bred by Steve, **Ch. Paraders Regal Lancer,** finished his title. Over the years, there was never a shortage of all-breed Best In Show wins, Group wins or Specialty Best Of Breeds. While today's Collie fanciers are well aware of Ch. Silver Ho Parader's remarkable siring abilities, few are aware of a splendid show career that ended with two all-breed Best In Show wins. The kennel's greatest show winner was **Ch. Parader's Bold Venture.** Not only did he win Best Of Breed at the National Specialty twice, but he was a multiple Best In Show and Group winner as well. In 1950, Steve was the breeder of the Best Of Opposite Sex, Winners Dog and Winners Bitch at the CCA National Specialty. At the 1965 National Specialty, he was the breeder and owner of both the Winners dog and Winners bitch. Wins at major shows were so numerous that to attempt a list would be an overwhelming task. Sometimes the only way to prevent a Parader win was to ask Steve to judge. Accompanying all the impressive show wins were numerous "Breeder of the Year" awards from the National breed club.

Altogether, more than 60 champions were bred by this kennel. Ultimately, Parader studs would be responsible for well over several hundred Collie champions. There is no way to estimate how many kennels have been influenced by this family of dogs. Nor is there any possibility of determining how many breeders received their start compliments of Parader stock. The influence is so far reaching that, during a span of 50 years, Parader dogs and bitches had a major impact on almost all Collie families. The Parader dogs came along at a time when temperament and soundness were desperately needed in the breed. They excelled in temperament and were known far and wide for their soundness, profuse coats and beautiful faces. Additionally, they were an extremely hardy family of Collies, known for being "good doers," as well as "easy keepers." Steve believed strictly in the principle of survival of the fittest and he practiced it relentlessly. He did not have the time nor the energy to waste on weaknesses and shortcomings.

Steve's personal contributions to the breed have been numerous and varied. He joined the CCA in 1946 and served the club in many different capacities, which included president, vice-president and director-at-large. He served on different committees, such as the Education Committee and the Breed Standard Committee. Not only was he a popular judge for more than four decades, but he was an accomplished writer and lecturer. His 40 years of teaching high school biology stood him in good stead. He has never been hesitant to share his wealth of knowledge. To this day, he not only greatly misses the dogs, but he loves talking about the good old days. His knowledge and understanding of the breed have been so remarkable that it would be extremely difficult to imagine the

Collie breed without his influence. He has rightly been called and will forever remain, **Mr. Collie.**

THE STORY OF TARTANSIDE

With grandparents who immigrated from Scotland and Ireland, it was no surprise to find that the Buddie household was always filled with Collies. It was in the early 1960s that a young John Buddie found a photo of his father's white Collie and a second-place ribbon from the Bloomingdale's dog show of 1929. Though it was nothing more than a "pet show," the idea of showing dogs intrigued John and, during the next few years, he spent all of his free time from school reading up on dogs and dog shows.

The name Tartanside came from John's fascination with the Scottish clans and the various *tartans*.

Tartanside Tiara would be the bitch who would lay the foundation. Sired by Ravettes Wayside Traveler out of Tartanside HiVu Classic, she combined the best of the families behind her. She had the long elegant head of her maternal grandsire Ch. Glen Hill Full Dress, and the beautifully rounded muzzle, and well-finished foreface of Bellbrookes Master Pilot and Ch. GinGeor Bellbrookes Choice. John's admiration for these three sires led him consistently to play their offspring back and forth in the creation of the Tartanside family.

Tiara's first litter produced two champions: a lovely tricolor bitch by the name of **Ch. Westgates Trace O'Tartanside** and **Ch. Tartanside the Gladiator.** "The Gladiator" would quickly become the foundation sire of the line and of several new families cropping up. The long head with beautifully turned muzzle, sweet eye and expression, coupled with a distinctive red mahogany color, set this proud-moving dog apart from the others. Finishing handily, he became one of the top-winning specials in the country. At the end of his specials career, he had amassed more than 100 Best of Breed wins, including a horde of specialties. For several years, he had been awarded the "Best in the East" award by *Collie Review* magazine; he was a multiple winner of the working Group, and amassed two all-breed Best in Show awards. But, among his highest honors would have to have been the three National Specialty awards—making him one of a very select group of individuals to achieve this honor. He broke more records at the CCA when he became the first Collie in breed history to top the breed from the Veterans Class in the largest entry of Collies ever assembled to that time. This was proof also of his lasting quality.

The early litters by this dog gave quick proof of his dominance as a sire. The very virtues that elevated him into a top-winning special were the characteristics that he seemed most prepotent for. The combination of beautiful head planes and rounded muzzle coupled with the correctly placed and shaped dark eyes became the distinctive features of his progeny. These were the same virtues that John wished to incorporate into the Tartanside breeding program, and which he wished to perpetuate in forthcoming generations.

In one of his earliest litters Gladiator produced a pair of champion tricolor sisters in **Ch. Tartanside Rosecrest Rani** and **Ch. Tartanside Japada Jasmine,** the latter beginning her show career with RWB at the 1973 CCA and ending her show career as the dam of five champions.

A beautiful Gladiator daughter named **Ch. Shenstones Touch of Gold** was bred back to her sire, with the choice male puppy returning to Tartanside, he being **Ch. Tartanside The Inheritor.** He, in turn, sired another CCA winner in **Ch. Aurealis Skylarking,** RWD at the 1979 event.

When the beautiful **Ch. Honeybuns Brown Sugar** was bred to Gladiator, the choice male pup in that litter was co-owned with Tartanside and the breeder Shirley Dowski, and this male would become **Ch. Honeybuns Blaze of Tartanside,** WD and BOW at the 1976 CCA— a dog which went on to become a Group winner.

By the age of eight, he was tied for Top Producing sire in breed history siring 44 rough and five smooth champions—a title he maintained for several years. His offspring won some of the highest honors and biggest shows in the country, but more importantly, they became foundations

From left: Ch. Tartanside Apparently; Andreas; Ch. Tartanside the Candidate; Ch. Tartanside Th' Critics Choice; Raleigh; Ch. Tartanside The Proclamation.

Left: Ch. Tartanside Rhapsody. Right: Ch. Tartanside Spellbound. (Photos courtesy of John Buddie)

Left: Am. & Can. Ch. Tartanside Apparently. Right: Ch. Tartanside Fringe Benefit. (Photos courtesy of John Buddie)

for some of the top kennels in the country today. His daughters had a great *nicking* capability, and seemed to fuse with a variety of other strains and families. Gladiator currently ranks in fifth position as a top sire in breed history.

As he was approaching old age, **Ravettes Tar N' Feathers**, who John considered to be one of the Gladiator's best daughters, was leased and bred to him, and the male puppy who resulted in this litter would be the next great producer in this prolific tail male line. This handsome sable was **Am. and Can. Ch. Tartanside Heir Apparent**. He was one of the first "puppy flyers" for Tartanside gaining his title with five majors at 10 months, but more importantly this dog became the real key to the Gladiator legacy, quickly proving himself to be Gladiator's top-producing son. He too would prove dominate for the beautiful expression his family was becoming known for. Numerically, he sired 22 American champions with a great many in Canada as well, but more important than the numbers was the definitive producing ability of his offspring. Some of the top producers in the history of the breed were sired by him, and many of his daughters showed strength in numbers by their champion get. Among his offspring were several Group winners, and in his 22 champions were three National Specialty winners: **Ch. Starrs' Uptown Girl**, B.O.W. at the 100th Anniversary show; **Ch. Tartanside Presentation**, WD at the 1985 event; and, **Am. and Can. Ch. Tartanside Apparently**, Best of Breed at the 1985 show.

Three important sons of Heir Apparent would carry on for Tartanside, and during that time a series of outcross bitches were brought in for them, with an occasional stud-fee puppy taken as well. It was about this time that David Supples joined the force behind Tartanside. The outcross selections to the three Heir Apparent sons were implemented for two reasons: first, to bring in some new blood and hybrid vigor; and second, to enable the crossing back and forth of this wonderful trilogy of Heir Apparent sons without becoming too intensely inbred.

Spellbound was eventually co-owned with Grace Kosub of Dallas, but not before siring **Ch. Tartanside Forest Night**, out of **Ch. Tartanside Fringe Benefit**, an Heir Apparent daughter. Before being exported to Japan, he had left behind 18 champion offspring here in the states, including a Best in South winner.

Am. and Can. Ch. Tartanside Apparently is currently the #9 sire of all time in breed history with 31 champions to his credit. A magnificent show dog, this dark mahogany won some of the largest specialties, along with a score of Group placements, on the East Coast during a brief campaign. But his most imposing win was in 1985 when he topped a formidable field of specials to go Best of Breed at the CCA. **Ch. Tartanside**

the Candidate was the son who would carry his name down through Tartanside winners currently being shown today. **Ch. Grandhill Heirloom**, an Apparently daughter, would continue in her sire's footsteps by taking BOS at the 1990 National, and she was the #1 Collie in the nation during that year.

The third member of the Heir Apparent trilogy was **Ch. Tartanside Th' Critics Choice**, who at this writing is currently the Top Producing Sire of All time with 60 rough and eight smooth champions to his credit. Like the other sires of his family, he continued a pattern of excellence in producing typey individuals who excelled in balance, elegance and, most importantly, the beautiful expression that the line became noted for. Among his 68 champion offspring were several national specialty winners.

The female side of Tartanside was equally as important as the tail male line, and certain bitches played very significant roles. Once able to determine which characteristics the young Heir Apparent was dominant for, an outcross bitch was sought who would, it was hoped, blend in well and continue to produce the desired characteristics. Ch. Tartanside Fairwind Fantasy was the bitch chosen with a smooth clean head with correct stop and backskull and the desired expression. It was no wonder that she nicked well when bred to Ch. Tartanside Heir Apparent. Her first litter produced four puppies and all of them finished. In that group was Ch. Tartanside Apparently. A repeat breeding was done, and once again four puppies resulted and another CCA winner came forth in **Ch. Tartanside Presentation**. Her third and final litter was sired by Ch. Tartanside Th' Critics Choice and only two pups resulted—one being **Ch. Tartanside Fanciful.** Although not producing a great number of puppies, Fantasy produced nine champions from 10 live puppies and through those offspring came a score of new champions.

Linebreeding continued down through the line crossing daughters of the three studs back and forth with great success. The Spellbound daughter, Tartanside Dominique would produce **Ch. Tartanside Wayside Wager** and **Ch. Tartanside Brookwood DeJeVu** when bred to Critics Choice. When another outcross was needed, Tartanside Caress was sent to Ch. Sealore Grand Applause. Caress was sired by Ch. Tartanside the Candidate, an Apparently son, and her dam was an Apparently sister, Ch. Eatons Tartanside Colleen. This was only a partial outcross since the dam of Grand Applause was an Heir Apparent daughter. From this breeding came **Ch. Tartanside Animation,** an exciting puppy who finished her title at eight months and promptly came in season. Her first litter produced **Ch. Tartanside Jubilation, Ch. Tartanside Trailwind Tally Ho, Ch. Tartanside Anticipation** and the CCA winning **Ch. Tartanside Imagi-**

nation. A repeat breeding produced **Ch. Tartanside Destination, Ch. Tartanside Sophistication,** and several others close to the title. To date she is the dam of seven champions.

Her daughter, Ch. Tartanside Imagination is currently the dam of five champions from her first litter.

Since the cross to Grand Applause had worked well the first time, another bitch was sent to him, this one being Tartanside Charisma, she by Ch. Tartanside Th' Critics Choice. This breeding produced the top-winning West Coast dog, **Ch. Tartanside Cinnamon Elijah** and his sisters **Ch. Tartanside Tenacious** and **Ch. Tartanside Unforgettable.**

One of the first champions produced by Ch. Tartanside Heir Apparent was **Ch. Tartanside Fringe Benefit.** Bred to Ch. Tartanside Th' Critics Choice, she produced **Tartanside Inspiration.** In an effort to once again bring in some new blood, she was crossed to Ch. HiVu the Enchantor. This breeding produced the impressive sire **Tartanside Preview.** Crossed with some of the best daughters of Ch. Tartanside Th' Critics Choice, this seems to be another cross that worked. In one of his early litters, he produced the Best In Show winning **Ch. Barksdale Blush** (BOB CCA 1995) and for Tartanside, he sired the important bitch **Ch. Tartanside Ballerina.** When Ballerina was bred back to her grandsire, Critics Choice, she produced the Group-winning **Ch. Tartanside Arabesque** and **Ch. Tartanside Ravishing.**

More than 200 champions have been produced using the sires and dams from this family. Tartanside studs have been awarded the Top Sire of the Year from the CCA in 1974, 1976, 1977, 1978, 1986, 1987, 1989, 1991 and 1993.

While breeding on a very limited scale, this kennel has served as a source of quality for almost 30 years.

THE STORY OF GLEN HILL

When the Glen Hill line of Collies was founded, I (then Pat Shryock) lived in a gray stone Victorian manor house on the classy Philadelphia Main Line. The stone gateposts to the place read Glen Hill 1881. A long drive lined with rhododendron led from the gates to the gabled old house. It was somewhat spooky, somewhat like Manderley in Daphne DuMaurier's great novel, *Rebecca.*

There in the early 1950s, I began to raise Collies. I had fallen in love with the breed when, as a child, I read the books of Albert Payson Terhune, such as *Lad: A Dog.* A dream of someday winning at Westminster in New York was a guidepost. As will be seen, this dream came true.

Ch. Tartanside Cinnamon Elijah.
(Photo courtesy of John Buddie)

Ch. Tartanside Destination, owned by
Pat Breuer. Diane Steel handling for
Judge J.D. Jones. (Photo by Patty
Sosa)

At this time, many notable kennels were within easy driving distance of Haverford, Pennsylvania, the setting of Glen Hill. And drive I did, visiting the famous Eastern breeders and soaking up information. The breeders, Mrs. Browning of Tokalon, Mary Beresford of Poplar, Bill Van Dyke of Honeybrook, Mrs. Ilch (owner) and Mike Kennedy (manager) of Bellhaven were gracious in sharing their knowledge and showing me their dogs.

I concentrated on asking such questions as: Which is the best one? Why is it the best? What do you look for in a show puppy? A show adult? How do you decide which dogs to breed together? and so on and on. These questions were answered most informatively.

I acquired a lovely bitch from Tokalon. This Collie was my wedding present from Dick Shryock. When asked what I wanted I said, "The best Collie bitch we can find. He asked, "Wouldn't you rather have a mink coat?" I answered "NO! The Collie." So we got **Tokalon Merrytime of Glen Hill**. She was lovely but never finished. Her two best progeny by Ch. Hylie Imperial Count each produced notable champions: **Ch. Glen Hill Excellence** and **Ch. Glen Hill Gwenivere**. In breeding Merrytime to the Imperial Count I was seeking to go back to the great Arken line, which was so strongly back of Tokalon. It took another generation, but it did the trick for me. I was on my way.

I also acquired a beautiful little bitch who appealed to me when I saw a weak, underfed, ungroomed pup at a match. To me, she looked like

John Buddie handling his Ch.Tartanside Arabesque, a consistent Best of Breed and Group winner. One of a long line of great bitches. (Ashbey Photography)

real quality. I acquired her and worked to get the puppy in shape. A few months later, this pup went Best of Winners and Best of Opposite Sex at the great Westminster show from the puppy class. She became **Ch. Glen Hill Dainty Miss**. Unfortunately, she died under a year of age. She was one of a long string of bitches who never had a live puppy.

I must have been driven by an indomitable desire to keep on after so many setbacks. Sometimes I think of the poet William Ernest Henley's words:

> Out of the night that covers me,
> Black as the Pit from pole to pole,
> I thank whatever gods may be
> For my unconquerable soul.

About this time I began to think I might create a line of Collies with a distinctive look. I wanted Collies that were upstanding dogs, high-headed, with long arched necks and regal carriage. I also envisioned Collies with long, lean elegant heads combined with well-rounded bodies, and lots of bone. It is hard to get that combination. However, over the years I have perfected that look. It is to be found in Glen Hill Collies of today. In addition, these dogs had to be soundly built and move with grace and drive. How marvelous to have a dream come true.

I was impressed by what I saw from Parader. I pondered on the combination that had produced the great Ch. Silver Ho Parader. That was

Glen Hill—the greystone manor house for which the Glen Hill Collies were named. It was the home in Haverford, Pennsylvania, where the author (then Shryock) lived and started the Glen Hill line. (Photo by Bill Roberts)

a breeding of a son of Ch. Honeybrook Big Parade to a Lodestone bitch. Coincidentally, I took a trip to the West Coast. On the way back I stopped at Steve Field's Parader Kennels. After much dickering, I was able to purchase a wonderful sable eight-month-old puppy. This became **Ch. Paraders Typesetter** a Best of Breed and Group winner. Also on the way home I purchased a little tri bitch puppy at Lodestone. She was **Dreamers Glen Hill Black Tea**. This bitch was later bred to Typesetter.

Black Tea and Typesetter produced a stunning sable male who became the top-winning Working dog in the United States. He was **Ch. Glen Hill Dreamers Nobelman**. This dog finished at Westminster one year, and won Best of Variety there the next year with me handling. He went on to place second in the Group. No rough Collie had placed that high in the Group at Westminster since 1961.

From Ch. Glen Hill Dreamers Nobleman came a string of Collies that in the late 1990s still carry the look I was seeking. There was a great triumvirate of **Ch. Nobleman** to **Ch. Glen Hill Emperor Jones**, to **Ch. Glen Hill Full Dress**. They were father, son and grandson. The blood of Full Dress is still close up in the pedigrees of many important Collies today.

When bred to one of Mary Hutchison's blue champions, Full Dress produced the beautiful **Ch. Glen Hill Blue Dress**. She in turn was the dam of the glorious **Ch. Glen Hill Blue Lace**. When Blue Lace was bred to her full brother, **Ch. Glen Hill Prototype**, history was made. There resulted what I still consider the most beautiful Collie I ever bred— **Glen Hill Dorian Gray**—a magnificent specimen who never finished because he hated the show ring. He may even be the most beautiful dog I ever saw.

Although this dog did not finish, his blood lives on through a tri son, greatly resembling his double grandsire, Ch. Glen Hill Full Dress. This was **Ch. Glen Hill Flash Back**. Flash produced many notable offspring. One litter contained two standouts. One was the adorable bitch **Ch. Glen Hill Campus Cutie**. This little doll took the National Specialty ringside by storm when she won Best American Bred in show and took home the famous Hunter Memorial Trophy. Her litter brother **Ch. Vaughn Glen Hill Ace O Spades** contributed to the line by siring **Glen Hill Floridian** (he of the magnificent coat) and great-producing bitch **Glen Hill Shelana Swan Lake**.

When Floridian was bred to **Glen Hill Promtrotter**, a daughter of Ch. Campus Cutie, another Westminster winner resulted, **Ch. Glen Hill Knight O' Round Table**, BOW Westminster 1950. He was the only sire with two progeny in the Top Ten at the CCA 1995. Also in this litter was a great-coated sable, **Ch. Glen Hill Top of the Line** (the cover dog).

Ch. Glen Hill Dreamer's Nobleman, foundation sire of the Glen Hill line. Note the perfect profile.

Glen Hill Floridian, one of Glen Hill's sire sources. He was the sire of Ch. Glen Hill Knight O'Round Table, Ch. Glen Hill Top of the Line and other champions.

The late Don Starkweather with Glen Hill Floridian as a puppy in 1981.

Ch. Bellvue Spring Lady Ann, three-time Top 10 winner, bred by Sayuri Harami and sired by Ch. Glen Hill Knight O'Round Table.

Glen Hill Pipi Longstocking (sitting) and Ch. Affenloch The Silver Laser, the sire and dam of five champions in one litter—shown with the author. Their get are Ch. Glen Hill Argent Quantum Leap, Ch. Glen Hill Lunar Eclipse, Ch. Glen Hill Ultra Violet Ray, Ch. Glen Hill Fazr To Stun, Ch. Glen Hill Argent Super Nova. They were bred by the author and Mary Dritsas. (Bill Meyer Photo)

Ch. Glen Hill Knight O'Round Table, Westminster winner and sire of BISS winner, Ch. Bellvue Spring Lady Ann. (Photo by Chris Menley)

The bitch, Ch. Glen Hill Campus Cutie, bred to Ch. Twin Creeks Headmaster, produced **Glen Hill Valedictorian,** a sire owned by Glen Hill. In addition to the Collies, I have bred many Boxer champions. This interest came through my late husband, Don Starkweather, one of the pillars of the Boxer breed. I have also bred Shetland Sheepdog champions and brought a great import from England. This was Ch. Lonesome of Nutbush, who finished his championship in one weekend in America.

I have also had some smooth Collie champions. I bought, with Heidi Mendez, a Valedictorian son, **Ch. Foxbride's Peterbilt.** He sired a tri champion, **Ch. Southstar's Majestic Prince,** the dam being top-producer Glen Hill Shelana Swan Lake. Prince is the sire of Mary Dritsas' Ch. Glen Hill As You Like It, Best of Opposite Sex at Westminster. From a son of Ch. Glen Hill The All American, I bred with Helen Williams, two knockout smooths, **Ch. Glen Hill American Hero** and **Ch. Glen Hill Lady Hero.** Glen Hill Shelana Swan Lake is the grandam of today's glorious blue champion **Ch. Glen Hill Ultra Violet Ray.**

So as you see, the lines from the early '60s through the '90s trace to the great triumvirate, Ch. Glen Hill Dreamers Nobleman, Ch. Glen Hill Emperor Jones, Ch. Glen Hill Full Dress, and so on down the line.

Many breeders throughout the country and in other countries have built upon Glen Hill stock. I cannot mention all of them but they include Tartanside, Briarhill, Antrum, HiVu, Sun County. Rubens Pinto in Brazil had a Full Dress daughter who produced 21 champions.

Collie history was changed forever when a stunning youngster was born in Joyce Avery's kennel. This was **Ch. HiVu the Invader,** and his dam was Glen Hill Cloth of Gold, a daughter of Ch. Glen Hill Full Dress. This dog blazed a trail of wins including Winners Dog at the National Specialty Show. His greatest contribution was when he was bred to John Buddie's Tartanside Tiara (a bitch with some Glen Hill blood). From this mating came the incomparable Ch. Tartanside the Gladiator. This sound, solid Collie with melting expression won the CCA Specialty three times. He also became the leading sire of his time and was so widely used that his blood courses through the veins of a large portion of the Collies of today. His grandson, Ch. Tartanside Th' Critics Choice, holds the all-time record for siring champions. He is out of a Glen Hill-Briarhill bitch.

Ch. Glen Hill The All American, winning one of many Specialty shows, with Judge Ted Paul and handler Diane Steel. He was owned and bred by the author and Heidi Mendez. (Photo by Bill Burt)

THE STORY OF FOXBRIDE

In 1979, Berlyn Yorkies was formed by Lynne Fox and Barbara Kilbride. It was a small kennel with high hopes and dreams of producing the Yorkie that had it all. Well, it didn't. It did however, produce several lovely champions.

They believed that they were committed to this breed, but in the back of Barbara's mind, remained the vision of her first and dearest love: her Collie puppy named Tokalon's Lead on MacDuff. Barbara's visit with Mrs. Browning in the '50s and remembrances of those magnificent Collies at Tokalon inspired Berlyn's transformation to Foxbride Collies.

The first page of their history begins on the first rung of a very tall ladder.

They purchased a sable merle rough male son of Ch. Tel Star's Cosmic Capers ex Foxfire Sea Sonnet. He was bred to Wagon Star's Magic Marker, and a 10-week-old tri, smooth puppy bitch was placed in their arms: she became **Ch. Wagon Star's Total Recall**. Her call name was Collette and she was the dam, grandam or great grandam of every Collie produced at Foxbride.

Glen Hill Valedictorian, sire of several champions, including Ch. Glen Hill The All American and Ch. Foxbride's Peterbilt.

With Collette as their sturdy foundation, her first breeding to Ch. Deep River's Time Lord allowed them to skip several rungs with the emergence of **Ch. Foxbride's Skip N' Go Naked**, called Music.

Music produced six champions and was a multiple Best of Breed winner and Group placer.

Not sitting idly by was her litter sister, **Foxbride's Fairly Obvious Who**, who, when bred to **Ch. Charmat's All That Jazz**, produced the incomparable smooth **Ch. Foxbride's McLaughlan**, called Max, and his specialty winner litter sister **Ch. Foxbride's Boogie On Down**, called Ria. Max, a puppy flyer, a teenage idol, now an admired senior citizen with more than 44 champions to his credit, provided the impetus to journey higher.

Continuing, Collette was bred to Glen Hill Valedictorian. Striving always for true Collie type and balance, they were elated with the results of this breeding: **Ch. Foxbride's Peterbilt, Ch. Foxbride's Spendabuck** and **Foxbride's Lead on MacDuff**. Each dog proved himself to be a sire of merit. Hence, shortening their trip up that very long ladder.

Ch. Foxbride's Starke Naked, dam of seven champions, was sired by the history-making Ch. Tartanside Th' Critic's Choice ex Ch. Foxbride's Skip N' Go Naked. Her name is Star and remained, in 1994, among the top-producing smooth dams. Both she and her tri rough litter sister, **Ch. Azalea Hills Foxbride Fancy**, offered that extra pizazz, elegance and undeniable Collie expression.

Ch. Foxbride's McLaughlan bred to Foxbride's Greensleeves, a tri rough Glen Hill Valedictorian daughter, produced **Ch. Foxbride's Kilkerran Calypso** (Scotty). This outstanding sable, smooth dog continued to stamp the look that they could not, would not, be without. Scotty's son, **Ch. Foxbride's West to Cherika**, H.C. was bred to **Ch. Foxbride's Boogie On Down**. The ultimate picture they had envisioned came closer to reality in **Ch. Foxbride's Hot Damn** (Della).

The ascent up the ladder was not an easy one and Foxbride was not without setbacks. Each step, although thoughtfully orchestrated, did not always meet their highest expectations.

They have bred more than 30 champions and truly find it difficult to concentrate on just a few. There have been several who didn't have the explosive career of others, but nonetheless, were of no less importance to Foxbride's growth. Their fervent hope is that what they started at Foxbride will continue to produce many meritorious Collies in the future while still reflecting the images of their past.

THE HISTORY OF TWIN CREEKS

In 1968, the first two Collies to carry the Twin Creeks prefix finished their titles and created a stir of interest along the way. When Ben and Joyce Houser bred Twin Creeks the Countess to Ch. Lick Creeks Drummer Boy, littermates **Ch. Twin Creeks Razzle Dazzle** and **Ch. Twin Creeks Razzmatazz** finished their titles, and along with their conformation titles came obedience degrees as well. The following year, another title holder appeared in **Ch. Twin Creeks Golden Boy**.

The 1970s appeared to be the budding period for this kennel, as a host of additional title holders bearing the Twin Creeks prefix garnered the name champion.

Overall balance and style seemed to be a key factor in the selec-

Ch. Foxbride's A Promise Kept, a rough champion bred by Lynn Fox and Barbara Kilbride. He was the winner of four specialties.

Ch. Foxbride's McLaughlan, 2nd Top Smooth Sire of All Time. (Photo by Kohler)

Ch. Foxbride's Hot Damm, great winning smooth bitch owned by Heidi Mendez and Debbie Batchelor. (Bonnie Gray by Tom)

Ch. Foxbride's Hot Damm at five months.

tion process at Twin Creeks, and while the early years were devoted to finding the nick that would work best for them, the selection process of individuals who would be housed at Twin Creeks shared these essential qualities, combining them with great temperaments and soundness. It is interesting to note how the importance of "eye appeal" was to the foundation of this family, as the Housers did a variety of outcrosses during the early years. They made purchases from several kennels, yet using their own keen eyes in the selection process, continually put out a group of winners who shared the same virtues. Joyce was also a professional handler, and her skill in the presentation of these fine individuals was the icing on the cake.

During the early 1970s, three sable bitches created quite a sensation in the Specials class. The first was **Ch. Twin Creeks Scrube Dube Da,** daughter of the aforementioned Ch. Twin Creeks Razzle Dazzle. She was a top contender at several prominent specialties and was BOS at the CCA. Another top contender at the specialties was **Ch. Twin Creeks Drummers Fancy** bred from Razzle Dazzles sister (Ch. Razzmatazz C.D.) to Ch. Two Jay Hanover Scrumptious, another popular winner at the shows and much admired by Collie breeders across the country.

Creating national attention during these formative years was a white by the name of **Ch. Twin Creeks First Frost,** who became the first white champion in breed history to garner a Best in Show.

The Housers credit Steve Field as a guiding light throughout their career in Collies, and a close friendship evolved between them. During their visits to Nebraska and the Parader Kennels, it was not uncommon for them to return home with a dog in tow. Two important males came to live at Twin Creeks and were used as strong influences during this time. These two males were **Paraders Top O' The Hill** and **Twin Creeks Mark of Excellence**—between them they sired numerous Twin Creek champions, as well as champions for other breeders.

Ch. Foxbride's Lead On MacDuff at five months. Owned by Lynn Fox and Barbara Kilbride. He was sired by Glen Hill Valedictorian ex Ch. Wagon Star's Total Recall.

Towards the latter half of the 1970s, the Housers were captivated by a beguiling tricolor bitch by the name of Ch. Lee Aires Amazing Grace. She was sired by Ch. Ransons Regency out of Ch. Lee Aires Live Wire, owned by Pat (Gorka) Forest and Gaye Niederst. The Housers expressed an interest to her owners in having one of her puppies, and, in 1976, a sable male from this litter came to live at Twin Creeks. History was made as this male turned out to be **Ch. Twin Creeks True Grit**, the strong foundation sire for a prepotent family that would follow.

The breeding program took a different turn with this young dog as they tried all three types of breedings to him (outcross, linebred, and inbred) with impressive results from all three.

Ch. Twin Creeks Nitty Gritty was the "Grit" daughter who would play a significant role in the continuation of the family. Considered by the Houser's as one of their favorites by this commanding sire, she would be bred back to Grit to produce the next great sire in the family in **Ch. Twin Creeks Post Script**.

When Rita Stanczik and Nancy Gustafson bred Braedoon's Hallelujah to Grit, a multitude of champions streamed forth—among them another favorite of the Housers, **Ch. Twin Creeks Stolen Property.** For Rita Stanczik and her Executive Collies came some very strong individuals for that family to build upon.

Ch. Twin Creeks Main Event was a flashy sable daughter of True Grit from this same combination out of Braedoon's Hallelujah. She would be used to try for some outcrossing and was sent to be bred to Ch. Carnwaths Evergreen. From that combination emerged **Ch. Twin Creeks Damn Yankee** who would make his home in Canada with the Pebblebrook Collies of Pete and Marion Liebsch, and would serve as a very strong sire in their own line of Collies.

Another Grit daughter who caught the Housers attention was a sable bitch called **Ch. Joius Amber Dream**. At the time, they were looking for just the right Grit daughter to breed to the inbred son, Ch. Twin Creeks Post Script, and this bitch seemed to fit the bill. Once again, the astuteness of a good eye made the Housers selections correct, as this combination produced **Ch. Twin Creeks Post Master, Capriole, Special Delivery** and **Love Notes.**

Ch. Twin Creeks True Grit, owned by Ben and Joyce Houser.

Ch. Twin Creeks Postscript, owned and bred by Ben and Joyce Houser.

The siring of True Grit became legendary and, from 1980 to 1984, he was Top Sire of the breed. It is interesting to note that he would relinquish this title to his inbred son. Ch. Twin Creeks Post Script who held the honor for two additional consecutive years.

I am sure that during the 1980s the Housers must have established some type of historical record by winning the coveted Breeder of the Year award for eight out of ten years—certainly these wins were a testimony to their dedication and perseverance.

Through the careful use of these two strong sires came a most definitive look known to all as Twin Creeks. Once the type was firmly in place, it was once again time to do the judicious outcross. Another sire line was sought hoping to retain the characteristics that they had worked so hard to achieve. An inbred Post Script daughter, Ch. Twin Creeks Love Notes (ex Ch. Joius Amber Dream) was bred back to her sire and this breeding produced **Ch. Twin Creeks Shady Lady**. Feeling she had the strength in phenotype and genotype, she was sent to the East Coast sire Ch. Tartanside Apparently, he too from a strong sire line through the Tartanside family. This breeding produced the exciting tricolor **Ch. Twin Creeks Tuff Guy**, who sired extremely well for them before being exported to Japan.

The line continues today from these strong individuals directly through Twin Creeks and through a wide variety of Collie families across the country who used these bloodlines to found and strengthen their own families of Collies.

LISARA KENNELS

Carmen and Larry Leonard began their love affair with Collies with the purchase of an eight-week-old smooth Collie, **Ch. Lisara's Merrytime Drambuie** (Merrytime Ringmaster ex Ch. Merrytime Felicity), bred by James and Frances Coleman of Merrytime. "Boo" sired 14 champions, six champions out of two litters from the sable rough, Tawny Miss of Glenayre (Kasan's Robin Locksley ex Shawn of Dunbarry), also owned by the Leonards. One of these puppies was **Ch. Lisara's Scheherazade** who became the number one smooth Collie in the mid seventies.

In 1975, the Leonards purchased a tri smooth female bred by Florence Lippman. She became **Ch. Lisara's Seavie Nightingale** (Wendy) who became the foundation for their line. Wendy's sire was the blue rough, Ch. The Blue Baron of Arrowhill and her dam a Ch. Black Hawk of Kasan's daughter, Ch. Seaview 's Lark of Kasan. Wendy was the dam of 13 champions.

It takes a few years to determine what look an individual wants to develop. To the Leonards, personality was very important. Collies have to have good temperaments, be able to face each new experience with gusto and yet be gentle, protective, showy, kind and sensible. They also had in mind the outline and look they felt depicted the elegant bearing that the standard calls for. The dogs must have good bodies, be pleasant to look at, have strong under jaws, round muzzles and a tight lip line.

Bred to Ch. Jim Pat Cooper Dust O' Merrytime, a littermate to the Leonard's first smooth Collie, **Ch. Lisara's Seaview Nightingale** produced seven champions in that litter. Among those champions were **Ch. Lisara's Cover Girl** who, when bred to Ch. Windrift's The Blue Knight, produced **Ch. Lisara's Afterknight Delight**, dam of 13 champions (12 smooths and one rough). Cover Girl was a lovely compact female who needed some head refinement which they hoped to accomplish by breeding her to the Blue Knight. They felt they had accomplished the head improvement they sought in a puppy from that breeding, Ch. Lisara's Afterknight Delight.

However, they still were not completely satisfied with the expression and pizazz and also wanted a better eye shape. Carmen was quite taken with and had handled in the show ring a young tri male called Ch. Sunkist Midnight Flyer (Ch. Stoneypoint Spartacus ex Ch. Sunkist Sweet Honesty) owned by Jan Grillo and felt that he had the expression and attitude they needed. Afterknight Delight (Dillie) produced 11 champions when bred to Midnight Flyer, including **Am. and Can. Ch. Lisara's Morning After**, also known as Dutch. Dutch is the dam of nine champions (3 rough and 6 smooth) and also the winner of nine All Breed Best in

Shows, 53 Group I, 24 Group II, 24 Group III, 16 Group IV, 16 Specialty Best of Breeds, 14 Specialty Best of Opposite to Best of Breed. Dutch was twice BOV at the National Specialty, twice BOS to BOV at the National Specialty and twice the top smooth all systems. At almost 15 years of age, Dutch lives in Illinois with the Leonards. All of their present Collies trace back to Dutch through Ch. Lisara's Seaview Nightingale, Ch. Lisara's Afterknight Delight and Dutch's sons sired by Ch. Lynridge Shades of Night.

With Dutch, they felt they had a Collie of the right size with good movement, a head with proper planes, muzzle, under jaw, tight lip line and corners to the skull, temperament, expression and the pizazz needed for the show ring. Yet Collie breeders are not happy to have produced one dog that pleases them, they want to produce those characteristics consistently.

When Dutch was two years old, they saw a photograph of Ch. Lynridge Shades of Night and were quite taken with his lovely outline and presence. Sight unseen, they sent Dutch to be bred to him and that resulting litter proved to be a cornerstone of their dogs.

Am. and Can. Ch. Lisara's Morning After's smooth blue son, **Ch. Aryggeth Lisara Liaison**, also known as Bear, at nine months of age was BOS to BOV to his dam at the 1984 National Specialty and went on to win two All Breed Best in Shows. Bear was the sire of Alan and Alice Cortner's Ch. Cortner's Two Timer O'Chriss Mik, also a BOV winner at the National Specialty. Bear also sired the BOS to BOV winner at the 1992 National Specialty, **Ch. Lisara's Once in a Blue Moon**, and won the stud dog class that year. He sired the BOV winner at the 1993 National Specialty, **Ch. Lisara's Music of the Night**, who was the top-winning smooth all systems for 1992 and 1993 and the winner of 10 Group I, 15 Group II, 11 Group III, eight Group IV and five Specialty Best of Breeds. Ch. Aryggeth Lisara Liaison was the sire of 23 Champions (2 roughs). One of his rough champion sons (Ch. Lisara's Kodachrome) is now producing a good number of champions for the Leonards. He is not the large Collie that Bear was but possesses the jolly temperament, balance and good movement of both his sire (Ch. Aryggeth Lisara Liaison) and grandsire (Ch. Lisara's Knighty Knight) who happen to be littermates from the breeding of Ch. Lynridge Shades of Night to Am. and Can. Ch. Lisara's Morning After.

Am. and Can. Ch. Lisara's Morning After's tri rough son, **Ch. Lisara's Knighty Knight** was the sire of the 1991 National Specialty BOS to BOB winner, the tri color rough, Ch. Glenorka's All Night Affair (owned by Rick and Syvie Lingenfelter), out of Glenorka's Champagne on Ice. He is the grandsire of **Ch. Lisara's Knaughty Knight** (Ch. Lisara's Quest ex Ch. Lisara's Hanky Panky), the BOV smooth winner at the 1992

Am. & Can. Ch. Lisara's Morning After. (Photo by Missy Yuhl)

Ch. Lisara's Music of the Night. (Baines Photo)

Ch. Lisara's Dressed in Blue Too. (Booth Photo)

National Specialty. Knighty Knight was the sire of 12 champions including **Ch. Lisara's Dubh Lin O'Collairine** (Pete and Judy Park); **Ch. Lisara's Close Shave** (Leslie Young); **Ch. Lisara's A London Fog** (WD smooth 1987 National Specialty); **Ch. Lisara's Quest** (blue rough); and, **Ch. Lisara's Chasing Rainbows** (blue rough dam of Ch. Lisara's Kodachrome). Whether inbred, linebred or outcrossed, Duncan's look and personality were evident.

Ch. Lisara's Shades of Morning, a blue, rough female, was somewhat more petite yet with good bone, good temperament, lovely outline, and the tight lip line which is so important. When bred to Ch. Lisara's Guest (A Ch. Knighty Knight son), she produced the lovely blue rough, **Ch. Lisara's Good Golly Miss Molly**.

Ch. Lisara's Dresden Blue was a substantial Collie with a flowing coat, beautiful expression and good movement. When bred to Ch. Lisara's Spellbinder (Ch. Sunkist Midnight Flyer ex Ch. Lisara's Afterknight Delight), she produced an elegant blue female who became **Ch. Lisara's Dressed in Blue Too** (Cricket). Cricket is a large Collie with a beautiful, long lean head, warm expression, good movement, pretty eyes and a flowing coat.

When bred to her blue, smooth son, Ch. Lisara's Blueprint (sired by Ch. Sunkist Midnight Flyer), Ch. Lisara's Afterknight Delight produced **Ch. Lisara's Merrytime Rainmaker** (Tiger), WD at the 1986 National Specialty. Tiger has produced 24 champions for owner Carol and Fran Coleman.

In 1983, the Leonards purchased a blue, rough female sired by Ch. Wyndfall's the Main Event out of Ch. Tamisett's Twilight Gong from Frank and Sara Novachek. Crystal became **Ch. Lisara's Crystal of Pinewynd**. They purchased her looking for yet another outcross and because they admired the elegance of her line. When bred to Ch. Lisara's Knighty Knight, Crystal produced **Ch. Lisara is Chasing Rainbows** (a blue rough named Diane) and **Ch. Lisara's Quest** (a blue rough). Quest lives with Fran, Carol and Julie Coleman who have used him extensively since he has produced so many nice winners for them. When bred to Ch. Aryggeth

Ch. Lisara's Once in a Blue Moon.

Lisara Liaison, Diane produced **Ch. Lisara's Scarlet No Hair** (dam of Bodyguard), **Ch. Lisara's Honorroll Debut** (from living with the Beddows in Maryland and providing them with an outcross), **Ch. Lisara's Grin & Bare It** (now in Canada with Dawn Klassen and producing winners), **Ch. Lisara's Tess Trueheart** and **Ch. Lisara's Kodachrome** (rough). Crystal also produced, when again bred to Knighty Knight, **Lisara's Whisper of the Night** who when bred to **Ch. Twin Creek's Don Juan** produced **Ch. Lisara's Fancy Free**, **Ch. Lisara's Love Hug** (now producing for Joe and Cellia Fouty in California), **Ch. Lisara's Love Dove**, all roughs.

When Whisper was bred to Bear, she produced **Ch. Lisara's Once in a Blue Moon**, **Ch. Lisara's Music of the Night**, **Ch. Lisara's Voodoo Chile** (owned by the Stancliffs in Texas) and **Ch. Lisara's Slick Chick** (owned by Louann Young and Debbie Price). When bred to Ch. Vennessee's Sculptured in Blue, Whisper produced their latest tri rough champion bitch, **Ch. Lisara's Untamed Heart**.

The Leonards are currently campaigning a blue, smooth male, **Ch. Lisara's Bodyguard** (Keven) whose dam, Ch. Lisara's Scarlet No Hair, is a daughter of Ch. Aryggeth Lisara Liaison out of a daughter of Ch. Lisara's Knighty Knight. His sire is Ch. Vennessee's Midnight Express owned by Joyce Weinman. Keven was #1 smooth all systems as of November 1995.

Some other smooth winners bred by the Leonards include, **Ch. Lisara's Hanky Panky**, WB at the 1986 National Specialty Centennial and the dam of 10 champions, her daughter (sired by Ch. Lisara's Quest), **Ch. Lisara's Oops a Daisy**, winner of many Specialty Best of Breeds, and **Ch. Lisara's Shear Madness** and **Ch. Lisara's Shear Magic**, who have helped their owner, nine-year-old Randi Moore, win many Best Junior Handler awards and 10 Best Brace in Show.

The Leonards were enjoying their smooth Collies so much that it wasn't until 1982 that they owned and showed their first rough Collie show dog, **Ch.**

Ch. Lisara's Love Dove. (Booth Photo)

White Cloud's Bewitchin Harvest bred by and co-owned with Linda Holden. Since then, out of 118 champions bred and/or owned by the Leonards, approximately 30 of those are rough Collie champions, six are Smooth Fox Terriers and the balance are smooth Collie champions. The Leonard's first smooth Collie completed his title in 1973. They have been fortunate to have multiple champions in their litters. They are dedicated to preserving the wonderful personality and faithfulness of the Collie in addition to its aesthetic beauty and continue to love, promote and enjoy the breed.

THE STORY OF CLARION

In the foothills of the Catskill Mountains is the home of the Clarion Kennels of Judie Evans. Judie's involvement with the breed dates back to the 1960s when, inspired by pictures of Ch. Tokalon Golden Ruler and his descendants in the Poplar and Brandwyne families, she became interested in breeding,

With the pictures of these dogs firmly ingrained in her mind, she set about to create a line of Collies who would share some of the virtues these dogs had.

She made two important purchases to establish a solid base. One was the purchase of the tricolor, **Ch. Valley Views Whirlaway**. The second, was the purchase of the Whirlaway daughter, **Kemricks Silver Satin**. These two would be the catalysts who would produce the type for Clarion.

The siring ability of Whirlaway was evident not only in Silver Satin, but in several other youngsters coming along, and at the end of his siring career he had produced an impressive 13 rough and three smooth champions. He himself began a show career at age seven, finishing his title in short order, winning two important Eastern Specialties.

Silver Satin was a show stopper, finishing her title with three five-point majors within a month, but her contribution in the whelping box overshadowed her impressive show career, and as the first Clarion homebreds hit the show ring their future looked bright.

In her first litter sired by Ch. Impromptu Ricochet, emerged one of the principal sires for the family in **Ch. Clarions Nightrider**. The blue **Ch. Clarions Blue Persuasion** was also in that litter, and a very influential tri bitch as well. Her name was **Lauriens Afterhours Blues**.

Ch. Clarions Nightrider had been sold as a show prospect, finishing his title quickly, and at age six was repurchased by Judie and offered at stud at Clarion. He sired 11 champions in the three short years that he

Ch. Kemricks Silver Satin, foundation bitch for Clarion, shown with John Buddie handling, Doris Werdermann judging. (Photo by W.P. Gilbert)

Above: Ch. Clarion the Platinum Minx was Best Puppy at the 1983 Collie Club of America Specialty. (Photo by Krook) Left: Ch. Clarions Color My World. (Photo by Krook)

sired for Clarion. Among these were **Ch. Clarions Light Up the Sky, Ch. Paradices Cloak n'Dagger, Ch. Milas Formal Sneakers** and Brazilian **Ch. Clarions All Night Long**. "Light up the Sky" sired 17 champions: among them, the exciting **Ch. Clarions The Platinum Minx**, Best Puppy CCA 1983, **Ch. Impromptu Banner Still Waves**, WD CCA 1984, and another key player in the Clarion family, **Ch. Clarions Too Much Heaven**. She would produce the next key sire in the Clarion program in **Ch. Clarions Color My World**, who was sired by Ch. Paradices Along Came Jones, a grandson of Nightrider.

Another important offspring of Ch. Light Up the Sky was **Clarions Touchstone**, the sire of **Ch. Clarions Touched by Poetry** whose offspring are currently creating new champions for the family. "Touched by Poetry," though four generations down from Silver Satin is a prime example of the positive value of close linebreeding. A most reminiscent example of Ch. Kemricks Silver Satin, she is possessed of the beautiful overall balance and elegance, the clean, light head, and the exquisite expression—the hard-to-get virtues that made Silver Satin one of the breed's finest. In her first litter she produced the puppy flyer **Ch. Clarions Careless Whispers**, who returned to the ring as an adult to top the breed at some of the prestigious Eastern specialties.

With such success from the breeding of Ch. Silver Satin to Ricochet, her next litter was a breeding to Richochet's sire, Brandwynes New Legacy, and this would give Clarion another CCA winner in **Ch. Clarions Midnight Sky**, Best of Opposite Sex to Best Puppy in 1972 and RD 1973.

The third litter for Ch. Silver Satin was an outcross, this time to the outstanding producer Ch. Tartanside the Gladiator, and while no champions emanated from this breeding, another important producer emerged in **Clarions The Silver Vixen**. She produced four champions, including **Ch. Clarions The Velvet Vixen**, by Ch. Nightrider, who followed in her dam's footsteps by producing four champions as well. The consistency in quality was deepening with each litter. From another breeding of Silver Vixen, to "Whirlaway" she produced **Clarions Misty Morn**, another prolific producer and the dam of five champions.

For the past 20-odd years, Clarion has continued to linebreed carefully, with the impact of the great Silver Satin always strong in the pedigrees.

The sire line at Clarion seems to extend from the first litter, beginning with Nightrider, to a son, Ch. Paradices Cloak N'Dagger to his son Ch. Paradices Along Came Jones to the Clarion Bred Ch. Clarions Color My World, who continues to produce in the family tradition. In a litter that doubled the blood of both Light Up the Sky and Along Came

Ch. Clarion Escapade pictured here with handler Donna Williams and Judge Evelyn Honig. (Photo by Kohler)

Below: Ch. Clarion Beyond Black. (Photo by SueS)

Above: Ch. Clarion True Colors, one of four champions by Color My World ex Clarion Cliché. (Photo by SueS)

Jones, by Color My World out of Paradices Clarion Cliche came **Ch. Clarion True Colors, Ch. Clarions Beyond Black, Ch. Paradices Mr. Stardust** and **Ch. Clarions Fade to Black**.

Clarions World Class, sired by Ch. Color My World, continues the sire line today. In one of his early litters he produced the exciting white bitch **Clarion Marmalade Skies**, RWB at the 1995 National Specialty, at eight months. Careful selection, judicious outcrosses and tight linebreeding to the original foundation dogs have given Clarion a distinctive look and a family of strong producers in the United States and abroad.

HIGHCROFT COLLIES

The Highcroft Collie Kennels, located just west of the Twin Cities in Minnesota, is, interestingly enough, a kennel more noted for its outstanding bitches rather than dogs. Although the husband and wife team of Donald and Leslie Jeszewski have bred and owned several exceptional males over the 30 years in breeding Collies, their bitches have been the more well-known winners and producers.

As a primary example, the Jeszewski's **Ch. Highcroft Quintessence** holds the current title of Top Champion Producing Rough Bitch of All Time. Not only did this lovely, normal-eyed, sable-and-white bitch, sired by major-pointed Twin Creeks Hot Property and out of Sarellyn's Adventuress C.D.X. (a Ch. Baymar's Coming Attraction granddaughter) produce 14 rough Collie champions, "Quin" also found time to finish her own championship title and pass her herding instinct test on the side.

Subsequent offspring of Ch. Highcroft Quintessence also became noteworthy winners, many of them winning classes at the CCA National Specialty shows. **Ch. Highcroft Double Essence**, sired by the Jeszewski's Ch. Highcroft Double Dare, placed second in the 9-12 sable-and-white puppy bitch class in Springfield, Massachusetts. **Ch. Highcroft American Classic**, also sired by Ch. Highcroft Double Dare, won the Best American Bred title when the CCA Specialty was held in Louisville, Kentucky, in 1990. Another Quintessence son, this time sired by the Jeszewski's Ch. Highcroft-Pizazz (a grandmother to grandson breeding) gained worldwide notoriety by winning multiple Best in Shows in the Orient.

Examples of Quintessence grandchildren that were also top winners and producers were **Ch. Highcroft Pizazz** and **Ch. Highcroft Shirley Temple**. Pizazz, a Ch. Twin Oaks Joker's Wild son, was Best of Opposite Sex to Best Puppy in 1990 at CCA. This dog sired eight rough champions in his first three litters. Ch. Highcroft Shirley Temple (Ch. Highcroft Pizazz x Heritage Hallion O'Highcroft, the latter being a Quin daughter) was the winner of the most heavily entered 9-12 sable-and-white puppy bitch class when the CCA National Specialty was held in Ontario, California. Shirley Temple went on to become the Top Winning Rough Collie Bitch for 1992, having won numerous specialty Best of Breeds, as well as having acquired three Group Firsts. This bitch also carried on her grandam's tradition of producing multiple champions.

Donald and Leslie Jeszewski frequently incorporated interesting outcrosses in their breeding program, firmly believing in taking advantage of the vast gene pool available. They were quite successful. The breeding of their Award of Merit winner, **Ch. Joius Highcroft Escapade** to **Ch. Claremont Cartloway Tristar**, produced a lovely, blue merle bitch by the name of **Ch. Highcroft Ultimate Parfait**, who was listed in the top 10 rankings for several different rating systems in 1994. Parfait's littermate, **Am. and Can. Ch. Highcroft Renaissance Blue, C.D., T.D.**, owned and trained by Judith Belloumini, achieved top 10 ranking for 1995. This same Collie is the youngest Collie on record to have achieved his tracking degree.

Another unique outcross was the breeding of a blue merle bitch, **Ch. Highcroft Special Favor** to Ch. Pebblebrook Showbiz, Winners Dog and BOS to Best Puppy at CCA in 1992. That litter produced **Ch. Highcroft Wyndlair Azure**, who also won multiple Group Firsts as well as Specialty BOBs. When Azure was outcrossed to the well-known sire, Ch. Vennessee's Midnight Express, she produced Winners Bitch, Best of Winners, and Best Puppy, **Ch. Highcroft Silver Sapphire** at the 1995 CCA Specialty.

An interesting aside in regards to the Jeszewski's Highcroft Collies, is that although they have had ample room on 43 acres to maintain a large number of Collies at any given time, they have always attempted to adhere to self-imposed limits of having no more than nine adults on their place. This fact lends encouragement to other breeders and fanciers, demonstrating that successful Collie breeding can be done with a limited, rather than larger number of dogs. Don and Leslie

Ch. Highcroft Double Essence finished at eight months of age. (Olson Photo)

*Ch. Highcroft Ulti-
mate Parfait, multiple
Specialty and Group
winner.*

*Ch. Highcroft Wistful Memory,
Specialty BOB winner.*

**Ch. Highcroft Strictly Business, mul-
tiple BISs in Orient.**

Ch. Highcroft Silver Sapphire pictured with handler Leslie Jeszewski, Judge Mrs. Harold Leek and presenter James Fredrickson. The 1995 Winners Bitch is owned by Don and leslie Jeszewski. (Photo by Kohler)

Jeszewski felt that by keeping fewer Collies, they could better maintain the "companion-level" relationship with their dogs, that spurred them into the fancy originally. To date the Jeszewski's have bred or finished over 44 rough champion Collies.

SPRING COLLIES

If Sayuri Harami of Spring Collies had to name the most influential dog in her kennel, it would be **Ch. Spring the Titan** (Ch. Tartanside Th' Critics Choice ex Bellvue's Black Ribbons). He is the sire of eight champions with "Vanna" Ch. Bellvue's Spring Fashion being the most famous. Titan is a very sound dog with a nice, clean head.

Another important Collie is a blue bitch Missa, **Spring Blue Mist of Dawn** (Ch. B.J.'s Yankee Blue ex Bellvue's Black Ribbons). Sayuri was frustrated to know that 85 percent of Collies are affected with CEA. When she heard that Bellvue Collies had a normal-eyed bitch for sale, she went immediately to get her. She became "Cookie."

Titan and Missa's daughter **Bellvue's Spring Lilac** was bred to Ch. Glen Hill Knight O' Round Table, a normal-eyed tricolor stud. Sayuri loved the elegance of the Glen Hill Collies and Knight had the normal eyes she was pursuing, along with other qualities. From this litter came **Ch. Bellvue's Spring Lady Ann** and **Ch. Bellvue Spring Sir Lance**. She has been in the top 10 of several rating systems for the past three years. She is a Specialty show and Group winner. Three of her littermates are nearing their championships. Sayuri says this was one of her best litters.

Titan's offspring from Bellvue's Savannah produced three champions who are important dogs for Bellvue's Collies. When one of the champions of Vanna was bred to Ch. Two Jay's Mountain Man she produced **Ch. Bellvue's Declaration of Spring**, a multiple Best in Show winner.

Missa was bred to Ch. Gambit's the Dragon's Roar, which produced two champion bitches. One is **Ch. Gambits Dawn on the Horizon,** the dam of **Ch. Gambits Chill Factor**, and grandam of **Ch. Gambits Freeze Frame**.

Bellvue's Spring Lilac winning Best of Opposite Sex at the Kennel Club of Beverly Hills in 1994 under Judge Mrs. J. Kay. (Rich Bergman Photo)

Missa was then bred to **Ch. The Meadows Notorious**. Sayuri loved the Meadows head piece and expression. Champions from this litter: **Ch. Bellvue's Spring Mojave** and **Ch. Bellvue's Spring Nightingale**, with multiple Group placements and a Group one.

There are many additional influential dogs that could be mentioned but her words are these: "I heard the voice of 70 last year (95) and decided to fade out from the Collies. There is so much in my life that I want to pursue yet. Most of my offspring are in good hands. I am very happy and contented that they will carry on.

"My heartfelt appreciation to John Buddie and Pat Starkweather of Glen Hill for their guidance all through my life in Collies.

"At the National in '91 when my Ch. Spring the Titan took the Stud Dog class with his beautiful offspring Ch. Bellvue Spring Sultana is one of my most important memories in my Collie life. I will treasure it forever."

Ch. Bellvue's Spring Sir Lance at the Inland Empire Collie Club in 1993 with Judge Mrs. Kodner.

Stud Dog Class Winner Ch. Spring The Titan with gets, from left, Ch. Bellvue's Spring Fortune, Ch. Bellvue's Spring Fashion and Ch. Bellvue's Spring Santana with Judge Pat Starkweather. Bred by Sayuri Harami and owned by him and Jody Ostrowski. (Rich Bergman Photo)

Ch. Bellvue's Spring Lady Ann, Top Winning Collie three years running.

PLEASANT HILL - ABBEHURST KENNELS

As a child, Billy Aschenbrener's family had Boston Terriers. When the monthly dog magazine arrived, he would turn to the Collie pages and admire the picture of Ch. Tokalon Blue Eagle in Mrs. Browning's ads. His first registered Collie was a birthday gift from his parents.

Billy's father would drop him off to spend the day at the benched shows in Portland, Oregon. One of the exhibitors who would let him groom and show her Collies was Mrs. Maude Abbey (Abbehurst Collies). Her first Collies were acquired from Mrs. Lunt's Alstead Kennels in 1920. Mrs. Abbey finished her first homebred champion and working Group winner **Ch. Abbehurst Picador** in 1926. She later purchased several Collies from the Saint Adrian Kennels of Mr. and Mrs. James Christie in Massachusetts. When Mrs. Abbey bred Saint Adrian Siverally to **Ch. Black Douglas of Alstead**, she gave Billy the best puppy, **Blue Douglas of Abbehurst**, who would become his first champion in 1946, and a co-ownership in the Abbehurst Kennels. Blue Douglas's most beautiful daughter and Mrs. Abbey's favorite was the homebred **Ch. Abbehurst Silvaire**, who finished in 1949. When this young, blue bitch and her near-champion sister Abbehurst April Showers were accidentally killed in 1950, Mrs. Abbey was so overcome with grief that she discontinued her Collie activities, but she remained loyal to the Collie breed until her death in 1960.

Another Collie breeder who took Billy under his wing and influenced him in the direction he would go with his Collies was Mrs. Grace Bardsley (Portland Collies). Her breeding stock was purchased from Dr. Bennett's Tazewell Kennels, and she named these Collies after the trains they arrived on from Chicago. Thus: **Ch. Pride of Portland, Portland Rose, City of Portland** and **Portland Heights**. She also purchased the champion sire Tazewell Trotyl from Dr. Bennett, as well as Collies from Mrs. Long (Noranda) and Mrs. Gray (Wooley's Lane). Mrs. Bardsley had a dislike for dog shows and seldom exhibited her Collies, but when she did they usually won.

From the foundation stock acquired from Mrs. Bardsley and then Mrs. Browning and her daughter Mary at Tokalon Kennels, Billy bred and/or owned many champions, first under his own kennel name of Pleasant Hill and later carrying on Mrs. Abbey's Abbehurst prefix. There were 10 working group winners and six all-breed Best In Show winners—a record in the Collie breed. The two tricolor bitches, **Ch. Pleasant Hill Enchantress** (Ch. Blackout of Tokalon ex Pleasant Hill Blue Horizon) in 1948 and **Ch. Pleasant Hill Torch Song** (Black Sheik of Cainbrook ex Pleasant Hill Highlite) in 1950 were the first two Collies to go Best in

Ch. Pleasant Hill Enchantress (left) and Ch. Pleasant Hill Torch Song with owner Billy Aschenbrener in 1953.

Ch. Frauluart Silver Smoke finished in 1960. He was bred by Louise Provancher and owned by Billy Aschenbrener.

Show, all breeds, in the Western United States. Enchantress was Best of Show the first time she was shown at eight months of age and finished her championship with a working group first. Torch Song made her championship in four straight shows, including a working group first, and finished at the 1949 CCA National Specialty show where she was Best of Winners and Best of Opposite Sex, over the Specials. Torch Song was also a Best in Show winner in Canada.

The other four Best in Show winners were: the sable bitch **Ch. Pleasant Hill Audacity** (Ch. Redberry Audacious Man ex Pleasant Hill Highlite); the blue bitch **Wind-Call's Whistle Stop** (Ch. Tokalon Blue Banner ex Wind-Call's Blue Lariat) who was Best In Show at six months of age, the first time shown; the sable male Ch. Pleasant Hill Star Addition (Ch. Addition of Lilac Lane ex Ch. Pleasant Hill Glenbrae's Star); and, the blue merle, **Ch. Lunette's Blue Print** (Ch. Three-Tree's Beau Blue ex Ch. Lunett's Chloe). Billy handled his own Collies and Blue Print was the last Collie he exhibited in 1968.

The last of the 13 Collie litters bred by Billy Aschenbrener during that period was in 1967.

Billy Aschenbrener is the only person who has judged the CCA National Specialty show five times. Still active in Collies, Billy resides in Sherwood, Oregon, where along with his partner, Dennis Day, share 60 wooded acres with several Collies, including the magnificent tricolor **Ch. Starr's Risky Business**, who was purchased by Billy in 1994, shortly after finishing his championship in the east.

Ch. Lunette's Blue Print shown here with owner/handler Billy Aschenbrener in 1967. (Photo by Robert)

Ch. Starr's Risky Business.

JAPAN

In June of 1996, I was privileged to judge dogs in Hokkaido, Japan. The hospitality shown to me was exceptional. I stayed on this lovely northern island for a few days and was shown the whole area "from the top." My host and hostess, Mr. and Mrs. Fukumoto, drove me around to see the beautiful lakes, the active volcano, the wonderful scenery which reminded me of Northern Michigan, or Scandinavia—towering pines and mountain hillsides were everywhere. Mr. Fukumoto is a famous international judge and has judged in the United States. He is president of Hokkaido Kennel Club.

From there I went to stay with the well-known couple, Yoshio Mori and his beautiful wife Mari. Mari is a professional photographer. In fact, she is the official photographer for the Japan Kennel Club. The Moris were incredibly kind to me. I had met them the previous year when Yoshio was judging in Texas at the same time I was judging there. Yoshio is a well-known judge and breeder of Collies and Shetland Sheepdogs, and he has judged often in the United States and other countries.

Mari Mori met me at the airport on two different occasions and struggled with the horrendous traffic of Tokyo. They put me up in their elegant home and drove me to two cities of great antiquity to see the glorious ancient temples there. Most of all, I recall the sitting Buddha, an

enormous statue in lovely *verde gris*. The unworldly beauty of the old cities and temples will remain with me forever.

From Tokyo, I accepted another gracious invitation and was driven to the country home of Hiroko Hiyama. Mrs. Hiyama had bought a lovely Shetland Sheepdog from me the previous year. She wanted me to see how beautiful he is now—a Japanese champion. Mrs. Hiyama's country place in the mountains was cool and charming, rustic in a sophisticated way. She had a large array of truly knockout Shelties.

From there I flew to visit Mrs. Nanae Takenoshita. Nanae is a tremendously successful breeder of Barclay Collies and Shelties. She has almost countless champions in each breed. Nanae had us driven around for two days to see her litters which were being raised mostly by co-owners. We have presented pictures of two of her great Barclay champion Collies. I visited her magnificent home overlooking Osaka, again hospitality was lavish.

From there, I was invited back to Tokyo and had the adventure of riding the famous bullet train. It whisked me back to Tokyo in the blink of an eye. I went to visit the famous judge and Collie aficionado Akira Kanda and his lovely wife. The Kandas have the BOQ Galleries, the most famous art gallery in Tokyo. Among the treasures there are some marvelous Collie prints in a semi-abstract style. The Kandas in their outstanding generosity gave me some of these prints as gifts. I find them to be superb works of art. One is reprinted on these pages.

Akira Kanda put together a lunch party for the members of the Musashino Branch of the Japan Collie Club at which I was Guest of Honor. A large and friendly group gathered at a beautiful downtown hotel. It was a charming affair. The hospitality of the Kandas over several days was something I will never forget. In fact, the friendship and hospitality shown me in my stay in Tokyo and other parts of Japan will be in my memory forever.

Yoshio Mori, famous Collie and Sheltie breeder-judge, showing Japan Ch. Glen Hill Firecracker.

At left is Mr. Akira Kanda addressing a luncheon in author's honor in Tokyo.

Nanae Takenoshita shown with one of her beautiful Barclay champions.

A top-winning champion of the Barclay Kennels in Osaka, Japan, owned by Nanae Takenoshita, shown here with her handler.

The author with Japan Ch. Glen Hill Firecracker and Hiroko Hiyama holding his sire Ch. Far West Toymaker. The dogs are Shetland Sheepdogs.

The author with the other judges at the Hokkaido Japan Dog Show.

Dog and bitch of Glen Hill background owned by Mr. Toshiyuki Shirai of Japan.

PART III.

THE COLLIE IN ACTION

U-UD Blossom Hill Rob Roy, UD, CGC, HC
performing the Utility directed jumping exercise.
(Photo by Sally Richardson Photo & Video)

Ch. Glen Hill Campus Cutie at the Atlanta CCA, handled by the author— proving the dog world keeps you young; she was in her late 60s in this picture. The judge is the late Laverne Walker. Cutie is the dam of top sire Glen Hill Valedictorian and grandam of Ch. Glen Hill The All American. Notice the proper single tracking. (Photo by SueS)

THE COLLIE AS A SHOW DOG

The operative word in *dog show* is *show*. The whole idea is to bring together the best examples of the breed and *show them off*. The competition is in some ways secondary. In exhibiting the very best each fancier has to show, the breed can be kept "up to snuff." No one wants to show a specimen that is inferior, so the exposure to the best makes each exhibitor want to produce the best. Since the *best* is a purely subjective matter, the idea of competition arose.

I can imagine in ancient England the farmers coming to town with their canines tagging along. Someone would say, "My, that is a handsome dog." Another farmer would say, "My dog is more handsome." Fist fights would threaten. In order to stop the competition by fisticuffs, the idea came about to have an outsider judge the animals. Some person with knowledge of animals would be appointed to decide which was the more attractive dog. From such lowly beginnings came the great dog show game, even the prestigious Westminster Kennel Club Dog Show and its precursor, Crufts in England. (See *The Great American Dog Show Game, Doral* Publishing, Inc.)

When I was first starting in dogs, I had a young friend who was already the owner of champions. This lovely girl has gone on to become one of the most famous names in dogs—Isabel (Mrs. Alan) Robson.

I asked Isabel whether she felt the training of the show dog was an important facet in success. Isabel said, and I have never forgotten it: "You put unlimited time, money and effort into getting your dog to the show. When you get in the ring you have only three minutes in which to impress the judge with your dog. Your dog better be perfectly trained, and all spiffed up, or he won't take the judge's eye."

As an exhibitor for many years, and a longtime judge, I am still impressed by her words. She sure knew what she was talking about. She has owned many great Best in Show winners, topped by her pointer Ch. Marjetta National Acclaim, Best in Show at Westminster in 1991.

The Collie is shown differently from most breeds. The standard states that the Collie should be shown standing freely on a loose lead. When trained properly, and when built properly, the Collie will show his heart out, standing in front of the handler, legs placed firmly, head up, and ears at attention. This effect looks easy to do, but it, like any other worthwhile endeavor, takes time and effort.

In another book, *All About Collies*, I stated that to me the picture of a good handler and a good Collie working together in the ring looks electric. The interest and concentration of one to another reminds me of a song: "I give to you and you give to me, true love, true love." Remember

Ch. Lisara's Body-guard winning Variety Group First at the South Dade Kennel Club in 1995. (Photo by Earl Graham Studios)

Ch. Aryggeth Lisara Liaison winning BIS at the Ingham County Kennel Club in 1987. (Photo by Phoebe)

Ch. Winover Silhouette handled by famous breeder-handler Tom Coen—winning as usual. Owned by Pat Breuer. (Photo by Chuck and Sandy Tatham)

Ch. Aurlealis Charidan Regina with Janine Walker-Keith of Incandescent Collies and Judge Pat Starkweather at the Bahia Sur Kennel Club in 1996. Co-owners Miriam Stempler and Debbie Falk. Breeder, Dante Fangon. "Gina" is #1 All Breed Winning Collie in the United States.

Bing Crosby and Grace Kelly singing that to each other? Too young? Too bad.

Some handlers do not show in the prescribed way, but they also do well. A Collie may be stacked and even have his ears propped up from the back. Some dogs even need to be handled that way. But the natural stance is preferable, and in most cases can be done.

Actually, not much is asked of the Collie. He must be trained to move freely on a loose lead. He should be happy on the lead and move with head up, and maybe even tail wagging. In my opinion, the best way to train a Collie to move that way is to take him for walks. Just walk him like a pet dog—the only requirement is that he stay on the left side. Play with him, pet him, give him tidbits. What ever it takes to make him "lead happy," do it. You will eventually give him instruction in such matters as moving with you in a triangle or a T. There is nothing to it if done with fun in mind. Remember, don't get too serious with your Collie or he may get "down in the mouth." A gay happy look is what we are after.

To get the dog to "show" for you, give him a little tidbit while he is standing free in front of you. He will learn to look to your hand for a treat. That is really all you need. After offering a treat, wait to give him the next one until he puts his ears up. When they come up on his head, properly at attention, reward him with the treat and a kind word, "Good Dog" is a fine phrase to use often. When said enthusiastically, your dog will learn to love the words. This early training must be repeated often so it becomes second nature to the dog. He will automatically look to your hand for food and raise his ears to attention. That is the look of a winner.

Some people try to use a squeaker to get the dog to look interested. This will usually work for a second or two. However, the Collie must stand at attention for long minutes. In a large show, the dog may have to hold his pose for half an hour or so. Nothing short of food will fascinate the Collie for that long.

You are far safer to rely on good old liver to keep the necessary alert look. Nearly all fanciers and handlers use liver as the attention getter. It is recommended to boil beef liver until thoroughly cooked. Then wash and dry it. It might help to dry it by putting it in the oven or the microwave. Some handlers sprinkle onion or garlic powder over the liver for additional flavor. The pungency of liver far exceeds that of others meats. (For a dog, that is).

If you are traveling a distance, or showing in hot weather, be sure to keep the liver in an ice chest. This food can spoil and harm your dog. Also, when traveling it is advisable to take your own water along for the dog. Many areas have water that is different from that which the dog is used to. A change of water can be upsetting to the dog's system. This can cause vomiting and diarrhea. Most of us will take along something to stop loose bowels. This symptom can cause dehydration which is very dangerous to the animal. You should also bring the food the dog is used to. These are creatures of habit and change can be damaging. While traveling, the dog should be offered water often, at least every two hours. Some dogs will go off their food and refuse to drink as well when on the road. Try to feed the dog at a quiet time and keep water available whenever you are stopped.

In another section, I have covered the lengthy description of how to groom a Collie for the show ring. Assuming all that has been done, your Collies should be clean, brushed out, and shining with anticipation. The true show dog loves every minute of his time in the ring. He is the star and he knows it.

I suggest you put the dog back in his crate or exercise pen after he is groomed. The dog will benefit from some rest before going into the ring. Some exhibitors take their dogs to the ring for long periods of waiting for the show time to come. I have seen potentially showy dogs get down and bored by the long wait. Give the pooch a break and let him snooze at ease until just before ring time. Then rouse him with an excited attitude, saying, perhaps, "Hey boy let's go." A pat on the back and a few fast paces to the ring will make him arrive lively and ready to go.

Once inside the ring, give your full attention first to the judge. Make sure you know where he/she wants you to be at any given minute. Follow directions to the letter. Many judges are quite annoyed by an exhibitor going the wrong way.

But keep your eye on the dog. Have him at full alert when the judge is looking. In a big class you can let the dog rest while the other dogs are being examined. While the judge examines *your* dog, be sure he stands firmly, with no shying or pulling back. This will have been drilled into the dog at home and at training classes. Most of all be sure the dog moves easily on a loose lead. Be sure he shows his ears when the judge is looking. That is about all there is to it.

THE COLLIE AS A HERDING DOG
by Lois Russell

The Differences between Collies and Border Collies
The second half of the 19th Century marked the division of the Collie as a herding dog in two separate breeds, the Border Collie, originally called simply the "rounding" dog, which we would call a "circling" dog, and the rough Collie, commonly referred to in that period as the Scotch Collie. At that time, the smooth Collie was considered by some to be a separate breed, but soon the two varieties were consolidated into one breed with two varieties that were shown together at the same shows but in different classes, as is done today.

One of the most profound changes in Scotland and Ireland initiated by the Agricultural and Industrial Revolutions was the substitution of large-scale sheep raising for generalized subsistence farming. In each county thousands of tenant farmers, who had rather densely populated most of Scotland and Ireland for centuries, were evicted and all vestiges of their dwellings destroyed during the Highland Clearances and the earlier Irish clearances.

The native farmers were replaced with a handful of solitary shepherds imported from England and the Border Counties, a few with their families and each with several thousand sheep. It took almost a hundred years to complete this ruthless cleansing of the land of its indigenous people and their life style. But the relatively few absentee landowners who claimed title to the entire land had few qualms and less sentiment about replacing people with sheep, especially since sheep farming on a large scale was so much more lucrative than the rents paid by indentured tenant farmers.

In Scotland, nonresident landowners, often titled Englishmen and successful industrialists, acquired the historic holding of the clan chiefs following the defeat of the Scots by the British at the Battle of Culloden on April 16, 1746, and the unification of Scotland and England. The properties were then sold or given to favorites of the English court, often as rewards for loyalty of service to the crown during the uprising. It has been estimated that at this time all of the Highlands as well as the Hebrides Islands were owned by fewer than 50 individuals.

As part of the Agricultural Revolution during the 18th and 19th centuries, landowners became aware of the desirability of making one's land economically productive rather than letting it serve for the subsistence of the tenant crofters. When it was discovered that sheep could indeed survive the winter out of doors and hardier strains were introduced that provided vastly increased wool production, the new owners converted their lands into enormous "hirsels." These were vast ranges of Scottish land kept exclusively for sheep raising and eventually as hunting preserves. It was the wool from the sheep raised on those hirsels that supplied the ever-expanding woolen mills in the British midlands, supported the extremely lucrative international trade in woolen goods and helped support Britain's wealth and power in the 19th Century. (K. J. Bonsar, in his book *The Drovers*, noted that in the period 1852-54: "The weekly average of animals passing through the streets[of London] to market was 69,946 almost all concentrated on two days.")

Ironically, less than 50 years after the last tenant farmers were shipped to North America and Australia, the shepherds who replaced them were themselves displaced as the vast estates were converted to hunting preserves—playgrounds for the wealthy. Most the of shepherds emigrated with their dogs to Australia, New Zealand, eastern Canada and western United States.

A single shepherd overseeing thousands of sheep scattered over a several-mile-square area needed a uniquely talented dog to share the work. Basically, this was a dog that would run out ahead of the shepherd and ferret out the widely scattered wild sheep. The dog would then gather sheep and fetch them in a group to the shepherd. The term "rounding" derived from the circular pattern of the dog's outrun.

Forest grazers do not need a dog that can drive or chase but one that can cast wide to locate a flock, or herd stray animals, then gather and hold them; and these are the precise qualities or instincts for which the modern "eye" dog like a Border Collie is famous.

Other authorities attribute the wide ranging outrun, rounding, and eye to the crossing of Collies with gun dogs such as Golden Retrievers during the 19th Century. There is little doubt of the enormous influence of the Golden Retriever on the Border Collie. For 55 years, from 1835 to 1890, Lord Tweedmouth's gamekeepers in Guisachan, Invernesshire, Scotland, maintained extensive kennels of Golden Retrievers right in the heart of the sheep-raising country. One can imagine how the local shepherds admired and coveted the talents of the Retrievers, their speed and determination, their gentleness and especially their retrieving instinct. So it was logical to cross the Collie and the Golden, and even today professional dog trainers can observe many shared traits and behavior characteristics unique to the two breeds—Goldens and Border Collies.

Edward Jones, the newspaper reporter, wrote in 1892 in his book, *Sheep-Dog Trials and the Sheep Dog*, that there were few instances of rounding dogs working in Wales in the years 1828 and 1873. About the later date, however they began to be widely available and many were directly attributable to a white bitch who had jumped off a train headed south from Scotland and was caught in the area of Abergwessin, the mid-Wales district, in 1862. She is referred to as the Kenarth bitch and the strain from that bitch "was kept more pure than any of the other ones, as the pups when grown up were 'kept up' to each other."

> The dog is a very prolific animal when circumstances favour its fecundity; and as the owners of the new breed would, doubtless, from interested motives, endeavor to rear as many young dogs as possible, with the view of supplying the demands of their neighbours, the consequence was that the new strain soon supplanted the native breed. and thus laid the foundation for future sheepdog trials...It may be safely assumed that the ("rounding") Collies owe their development and perfection as sheepdogs to the requirements of their duties and the influence of their surroundings, acting in the way of natural selection through an untold number of generations-the result of this process being an inherent instinct or capacity for working sheep. If their relative, the common cur or chasing dog (the traditional "Scotch Collie) has continued in this original and comparatively undeveloped condition, it is doubtless, owing to the circumstance that the necessity for his improvement was not so urgent as in the case of (these) Collies.

Working young stock is much more difficult for a dog than handling mature animals that are familiar with the herding routines. Here Ch. Starr's Midnight Hour, CD, HT, is sorting lambs. (Photo by Hildegarde Morgan)

James Hogg, "the Ettrick Shepherd," the poet and author son of a shepherd, gave a revealing picture of the difference in the behavior of the shepherd's rounding dog and the farm Collie in *Blackwood's Magazine* in the early 19th Century:

> It is a curious fact in the history of these animals that the most useless of the breed have often the greatest degree of sagacity in trifling and useless matters. An exceedingly good sheep dog attends to nothing else but that particular branch of business to which he is bred. His whole capacity is exerted and exhausted on it, and he is of little value in miscellaneous matters, whereas a very different cur, bred about the house and accustomed to assist in everything will often put the noble breed to disgrace in the paltry services. If one calls out, for instance, that the cows are in the corn or the

hens in the garden, the house colley needs no other hint, but runs and turns them out.

The shepherd's dog knows not what is astir, and if he is called out in a hurry for such work, all that he will do is to break to the hill and rear himself up on end to see if no sheep are running away. A bred sheep dog, if coming hungry from the hill and getting into the milk house, would most likely think of nothing else than filling his belly with cream. Not so his initiated brother; he is bred at home to far higher principles of honour. I have known such to lie night and day among from ten to twenty pails full of mild and never once break the cream of one of them with the tip of his tongue, nor would he suffer, rat, cat or any other creature to touch it. The later sort are far more acute at taking up what is said in a family.

The Shepherd's Dog

Interesting that Hogg takes note at this early date of the difference in attitude between the intensity of the hill shepherd's dog—the Border Collie type—and the more relaxed but very versatile farm Collie who companionably shadowed his master as chores were done—ever ready to assist and respond to spoken or signaled directives. Farmers could ill afford to keep dogs as pets in that period, so their dogs provided a multitude of useful services: herding the livestock from one grazing to another; chasing them out of the crops on the unfenced cultivated land; baby-sitting children; frightening away intruders; flushing deer or retrieving a bird or two during an illicit nighttime hunt. Collies were even used to run the treadmills that pumped water and ground grain.

Although such dogs did spend a certain amount of time, as they still do, just lying around the house snoozing, they readily adapted to the routine of the farm and, once familiar with that routine, performed their customary functions efficiently and often without supervision.

Livestock of all species, including poultry and fowl, also learn the farm routine which is, after all, based on their needs and they will cooperate in executing that routine. Often they will anticipate what they are expected to do at a certain time and will be waiting at the gate when it is time to return to the barn at the end of the day. When the gate is opened, they will calmly file out, head for the barn and go to their respective stalls or milking stanchions without any guidance. Dogs herding such well-trained stock would naturally be scorned by a hill shepherd, and Hogg no doubt picked up the unfortunate word "useless" from his father. It is rather incongruous for him to describe a "useless" dog performing such useful services, and the above quote does not begin to mention the other helpful tasks that the ever-loyal farmer's dogs performed.

The next piece in the puzzle is sheepdog trials, since that is where the most talented and best-trained sheepdogs actually demonstrated the skills they used in their day-to-day-work. There were two very different forms of sheepdog trials reflecting the two separate groups of herding Collies, one an outrun course for rounding dogs and the other a driving course for the all-purpose farmers' and drovers' dogs. The first sheep herding trials were held in Bala, North Wales, in 1873, and this sport of shepherds eventually spread throughout England, Scotland and Ireland during the succeeding 20 years. Edward Jones described in detail the early trials:

> Sheepdog Field Trials are of very recent origin. That such should be the case is somewhat surprising considering the extent to which the practice of testing the superiority of almost every kind of skillful or athletic performance, whether human or animal prevails by the ordeal of competitive contests, and how rapidly they spread from place to place immediately after being started...
>
> Shepherds as a class, are almost entirely removed out of the influence of rivalry, owing to the isolation which characterizes their daily avocations. But probably the best explanation as regards Wales is the fact that the introduction of the present improved strain of sheepdogs is of recent date-Collies or "rounding dogs" being first introduced into the country about 60 years (1830). Certainly they were "few and far between" within the recollection of the present generation-the prevailing type of sheepdog being one that would merely chase sheep and catch or take hold of them if required to do so...The services of such a race of dogs were of much value, although they fell far short of the services rendered by the improved strain of shepherd's dogs, which has now-a-days almost supplanted them. The progenitors of the improved breed were, undoubtedly, obtained from Scotland-some by purchase, others by the immigration of Scotchmen accompanied by their native dogs.

Starr's Classic Gold driving sheep and learning to keep a proper distance behind the stock so that the flock does not become agitated and start to flee. (Photo by Hildegarde Morgan)

At herding trials, all the functions that a herding dog normally performs around the farm are put together to form a trails course. The first required exercise is that the dog fetch the stock to the handler who must remain stationary at a fixed spot. Here, Ch. Balmoral Standing Ovation, CD, HI, HC, TDI, CGC, fetches the sheep to his owner Pat Rawitch. (Photo by Lori Herbel)

Ch. Cannondale Carnival returns the sheep to the pasture following the shearing. (Photo by A. David Russell)

Ch. Montara's Beyond the Blue Neon, PT, holding the sheep waiting to be sheared. (Photo by Hildegarde Morgan)

The smooth tri moves the goats through the chute on the course. (Photo by Lori Herbel)

Jones elsewhere described the various types of Collies prevalent in Wales at that time and noted that there was a popular strain of blue merle dogs, also called harlequins, that differed from other Collies only in the color of their coats. It is unclear whether or not this was the strain referred to by others as "Welsh heelers," or if they might be linked to the Australian Blue Heelers, now known as Australian Cattle dogs.

The relaxed and comparatively slow-paced working style of the farm and droving Collies that were by that time firmly established in the northwest and midland English pastoral regions were ideally suited to the nature of the local stock and clearly reflected the contrast in the agricultural practices in the two areas. Collies in England, both rough and smooth coated, were also employed as often for moving cattle as for sheep. This fact can be deduced from the requirement of the sheep-herding trials held in that area of England where the ancestors of our Collies lived.

In 1878, the North-West Counties Sheepdog Trials Association inaugurated the very popular and successful series of trials in the counties of Cumberland, Westmorland and Lancashire in England. The trials continued for several decades and were still well supported at the turn of the century. When comparing the course offered in Wales with the English course both stock and dog were expected to move at a steady, sedate pace of about three to four miles an hour as compared to the nine miles an hour or faster expected on the Welsh courses.

The fact that sheepdog trials in England were exclusively of the driving type further implies that the skills of the dogs competing did not include a strong rounding tendency. Nor did large herds of domesticated breeds of sheep with strong flocking tendencies grazing in enclosed pastures need that talent to any appreciable extent.

It is worth noting that the course offered for the International Collie Trials held at the Philadelphia Centennial in September 1880, probably one of the first sheepdog trials held in this country, almost duplicates the course used by the North-Western Counties Sheepdog Association in England. The course was in the form of a horseshoe about 60 yards wide and 700 yards from one end to the other. There was a pen at each end. The track that the sheep were to follow was 60 feet wide, marked on one side by a four-foot-high fence with a single rail placed on top of the posts.

The dog was to take a group of five sheep out of pen No. 1, drive them around the track, through a line of flags and pen them in pen No. 2. Prior to the start of each run, the shepherd was permitted to walk the course with his dog. Once the run began and the sheep were on the course, the shepherd was permitted to precede or follow the sheep, as he chose, but was not permitted to assist the dog except by signal or voice. At the end of the regulation competition, each shepherd was given the opportunity of exhibiting the particular talents of his dog by performing a demonstration of his own choosing. He was also encouraged to show the training of his dog for other practical purposes as a farm or house dog. At no time during this competition was there any test of "rounding" skill.

The Collies that competed in Philadelphia were closely related to those of the north and midland counties of England since the majority of them were importations from those areas. They were only a generation or two, if that, removed from the all-purpose farm dogs acquired by the drovers and resold to midland farmers and livestock grazers.

Victims of the inevitable march of progress, by the 1890s Collies were rapidly losing their place in the agricultural scheme in Britain. The Highland Clearances had ended the kind of farming that produced the Collie. Although droving flourished until near the end of the 19th Century, it was only a matter of time before the steam engine and the railroads would put the drovers out of business. The turn of the century marked the end of a long and distinguished career as an all-purpose herding dog for the versatile Collie. Had it not been for the dog-show fancy, the Collie as we know him would probably have become extinct.

We do know that most modern Collies in this country are derived primarily from a handful of dogs bred during a 20-year period in England, Ireland, Scotland and perhaps Wales. The period extended from 1867, the year the first significant show Collie, Cockie, was whelped, to the mid-1880s—when Collies were imported into the United States and the newly formed AKC began registering them.

When Collies are first exposed to livestock, remember that, in most cases, they are exhibiting instinctive behavior of the original farmer's

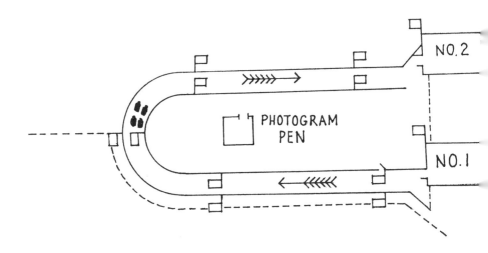

herding dog, not the more sophisticated and specialized reflex reaction of the improved rounding dog.

The Collie today has had little done to enhance his original herding skills—simple skills that sufficed for small farmers with a few head of assorted livestock that led an ordered daily existence. Those were the same herding skills specifically sought out by drovers who selected from farmers' dogs those who appeared to have the additional strength and endurance to travel over rough terrain in all sorts of weather. What both farmers and drovers needed were dogs capable of keeping stock flowing sedately toward their destination, patient enough to permit the stock to snatch an occasional mouthful of grass, and astute enough to use their own initiative to bend the flock or herd away from danger along the way.

The conformation of the Collie, quite similar to the early European "tending" dogs, clearly demonstrates the role the breed was designed to play. The Collie is built to provide strong, steady, forward movement with little need for great speed or rapid shifts of direction. The nimble and speedy Border Collie, on the other hand, with its exaggerated hindquarters and crouching forehand closely resembles the great African cats, the fastest and most agile animals on earth over relatively short distances. This is precisely the conformation needed by dogs who must control individual wild sheep in steep, rocky hill country, as well as manage several hundred such animals being hastily removed from their native habitat at shearing time.

Considering the genetic make-up and conformation of the Collie, it should not be surprising if the majority of today's dogs do not show much instinct for a fast, far-ranging outrun or for fetching. Most of today's dogs are direct descendants of extremely competent farm and droving dogs. The miracle is that the instinct to herd livestock in any fashion survives apparently undimmed by time. With training, Collies should be able to execute adequately, if somewhat casually, the functions performed so quickly and adroitly by the amazingly talented modern version of the Border Collie, and often a Collie with excellent stock sense will have no concept of an outrun at all. Nor will the average Collie necessarily exhibit a strong desire to keep stock grouped closely around the shepherd or handler. Instead, he will usually prefer to work between the handler and the stock, or beside the stock, pushing the stock ahead of the handler. These are tendencies that may be confusing to a handler more familiar with working Border Collies.

With the exception of the few dogs imported to run in the Philadelphia Centennial trial, little consideration was given to working ability. Contemporary authors, however, never failed to mention the herding feats of the dogs they discussed. Fortunately, subsequent generations have served to carry on the genes apparently unimpaired. James Watson sent several of his show winners to the Chicago area where they became invaluable workers in cattle operations. One well-known winner was, in fact, loaned to a cattleman who found her so valuable that he refused to return her for the next show season. Watson never specified whether the bitch worked in the stock yards or on a farm, but he hastened to explain that she learned her complicated job in three days and subsequently trained all the young dogs that followed her.

How typical of the Collie to see a need and fill it. This trait of almost immediately and permanently imprinting on first experiences is another facet of Collie character that makes it important to ensure that when a Collie, if first exposed to livestock, be given ample opportunity to express his natural instinct without being permitted to develop bad habits. Instinct testing the ever-gentle Collie can be touchy business. As an example, a dog who is first allowed to chase stock out of control will probably need such firm corrections to cure that bad habit that the dog may be completely discouraged from any further attempt at herding.

Although the emphasis among East Coast fanciers has always been on showing, further west, especially in Wyoming and the mountain states, several important stud dogs such as the sons of Ch. Tokalon's Blue Banner, CD, were selected for their working ability as well as their ability to win in the breed ring. Over a period of 30 years, Glen Twiford's Wind Call Kennels produced a significant number of accomplished stock dogs that were also breed champions. The style of herding practiced on the Twiford ranches closely resembled droving or tending with flocks of two or three thousand sheep constantly being moved from one grazing area to another by a mounted shepherd accompanied by two Collies.

The American Kennel Club herding program offers the fancy an important opportunity to preserve the rich heritage of the breed and insure that future generations of Collies continue to be the unique animals we know and love. Given a favorable opportunity to ignite their latent instinct most Collies will approach working stock with unqualified joy. Whether rounding dog, droving dog, or patrolling dog, they all certainly "perform the useful functions for which they were originally bred."

Whatever their working style, they all carry on their distinguished heritage and are a credit to the breed. Few breeds of dogs have had such a remarkable impact on the course of human history as the Collie, and sadly little acknowledgment has ever been given to these accomplishments. However, it is certain that the Collie will continue to be loved and cherished for all his virtues by a dedicated fancy for many generations to come.

THE COLLIE IN OBEDIENCE
by Carol Knock

Changes in dog obedience training have been very positive. When we began obedience training in the 1930s, the rule of thumb was to purchase a leash and a choke chain. There was seldom a reference to lead width, what the lead or collar was to be made from, nor how to size a training collar. These tools were sometimes loud, uncomfortable and distracting to the Collie. As the years passed, we became wiser. Soon we learned our Collies did not learn well through force, but learned through good communication and kindness. Trainers began teaching obedience training with user-friendly tools.

Training instructors have attended seminars all around the world bringing back new and unique techniques. Obedience instructors have been educated on how to understand the many canine and human personalities. Knowing how to resolve canine behavior problems and human emotions has made it possible to develop the most potential of the Collie and his owner/trainer. We have come a long way from the crash-bang-forced obedience training. Various methods of communication, compassion and kindness have enhanced the Collie's attitude and thirst for learning. We have been enlightened by: trainers of facilities, such as Sea World who does "operant conditioning;" groups such as National Association of Dog Obedience Instructors (NADOI) who have helped develop better-educated dog obedience training instructors;, and many well-known dog psychologists, veterinarians, and commercial schools.

Mysti fetches the ducks to the handler. It appears that the flock has started to split, a serious error, but Mysti has shifted her direction slightly in order to regroup the ducks before they split further. (Photo by Bonnie Young, courtesy of Suzanne Schwab)

Dog obedience magazines, newsletters, and dog obedience clubs were formed. The world of computers has come into our lives. Computers have made training education more accessible because of the Internet. We now can have an E-Mail address and talk to other obedience enthusiasts throughout the world. Because of the vast knowledge we have gained in the past 60 years, Collies have not only scored high in competition, but have become a better understood breed as a pet.

Collies have Companion Dog and Utility Dog titles, along with Tracking, Herding, Agility, Versatility, and Canine Good Citizen certificates.

Obedience training expanded into more than just a sport earning AKC obedience titles. It found new ways to have fun with Collies. Some of those activities included Frisbees, Flyball, sledding, herding, carting, tracking, backpacking, swimming, bicycling, walking, jogging, relay racing, agility, Canine Good Citizenship programs, Temperament Testing, assistant dogs, and social/therapy dogs.

Tracking

Who ever heard of a Collie tracking, we were told by past trainers. Surprise! They were as good if not better than other breeds being trained. Tracking clubs were formed. It is exciting to try this new adventure. And what do you know, we have numerous tracking Collies. For further information on Tracking with your Collie, contact the CCA for the Tracking Committee Chairman.

Relay Racing

What great fun for Collies to race against another team over a series of four jumps to retrieve a scented dumbbell out of a group of four dumbbells. We made special jackets for our Collies with team colors and team numbers.

Controversy over jump height for the Collie became evident as the years passed. After considerable rhetoric, the AKC allowed the Collie's jump height to be lowered. In 1996, jump height is once again being investigated and possibly will be lowered. Many other AKC rule changes have taken place. New rule books may be ordered from the AKC.

Competition Obedience

When competing in an AKC obedience trial, you have the opportunity to earn a "leg" which eventually earns an obedience title. This is accomplished by earning a qualifying score. If you earn a qualifying score under three different judges, you are eligible for an obedience title. The first title earned at an AKC obedience trial is CD. CD stands for Companion Dog and is earned in the Novice class. The Novice class consists of heeling with dog on and off lease, a figure eight, stand for examination,

Above: U-CD Sunrise Diane Duo Delight, UD, perform-
ing the Open broadjump exercise. Below: She is per-
forming the flip finish. Owned by Diane Hemphill

Sunrise Diane Kentfield Gold, HIC, performing the retrieve over the high jump, an Open exercise. Owned by Anita Gaeta.

a recall, and a long sit and long down. Your second title is a CDX and is earned in the Open class. CDX stands for Companion Dog Excellent. The Open class consists of heeling off leash, figure eight off leash, retrieve on flat, retrieve over the high jump, drop on recall, broad jump, and long sit and down out of sight. The title at an AKC obedience trial is the UD and is earned in the Utility class. CD stands for Utility Dog. The Utility class consists of hand signals, heel from stand, directed retrieve, directed jumping, scent articles, and long stand.

Besides accumulating legs to earn a title behind your Collie's name, you now have the opportunity to earn an Obedience Championship. If you have the placement wins according to the AKC rule book, you will earn points toward your Obedience Trial Championship (OTCH). Once this title is earned, you place it in front of your Collie's registered name.

Canine Good Citizen

Obedience competition isn't the only event taking place for your Collie. We now have an activity called Canine Good Citizen (CGC). The CGC was designed in response to the anti-canine sentiment gaining mo-

U-CD Sunrise Check It Out, CDX, performing the go-out, a part of the Utility directed jumping exercise. Owned by Diane Hemphill.

mentum in society today. The purpose of the CGC test is to demonstrate that the dog as a companion of man can be a respected member of the community. The CGC involves taking your Collie to a CGC event where they have set up various situations. These situations test your Collie's confidence and control. At the present time, your Collie will be tested in 10 different situations. They are: 1) accepting a friendly stranger; 2) sitting politely for petting; 3) appearance and grooming; 4) walking on a loose leash; 5) walking through a crowd; 6) performing the sit and down command/staying in place; 7) accepting praise/interaction; 8) reaction to another dog; 9) reactions to distractions; and 10) supervised isolation. Writing to the American Kennel Club will give you the most recent rules and regulations needed to perform the Canine Good Citizen Test.

Agility

One of the most exciting events is Agility. This sport has become popular not only with obedience enthusiasts but also the public. Your Collie is required to go through a course of objects that test the athletic ability and willingness of your dog. Your Collie must go over a series of jumps, across a dog walk, through open and collapsed tunnels, through a tire jump, weave in between weave poles, across a teeter totter, jump up on a pause box, and climb up an "A" frame, not necessarily in that order. If you qualify according to the rules of the sponsoring organization, you will earn titles to be placed behind your dog's name. There are different levels of Agility. Each section becomes a bit more challenging. Not only does your Collie have to be physically fit but so does the handler. For more information on Agility, write to the American Kennel Club for their Agility rules and regulations.

There is another organization known as the USDAA (United State Dog Agility Association). This organization's rules differ from the AKC. No matter which group you choose to be a competitor, the excitement for you and your dog is phenomenal.

Herding

One area that should never be neglected is the Collie's instinctive nature to herd. We now have Herding Instinct tests. These tests determine if your Collie has an instinct to herd. If this activity intrigues you, you can go another step further, and begin to train your dog to herd. At that point you can seek out herding competitions to become involved in. For further information on herding with your Collie, write to the Collie Club of America for the most current name and phone number of the Herding Committee Chairman.

Am. & Can. Ch. OTCh. Shoreham Dubious Delight, TD, Can. CD, owned by Jennifer Julander, having fun jumping over Jennifer's husband Harold. (Photo by Rich Bergman)

Social/Therapy Dog and Assistance Dog Programs

Therapy dog programs have cropped up throughout the nation. Your Collie has to follow criteria to be able to present himself in a hospital or nursing home situation. Although therapy dogs have been recognized since the 18th Century, we have fine-tuned the procedure so that Collies may be good canine citizens to those in need. Collies are assistance dogs for the blind, assistants to individuals who are afflicted with seizures, hearing impaired, as well as other types of disabilities. For more information of Social/Therapy Dogs and/or Assistance Dogs, please contact the Collie Club of America.

As you have read, obedience training has come a long way. Many years ago, trainers would spend a two-day weekend with a well-known trainer to update their skills and knowledge to instruct or to be better handlers. Today, we have two-to-seven-day Dog Scout Camps, Canine Behavior and Training Camps, seminars and other gatherings throughout the world. They teach you not only how to understand your dog but also how to have fun and truly enjoy your Collie as a companion.

We have NADOI, a well-known worldwide organization that continually assists instructors with new and innovative training techniques, behavior modifications, upcoming workshops, seminars, camps and just plain fun. NADOI has currently compiled an Internet address book. Check with your local kennel club for a NADOI obedience instructor near you. If you cannot find a NADOI instructor in your area, contact the Collie Club of America Obedience Committee Chairman who will help you find a Collie obedience person near you.

There are video tapes on competitive obedience, behavioral solutions, positive training methods with food, and your dog's athletic ability. Audiotapes, books, and magazines have every conceivable piece of information you ever wanted to know about your dog. Go to your local library, book store, or local pet supply retailer and look for dog magazines, books, and videotapes. If you need a specific address on a specific area of training, please contact the Collie Club of America. It would be more than happy to put you and your Collie on the right track. No matter which area of training you choose, it will open the door to a whole new world with you and your Collie. Good luck and enjoy every minute.

American Working Collie Association

by Jean Levitt, president

Dedicated to the promotion and preservation of the Collie as a working dog, the American Working Collie Association (AWCA) was established in 1979 by founder Cindy Dorsten. It consisted of a small group of Collie owners scattered across the country who shared the conviction that the multi-talented Collie ought to have the opportunity to demonstrate, develop and receive recognition for the many latent working instincts inherent in the breed, particularly herding.

By 1984, a Versatility program was established. It awards the Versatility Companion (VC), Versatility Companion Excellent (VCX), Versatility Championship (VCH) to Collies that have demonstrated a wide range of skills as working dogs.

The VC title, awarded to many dogs and placed after the dog's name, indicates that at least five titles and certifications in at least three categories have been earned (one point for each title and certification).

The VCX title, awarded to quite a few dogs is also placed after the dog's name, indicates at least 10 titles and certifications in at least five categories have been earned. It is quite an achievement and requires considerable training and teamwork between handler and dog.

The VCH title, awarded very sparingly and placed in front of the dog's name, indicates that at least 15 titles and certifications in at least six categories with at least two titles from two different categories have been earned at the intermediate or advanced level. The categories are: stock work, obedience, soundness, scent work, protection, draft work, assistance work, canine sports, conformation ring and miscellaneous.

Four Collies have been awarded the Versatility Champion title:

1. Ch. VCH **King's Valley Select**, Cole (known as Gentleman Cole) HC, BPDX, WKD, AD, Registered Service Dog for the Disabled, owned by Jean Levitt, bred and trained by Eva and Leslie Rappaport.

2. U-UO, Can, Otch, VCH, **Mo's Superstar** (Bobby) Am CDX, VB, TT, VCX, HC, STD dsc, OTD-d, HTDX, HTD, TDI, CRT owned by Monike Hole and Ray Meisch.

3. Ch. U-CDX, VCX, HTCH **Sunbrier Spectre** CDX, HS, CRT, HTDX, ATDd, STD sc, RD, TT, TDT owned, bred and trained by Kathy Stokey Dillon.

4. Am/Can Ch VCX, Can OTCH, U-UD, Hi, VU, **Black Bart**

Above: Markos Aatuk Blue Austin (Sir Austin) and Jean Levitt. Below: Ch. & V. Ch. Kings Valley Select and Jean Levitt. As service dogs, they backpack, pull carts and are Walker Dogs for Jean. (Photos by Barry Levitt).

the Sky Hawk, UDT, HT, AG-11, VX, TT, TRI, CgC owned and trained by Jim Smotrel; bred by Mary M. and Kareb Hutchinson.

Collectively, these four Collies have won *Dog World Awards*, been featured repeatedly on television and in books, magazines and newspapers. They have appeared publicly to give demonstrations, to educate, to raise money for the homeless and disabled, and Collie Rescue. They have modeled for print advertisements and television commercials. They have made hundreds of social therapy dog visits. They have performed farm work, backpacked, pulled luggage on travois, carts and sleds, sired champion offspring, rescued people, and toured the White House.

The American Working Collie Herding Program, which includes Herding Instinct Certification and several levels of herding trials titles, demonstrates trained Collies utilizing their herding abilities.

This particular type of herding program evolved into what is now the American Kennel Club Herding Program. This program, according to Cindy Dorsten, was designed to help encourage, preserve and protect the natural and innate herding abilities of the Collie, and to promote the Collie as a trained working dog and stock dog, and herding trials competitor.

The association offers a draft Work Program that includes sledding, weight pulling, backpacking and the popular carting. A backpacking BPD dog and BPDX, backpacking Dog Excellent titles are offered. And, Carting, CRT and Carting Excellent titles are offered.

Temperament certification tests are sanctioned AWCA, utilizing the Temperament Certification program of the German Shepherd Club of America.

The AWCA newsletter, *Collie Connection*, edited by Vice President Terry Thistlewaite, contains educational articles, news, original working Collie sketches by Terry, and updates on new titles earned by American working Collies.

For more information about the association or its programs, please send a business-size envelope to: Gail Jay, AWCA secretary/treasurer, 2100 Fiero Avenue, Schnectady NY 12303.

PART IV.

BREEDING

*Ch. Tartanside Th' Critics Choice,
Top Producing Sire of All Time in
Collies as of 1996. Shown here at the
age of 13.*

Creating Families and Strains
by John Buddie

Since the demise of the really big kennel operations back at the early part of the century, the picture of the Collie lines and strains has undergone great transition. While some kennels are still able to work with large numbers of dogs on a larger scale, they are the exception to the rule for the most part. Working on a larger scale, one is able to achieve homozygosity among individuals in a shorter amount of time due to the number of breedings that can be accomplished at one time.

When the big kennels were in their heyday, each had characteristics that they deemed of great importance and each and every generation produced individuals that were strong in these areas. Once certain characteristics were firmly in place, they became "typical" of particular families and each family became known for the strong characteristics that seemed to be synonymous with that family. These characteristics were important to good breed type as well. These breeders made their way into that realm of top breeders. Their lines were well respected. Often serving as foundations for new lines or as complementary crosses.

Today, the majority of the breeders are forced to work on a smaller scale and achieving a new strain of Collies or a new family look is a long and ambitious process. As families evolve, certain individuals within the given family stand out. These individuals chosen carefully by the breeder serve as the fountainheads of the lines. Judicious outcrosses are sought and complementary linebred dogs introduced, but the key to success always lies in the selection of the right individuals. There is no magic formula for success. The eye of the breeder is truly the key to success and each breeder approaches this task with a different formula.

So You Want to be a Breeder
By Dr. Cindi Bossart

For the past 17 years in veterinary practice, I have been approached by many people who for one reason or another have decided they want to breed their dog. When they ask my advice I spend the next 10 to 15 minutes explaining all of the tragedies that may occur: stillborns; cesarean sections; bad milk; fading puppies, etc. If, after my attempt to dissuade them breeding their dogs, they still want to have a litter of puppies, I will present my DOs and DON'Ts of "So you want to be a breeder."

Prenatal Care

Choosing a mate for your dog requires careful consideration. Phenotype is what the animal looks like. Genotype means the genes that make up this animal. Before choosing a mate, you must look at the pedigree of your dog and the pedigree of a potential mate to make sure you are not doubling up on a problem, such as progressive retinal atrophy or hip dysplasia. With the AKC pedigrees that list CERF and OFA numbers this has become easier.

The reproduction history of your dog should be studied. If you have a bitch, how were her mother, grandmother and aunts as far as heat

Ch. Affenloch The Silver Laser was imported to the US from Canada by Dr. Cindi Bossart. He finished his American championship as a youngster. In his first litter, when bred to Glen Hill Pipi Longstocking, he produced at least five champions. He promises to be an important addition to American bloodlines. His pedigree is derived almost entirely from Glen Hill and Tartanside lines.

cycles, conception, live births and nursing. If four out of five bitches in the litter have not gone into heat at two years of age, I would look at another line of dogs for my potential bitch. Then again, if all the males in the last litter were sterile, I would not buy a male pup from the repeat inhouse stud dog.

As far as physical condition prior to breeding, I like to see both bitches and dogs be of normal weight, not too thin and, by all means, not obese. They should be exercised routinely to keep in excellent physical condition. A male in good physical condition will have a better libido, and a female in good physical condition will have an easier time whelping in nine weeks.

Examination Prior to Breeding

The Bitch: Prior to breeding, bitches come into my office for a good physical examination. The entire body is examined to check the outward health of the bitch. An internal exam, or vaginal, is performed to check for any abnormalities, such as the presence of a persistent hymen (a band of tissue across the vagina) or the presence of an osclitoris (a small bone in the clitorus, which is usually indicative of a "termaphrodite"), and that bitch should be studied more carefully before becoming a part of any breeding program. Examination of the cervix may reveal lesions indicative of infection.

Laboratory tests on the bitch include vaginal cytologies, culture and sensitivity of the cervix, mycoplasma cultures, serum brucellosis tests, complete blood panel on any bitch over six years of age and a thyroid test. A parvo titer may be done to make sure the bitch has antibodies to parvovirus that she will pass on to her pups for early life protection. An ICG target test is performed to determine the time of ovulation on a bitch in heat. This determines the proper time to breed the bitch successfully.

Problem bitches may require surgical evaluation of the reproduction tract. This can be done with laparoscoy or by an exploratory surgery.

The Dog: On physical examination any abnormalities are noted. Are there two testicles? Do the testicles feel the same? Are they painful or hot? The penis is extruded from the sheath to examine for signs of infectious lesions or physical abnormalities.

Lab tests start out with a semen sample. Semen is collected from the male. At this time, his libido and ability to make normal pelvic thrusts is examined. The penis is examined during ejaculation to make sure the bulb of the penis enlarges normally to insure a "tie" during a natural breeding. The semen is then examined for the volume of all three parts (the pre-sperm, the sperm, and the prostatic fluid). The second fraction is examined for the number of sperm per cc, the appearance of those sperm and their motility. Culture and sensitivity and mycoplasma culture are performed on the semen sample.

Two additional lab tests are brucellosis evaluation and testicular biopsy. The latter is used in dogs with infertility or decreased fertility to determine the cause of the change in fertility and the possible treatment. Dogs with no sperm production or abnormal sperm production are not considered sterile without first having testicular biopsy. When performed under a sterile surgical environment, this is a very safe diagnostic procedure.

Breeding

Now that the bitch and dog have been evaluated for their breeding soundness, we are ready to commence breeding. Determination of the correct days to breed a bitch has been simplified with the advent of progesterone and LH testing done in the hospital on blood samples taken from the bitch. There is an abrupt change in hormone status that occurs in the bitch four to seven days prior to ovulation. This abrupt change in the blood allows proper timing for successful insemination by the dog. If chilled semen is to be sent from Los Angeles to Washington, D.C., this change in hormones allows the breeder in California to know when to ship sperm to the East Coast bitch. If the bitch and dog are both in Washington, D.C., the abrupt change of hormone in the blood tells us when to conduct insemination. New, more accurate determinations of ovulation are becoming available on a day-to-day basis. Veterinarians who deal in reproduction keep abreast of the new technologies.

Vaginal cytologies determine the change in the environment of the vagina. Increased cornification of the vaginal wall *usually* coincides with ovulation timing, the more cornified (a distinct change in type of cells) the closer to ovulation.

A dog's libido is a good indicator of the proper time to breed. The only problem arises with the male who will breed even when a bitch is not in heat and the bitch that stands when she is not in heat.

Presently, the most accurate determination of the best time to breed is blood hormone testing.

Techniques for Breeding

The traditional "doggie style" of natural breeding is a very successful mode of insemination. As long as the bitch and dog are well behaved, physically fit and free of infectious disease, this is a totally acceptable method.

Vaginal or cervical insemination takes the worry out of being close. This method insures that the semen is introduced to the proper part of the bitch. Some inexperienced males when bred traditionally will ejaculate prior to putting the penis inside the bitch. Many a breeding has been lost on the kitchen floor. If there is a discrepancy in size of the bitch and dog or if the dog is not on the premises (i.e., chilled semen), this method of insemination is safe and effective.

Surgical insemination is used for problem bitches. If we feel there is a problem with vaginal insemination, we will surgically inseminate the bitch. Frozen semen is routinely surgically inseminated. Veterinarians who are involved in reproduction can instruct you on frozen semen collection, storage and insemination.

Pregnancy

Pregnancy determination is accomplished presently by one or all three methods: 1) by palpation of the uterus: an experienced hand can feel the uterus and small marbles inside the uterus (baby puppies between 21-25 days after the last breeding; (2) ultrasound can pick up puppies starting at 19-22 days; and (3) ICG (International Canine Genetics) has an actual "pregnancy test" done on blood that is accurate from day 30-35 after the last breeding.

Even before pregnancy is determined as positive, we treat a bitch as though she were pregnant. For the first three weeks (first trimester, as most pregnancies are about 9 weeks long), we start the bitch on a good growth formula of food. Exercise is regulated on a daily basis. Swimming is not allowed, but good, organized exercise is encouraged. During the second trimester, pregnancy is determined. If positive, we increase the food ration by 20 percent to 40 percent depending on the activity of the bitch. This increase may be in the form of the growth food ration, balanced pregnancy diet supplement, or other supplements such as cooked hamburger and cottage cheese. During the beginning of the second trimester, most bitches will go off feed for a day or two. This coincides with changes that are occurring in the uterus. Breeders refer to this change in behavior as "morning sickness." Bitches should be encouraged to eat.

In the third trimester, most of the bone growth and "body tissues" that make puppies look like puppies occurs. Throughout pregnancy the bitch's weight with puppies will increase approximately 30 percent with most of the weight gain in the third trimester. Multiple feedings will allow the bitch to consume the nutrients she needs to whelp successfully. Do not, however, allow the bitch to become fat.

As far as pharmaceutical supplementation, any drug that is administered to a pregnant bitch must be safe for her and her developing puppies. An experienced veterinarian and/or reading the drug insert will let you know if a particular pharmaceutical is safe during pregnancy.

Radiographs of a pregnant bitch can determine normalcy and number of puppies. The puppies' skeletons show up on radiograph initially around 45 days of pregnancy. Skeletal tissue forms in a predictable order, first the head, then the front legs, rear legs, ribs and finally the teeth. Radiology helps with whelping by determining how many puppies should be delivered and whether the bitch's pelvic canal is large enough to deliver the puppies or whether a cesarean section should be planned.

If natural whelping is preferred, you must be prepared (lots of friends and supplies at hand). Again, progesterone testing will accurately determine when delivery will occur. If this is not feasible, taking the bitch's temperature three times daily for one week before the first due date and up to delivery will *usually* show a drop in body temperature of the bitch to about 98° between 12-36 hours before whelping. Most, but not all bitches will go off feed 12 hours before delivery. Most bitches will also start nesting behavior 6 to 24 hours before whelping. Remember not all bitches "read the book." Some bitches have normal temperatures throughout pregnancy and deliver puppies while eating dinner.

Normal delivery starts with slight uterine contractions with or without voluntary abdominal contractions. This stage of whelping may last 12-72 hours. The actual birthing starts with uterine contractions accompanied by voluntary abdominal contractions of the bitch. Hard continuous contractions should produce a pup in five to ten minutes. The interval between pups may be as long as three hours or as short as two seconds (that's why it's important to have friends around). If three hours pass and the next pup has not been delivered, contact your veterinarian. The bitch may need oxytocin and/or calcium supplements. She may even need a c-section. Three hours between puppies should be a rule of thumb for deciding when to ask for assistance from your veterinarian. Some bitches may go six hours between puppies, but after three hours the bitch should be examined to make sure everything is proceeding normally.

At the end of whelping, the bitch should be checked to make sure all the puppies have been delivered. She should get a clean-out shot of oxytocin to remove any retained placentas that were not delivered as the pups came out.

Neonatal Care

Some bitches on delivery do exactly what they should. This "perfect bitch" pulls each individually wrapped pup out of the vagina. She removes the placenta from around the puppy, then eats the placenta. This stimulates more uterine contractions and milk let down. She licks the puppy clean and nudges the pup up to her nipples then encourages the pup to nurse. In this "perfect" situation, we can just sit and observe.

Unfortunately, this doesn't always happen. At this point, we have to intervene. We take the pup out of the placenta, clear the throat with a small ear bulb syringe. We rub the pup in a soft warm cloth, shake it gently to clear the lungs, then stimulate it to breathe. After he's breathing well, we attach the pup to the bitch's nipple. Once the puppy starts its rooting behavior we can take a breather until hard uterine contractions start again. At this time, we remove the nursing pup to a critter box (an infant incubator) and prepare to deliver and tend to the next puppy.

In the first few days of life, the number one killer of newborn puppies it hypothermia or low body temperature. Puppies do not have the internal ability to regulate body heat at this early age. If for some reason a pup gets away from the body heat of the bitch or is not in his warm toasty infant incubator, his body may super cool. Any milk that may be in the intestines will curdle. The pup will have no energy to breathe, then his heart will stop and the pup will die.

A puppy's temperature can be taken with a rectal thermometer right after birth. The rectal temperature should be 97° to 99° for the first three days of life. Body temperature should slowly increase over the next week to 10 days to 100° to 101°.

If the bitch is not "sitting tight" and leaves the puppies often, a heat source should be provided to keep the puppies from super cooling when the bitch is away. If the bitch is a "bad" mother and continually pushes her pups away, it may be wise to attach the pups every hour, let them feed, let the bitch stimulate the pups to urinate and defecate, then put the pups back in the infant incubator until the next feeding.

In some instances, the bitch may not be able to take care of the pups. For some reason, she tries to destroy them when they are near her (in that case, if the pups are normal, a second litter from this bitch would be questionable). If she has toxic milk from infection, or she has eclampsia (a calcium imbalance that may be corrected before the bitch can safely continue to nurse), it may be necessary to hand rear the puppies temporarily or completely.

Hand rearing puppies takes time and patience. The methods of feeding the types of milk replacers may vary. But the art of hand rearing (and any breeder who has successfully hand reared a litter will concur it is an art) does not vary. You must control the environment, supply enough nutrition and stimulate the normal body functions. In newborn pups, the normal body functions are rooting for food and eliminating. A baby bottle nipple to the roof of the mouth will stimulate rooting. A baby wipe to the bottom will stimulate urination and defecation.

When you get to this point and you find yourself hand rearing a litter, it's time to call in all the help of those you know with experience. Most of the disasters that a first timer may be having have already been encountered by other breeders.

The most important thing you can do to maximize your success in caring for newborn puppies is to be prepared. Supplies needed include feeding supplies, appropriate environmental supplies and nursing care essentials. Choosing a formula is a complicated task. Many homemade recipes abound and you'll get lots of conflicting advice from breeders and veterinarians alike. We have raised orphan puppies on the commercially prepared diet of *Havolac* at a dilution of 50:50 with lactated ringers' solution. We have also used goat's milk as a supplement for puppies being suckled by the bitch. Cow's milk has nearly four times the amount of lactose as bitch's milk and can cause diarrhea when used as formula. The formula fed puppies by us is divided into six to eight feedings daily. For puppies less than one week old, we feed approximately 20 ml (i.e., two-thirds of an ounce) per pound of body weight per feeding. Frequent weighings are required to adjust the amount fed accordingly. A rule of thumb is that a pup should gain 5 to 10 percent of birth weight each day. For example: a 10-ounce puppy at birth should gain about one ounce per day. Puppy weights should be doubled by 10 to 14 days of age. Use an accurate scale at these low weights. Be sure to purchase a baby bottle that has measurements on it in milliliters (mls) and ounces. An assortment of nipple sizes is also handy to accommodate puppy preferences thus encouraging suckling. Keep the pups in a secure area from other household animals and out of cold, drafty or wet areas.

Remember the pups' nervous systems are still developing for the first three to four weeks. Rooting reflexes (nuzzling a cupped hand) are present in normal newborn. Eyes open usually between 10 and 14 days but retinas are not fully developed until about four weeks of age. Ear canals usually open somewhere around 14 days, but most pups don't hear like an adult until they are four weeks of age.

Preparing yourself for supportive care of newborns can ease the strain and tension associated with the demands of your new charges. Following these simple tips can make the experience a rewarding and successful one.

If you have any questions or would like to discuss breeding dogs, contact your local breed club, or a veterinarian who has a special interest in reproduction.

Genetics

The study of genetics can be complicated and difficult to understand, but in the breeding of any animal, the background is extremely important. The more one knows about the ancestors of an individual dog, the more one can predict the qualities of its offspring. Pedigree study can be instructive as to desired qualities, such as cleared eye conditions, good hip status, and if you are really familiar with the dogs in the background, you will know about temperament, color, good or bad structural points and such important things as coat, style, expression, head, feet and beauty. Certainly the more information you have about ancestral qualities, both good and bad, the better you can plan a breeding program. There is one advantage of advanced age for a breeder: One can usually remember that old Ch. What's His Name back in the fifth generation was a good-looking dog, but produced a lot of problems.

Consistent breeding of show quality dogs should be considered an art. To some breeders it comes naturally. Others have to learn this art. Still others will never achieve success in this vital and important facet of purebred dogs.

To some breeders having an eye for a dog is second nature. Breeders lacking this natural talent can become self-taught provided they have the intelligence and motivation to discern between the good and poor examples set before them.

Consistent breeding of show-quality specimens depends on important factors beyond the natural or acquired talents of the breeder. The breeding stock itself is of prime importance and should be the very best the breeder can obtain. Many breeders still operate under the illusion that second best will produce as well as the choice specimen, pedigrees being equal

Another important element contributing to the success or failure of any given breeding program is that of chance. Everything else being equal, sex distribution, puppy mortality, timing, transmission of the best factors (or the poorest), etc., all depend to a great extent on chance.

There is no shortcut to breed improvement, no miraculous or secret formula that can put Mother Nature out of business and place the breeder in full control. There are, however, many do's and don'ts that can be used to minimize the chances of failure and to encourage the chances of success. These do's and don'ts are axioms of our breed, yet there are breeders who ignore and bypass them.

The first step in your breeding program is to decide what is ideal. Until a breeder knows what kind of specimen he wants, he is stopped cold and can neither select the best nor discard the worst. This is where the breeder's capabilities and talents come into play. For this is the basis of selective breeding, and the backbone of any breeding program.

Characteristics such as height and coat color are known as inherited traits. They are traits that offspring inherit or receive from parents. Inherited traits are passed along from generation to generation. As a result of heredity, each generation is linked to older generations and to past generations. For example, a dog may resemble his parents with respect to height, head shape and coat color. His grandsire or great grandsire may have also possessed the same identifying features.

A whole science known as genetics has grown up around the study of heredity. Specifically, the science of genetics is the study of how the reproduction process determines the characteristics of an offspring and how these characteristics are distributed.

According to Anthony Smith, writing in *The Human Pedigree*:

Gregor Mendel, a nineteenth-century monk living in Czechoslovakia, is credited as the founder of genetics. Basically, Mendel's work had proved that traits can be passed from one generation to the next, both with mathematical precision and in separate packets. Before this time, it had been assumed that inheritance was always the result of being colored water of a weaker hue. Mendel foresaw genes, the differing units of inheritance (that are named, incidentally, after the Greek for race). Genes remain distinct entities. They do not blend, like that of colored water. They produce, to continue the analogy, either plain water, or colored water or a mixture between the two. Moreover, assuming no other genes are involved to complicate the story, they continue to create three kinds of product in generation after generation. The packets remained distinct.

The mathematics also has a pleasing simplicity at least in the early stages. The human blue-eye/brown eye situation is a good elementary example. There are genes for brown and genes for blue, everybody receives one of each from each parent. To receive two browns is to be brown-eyed. To receive two blues is to be blue-eyed. To receive one of each is also to be brown-eyed because the brown has the effect of masking the relative transparency of the blue.

This also signifies that brown is dominant over blue and will always cover over the recessive blue color. Blue will only be expressed when it, as a recessive, is inherited from both parents.

The clarity of Mendel's vision certainly helped science. It was assumed that all of inheritance was equally clear cut, with a ratio of 3:1, or his equally famous ratio of 9:3:1 (involving two characteristics) explaining all of our genetic fortunes. So they do, in a sense, but the real situation is much more complex. Only a few aspects of inheritance are controlled by a single pair of genes. Only a few more are controlled by two pairs. A feature like height, for example, or coat color may be organized by 20 or so pair of genes. Each pair is working in a Mendelian manner, but the cumulative effect of all of them working together is a bewilderment.

There are literally thousands and thousands of paired genes within each animal. There are enough of them, and enough possible variations, to ensure that each specimen is unique. Never in history has there been a duplicate of any specimen. Never in all of future history will there be another one just like it again. Each dog is a combination that is entirely individual and yet his genes are common to the population they live in. There is nothing unique about them.

Piggybacking now upon Mendel's work and that of later scientists, let us look at how breeders can use this knowledge and breed better dogs.

Each dog contains a pair of genes in each of its cells for each trait that it inherits. One of the genes is contributed by the sire and the other by the dam. For a discussion regarding color, see Chapter 1, section on Color.

Though the color of a dog's coat may be determined by a single gene or by a pair of genes, the skeletal structure of a dog is determined by the interaction of a large number of genes. It should be easy to understand why something as highly complex as the structure of a dog's head or body is controlled by the actions of multiple hereditary factors.

Movement is a good example. No one gene labeled gait has the ability to determine whether an individual puppy will move properly or improperly. Rather, there are countless genes, working in concert which determine these facts.

What factors enable an individual dog to move in a way that has been designated as correct for its particular breed? Every breed has a characteristic gait, which is determined by its structure—not the structure of the legs, or the feet, or the hips, or the shoulders, but the structure of all the parts working in concert for this breed. Thus, the Chow Chow moves with short steps and stilted action, the Pekinese and Bulldog roll along, and the German Shepherd Dog covers ground rapidly with far-reaching steps and a smooth action. These differences in gait are the result of differences in structure—the manner in which all the body parts are assembled in an individual.

Any attempt to explain multiple-factor inheritance fully would prove to be a real puzzle, for most dog breeders have no formal training in advanced genetics. However, the following facts may serve to give a better understanding of this complex subject:

1. What is seen and described as a single characteristic (leg, foot, tail, etc.) is often affected and influenced in its development by a large number of different and unrelated genes that are capable of independent assortment.

2. It is extremely difficult to sort out the various genes that influence a particular characteristic and to determine the specific effect each has on that characteristic. In other words, just how important is a given gene in the development of a particular characteristic?

3. Some genes have a direct, complete influence on the development of a characteristic (dominant genes). Some have only a partial effect, being neutralized to some extent by the action of the opposing member of the pair of which it is one (incompletely dominant genes). Some genes are completely masked and have no effect unless such genes comprise both members of a given pair (recessive genes).

4. The combination of multiple-gene effects together with environmental influences is the rule rather than the exception in such characteristics as body length, height, weight, head and muzzle development, tooth characteristics, foot size and shape, muscle and bone development, and such recognized faults as loose shoulders, flat ribs, cowhocks, weak pasterns and splay feet. As an example, body size depends upon some genes that affect all the tissue and upon others that influence only certain regions, such as the legs, neck, head or tail. In addition, diet, exercise and other environmental influences determine the degree to which genes are able to stimulate and produce growth of the different tissues, organs and body parts.

There are some 140 breeds eligible for registration with the American Kennel Club. None of the breeds is purebred in the true genetic sense of the word. All of them are subject to variations of form and type which may account for considerable differences in appearance between specimens of the same breed. Unlike certain strains of laboratory mice, which have been standardized by inbreeding and selection, no breed of dog exists which duplicates its own kind without variation.

Major differences between breeds are probably due to independent genes that may be found in one breed and not in another. To understand the manner in which complex parts such as the body, legs, head, and other structural parts are inherited, the following will be necessary:

1. Observations of a large number of animals, resulting in careful and accurate records of the differences in structure which exist within the breed.

2. Accurately recorded breeding tests between the animals of contrasting structural types, and recorded observations of their resulting offspring. This may well require the crossing of breeds at one or more genetic research laboratories, as was done in the controlled experiments done by Dr. C.C. Little at the Jackson Memorial Laboratory of Bar Harbor, Maine. In this way, extreme types can be compared and the inheritance of marked differences in structure can be studied.

3. The making available of these records to scientists who are qualified to analyze them. The task of breeding and raising a large enough number of animals representing different breeds, the recording of observations of their structural types and the types of their offspring, is beyond the finances and ability of any one person or any one institution. However, such data could be collected by breeders at no additional expense and a small amount of additional work. Each breeder's records could be sent to a central laboratory for analysis and any resulting conclusions could, in turn, be made available to breeders.

What kind of questions pertaining to inheritance in dogs can geneticists answer right now? Information pertaining to a great variety of subjects is available, including: color differences found in the coat, eyes, and skin of most breeds of dog; differences in the length, quantity, texture and distribution of hair; various reproductive problems, such as fertility, fecundity, the production of stillborn or non-viable young, monorchidism; various abnormalities of the eye, malformations resulting from arrested development, such as harelip, cleft palate, cleft abdomen, etc.; diseases as hemophilia and night blindness; differences in ear, eye, nose, jaw, foot and tail characteristics; differences in head size and shape; and numerous physiological differences resulting in characteristic patterns of behavior.

Many breeders have practiced line breeding by grandfather to granddaughter breeding, but have only skirted the edges of inbreeding which might include full brother to sister matings shying away from carrying it to its full potential. As a means of finding out which animals have the best genes, inbreeding deserves more use than it has received. Not only does it uncover recessives more surely than any other method, but it increases the relationship between the inbred animal and its parents and other relatives so that the animal's pedigree and the merits of the family to which it belongs become more dependable as indicators of its own genes.

Considerable inbreeding is necessary if family selection is to be very effective. The gene is the unit of inheritance, but the animal is the smallest unit that can be chosen or rejected for breeding purposes. To breed exclusively to one or two of the best specimens available would tend to fix their qualities, both good and bad. In fact, that is the essence of what happens under extreme inbreeding. Moreover, the breeder will make at least a few mistakes in estimating which animals have the very best inheritance. Hence, in a practical program, the breeder will hesitate to use even a very good stud too extensively.

The breeder also is far from having final authority to decide how many offspring each of his bitches will produce. Some of his basic stock may die or prove to be sterile or will be prevented by a wide variety of factors from having as many get as the breeder wants. Bitches from which he wants a top stud dog may persist in producing only females for several litters.

The ideal plan for the most rapid improvement of the breed may differ from the plan of the individual breeder chiefly in that he dare not risk quite so much inbreeding deterioration. If the object were to improve the breed with little regard for immediate show prospects, then it would be a different story. This is an important point and deserves more attention.

Inbreeding refers to the mating of two closely related individuals. Most breeders practice inbreeding to a limited extent, even though they may call it close-line breeding. Actually, the breeding of half brother X half sister, as well as niece X uncle or nephew X aunt is a limited form of inbreeding. For purposes of this discussion, however, inbreeding will refer to the mating of full brother X full sister, father X daughter, and son X mother. Most breeders probably consider these three categories representative of true inbreeding.

It would certainly be interesting to know exactly what percentage of inbreeding takes place in various breeds and what results are obtained. Speaking in generalities, it would probably be safe to say that only 1 or 2 percent of all champions finishing within the past 10 years were the products of inbreeding. On this basis, it would be reasonable to conclude that the practice of close inbreeding on these terms is relatively rare.

In the breeding of domestic animals, such as cattle, chickens, etc., as well as plant breeding, inbreeding is regarded as a most valuable tool to fix a desired type and purify a strain. This raises the question as to why inbreeding has not gained more widespread acceptance among dog breeders. By combining inbreeding with the selection of those individuals most nearly ideal in appearance and temperament, the desired stability of the stock is quickly obtained.

Breeding the offspring of the father X daughter or son X mother mating back to a parent is called backcrossing. To illustrate this, suppose an outstanding male specimen is produced and the breeder wants more of the same type: The male is bred back to his dam, and the breeder retains the best bitch puppies in the resulting litter. By breeding these back to the excellent male (backcrossing), there is a good chance that some of the puppies produced as a result of this backcross will resemble the outstanding sire. In backcrossing to a superior male, one may find some inbreeding degeneration in the offspring, but this is improbable according to Dr. Ojvind Winge in his book, *Inheritance in Dogs*.

The mating of brothers X sisters is far more likely to produce inbreeding degeneration. This is because a brother X sister mating is the most intense form of inbreeding. Studies show that those breeders who have attempted to cross full brothers and sisters, for the purpose of fixing good characteristics in their stock, give very contradictory reports of their results. It has been found that the mating of brother X sister results in somewhat decreased vitality in the offspring.

It may happen that abnormal or stillborn individuals are segregated out in the litter if special genes are carried in the stock. Everything depends upon the hereditary nature of the animals concerned. Inbreeding degeneration is of such a peculiar nature that it may be totally abolished by a single crossing with unrelated or distantly related animals. However, if it had made its appearance, the breeder should know it was present in the hereditary make-up of his stock.

Most of the studies on inbreeding are in agreement. The decline in vigor, including the extinction of certain lines, follows largely the regrouping and fixing (making alike) of recessive genes that are, on the whole, injurious to the breed. However, along with the fixing of such recessives, there is also a fixing of gene pairs that are beneficial and desirable. It is a matter of chance as to what combination gene pairs a family finally comes to possess, except that selection is always at work weeding out combinations that are not well adapted to the conditions of life. There is a common belief that inbreeding causes the production of monstrosities and defects. Seemingly reliable evidence indicates that inbreeding itself has no specific connection with the production of monstrosities. Inbreeding seems merely to have brought to light genetic traits in the original stock.

One of the most interesting and extensive investigations of inbreeding in animals was done by the U.S. Department of Agriculture. Thirty-five healthy females were selected from general breeding stock and mated with a like number of selected males. The matings were numbered and the offspring were kept separate and mated exclusively brother X sister. Only the best two of each generation were selected to carry on the succeeding generations.

Each family became more like itself, and while this was going on, there was a gradual elimination of sub-branches. There was a decline in vigor during the first nine years, covering about 12 generations. This decline applied to weight, fertility and vitality in the young. During the second nine years of inbreeding, there was no further decline in vigor of the inbred animals as a group. This stability was interpreted to mean that after 12 generations, the families had become essentially purebred—that is, no longer different with respect to many genes.

What does all this mean in relation to breeding good dogs? Inbreeding coupled with selection can be utilized to fix traits in breeding stock at a rapid rate. These traits may be good or they may be undesirable, depending entirely upon the individual's hereditary nature. Inbreeding creates nothing new—it merely intensifies what is already present. If the hereditary nature of an individual already contains undesirable traits, these will naturally be manifested when the recessive genes become grouped and fixed. This applies to the desirable traits as well.

The term genotype refers to the complete genetic make-up of an individual, in contrast to the outward appearance of the individual, which is called phenotype. In selecting puppies to retain for breeding stock, breeders must rely on phenotype because they have no way of knowing an unproven individual's genotype. Inbreeding can reduce genotype and phenotype to one common denominator.

Suppose that an outstanding specimen appears as the product of inbreeding. What would this mean in terms of breeding? It would mean that this specimen has a greater chance of passing on his visible traits rather than possible hidden ones. Prepotent dogs and bitches are usually those that are pure for many of their outstanding characteristics. Since such a limited amount of inbreeding has been carried on in most breeds, prepotent specimens have become pure for certain traits more or less by chance, for they have appeared in most breeds as products of outcrossing, as well as by line breeding. Since line breeding, especially close line breeding, is a limited form of inbreeding, the same good and bad points apply to line breeding but in a much more modified degree. The practice of inbreeding appears to be extremely limited in dogs, so one must assume that breeders are willing to trade slower progress for a lower element of risk with respect to degeneration.

Assume that you have selected a bitch to be either line bred or outcrossed and the proper stud dog who complements her has been selected. The breeding has been made, the puppies have begun to grow up. Hopefully, it will be a good breeding and the results will yield several good prospects, all carrying the dam's good traits but showing a great improvement in the areas where she needed help. What if it doesn't turn out this way? What if the breeding results in general disappointment with none of the puppies showing much improvement? You might well ask how this can be possibly happen when all the proper aspects were taken into consideration in planning this breeding.

Remember the concept of dominance? Test breeding is the only true way of determining whether a dog or bitch is especially dominant. Here again, line breeding comes into play, for the closely line-bred dog or bitch has a much better chance of being dominant by virtue of a concentrated bloodline than the dog or bitch that is not line bred. When selecting a stud to complement your bitch, take into consideration the qualities of his parents as well. For example, suppose a stud is sought to improve the bitch in head. Obviously, a dog with a beautiful head is chosen, but it is also important that his parents had beautiful heads. Then the stud can be considered homozygous for this trait. If the dog selected does not have parents with beautiful heads, or only one parent had a beautiful head, he is said to be heterozygous for this characteristic and his chances of reproducing it are diminished. Dominant dogs and bitches are homozygous for more of their traits, while less dominant dogs and bitches are primarily heterozygous in their genetic make-up.

A great majority of dogs and bitches are probably dominant for some of their traits and not especially dominant for others. It is up to the breeder to attempt to match the proper combination of dominant traits, which is why the dog and bitch should complement each other—the best practical way of attempting to come up with the right combinations. There are some dogs and bitches that are completely non-dominant in their genetic make-up when bred to a dominant partner, so good things result provided their partner is of top quality. When a non-dominant bitch is bred to a non-dominant stud, the resulting litter is bound to be a disappointment. When a dominant bitch is bred to a dominant stud, it is possible that the resulting litter will be a failure. This explains why some "dream breedings" result in puppies that do not approach the quality of either parent.

There are some dominant sires that pass on their ability to their sons that, in turn, pass on their producing ability to their sons, etc. Likewise, there are dominant bitches that pass on their producing ability to their daughters, granddaughters, great granddaughters, etc. Thus, some lines are noted for their outstanding producing sires and/or bitches. Such a line is a true producing bloodline. A producing bitch, usually with a heritage of producing bitches behind her, bred to a proven stud dog will usually come through with those sought after champions. To this, only one additional qualification need be added— that the breeder exercise some degree of intelligence.

Much discussion between breeders has centered on the subject of which parent contributes the most, the sire or the dam. As we have seen, each contributes 50 percent of their genetic heritage or an equal amount; but by so doing, their respective factors of dominance and recessiveness are brought into play. Thus, in reality, there is not an equal contribution. If there were, there would be no outstanding producers.

The producing bitch is a very special entity. Those fortunate enough to own or to have owned one will surely attest to this. When a bitch has produced champion offspring, she is singled out for recognition. While the stud dog's production is unlimited, depending upon his popularity, this is not true in the case of the bitch. Many stud dogs, in achieving a producing record, have sired hundreds and hundreds of puppies. The average bitch will produce between 20 and 30 offspring in her lifetime, which drastically limits her chances of producing champions in any great numbers. Taking this limitation into account, it becomes quite obvious that bitches who produce quality in any amount must possess an attribute different from the average. That attribute is dominance.

The producing bitch may or may not contribute the qualities she herself possesses. Her puppies will, however, bear a resemblance to one another and to subsequent puppies she will produce, regardless of the sire. Whether closely line bred or outcrossed, whether bred to a sire of note or to a comparative unknown, the consistency of quality and type will be apparent in the offspring.

Occasionally a bitch will come along with little or no producing heritage, yet she will be a standout in producing ability. We must assume that such a specimen inherited a genetic make-up different from that of her immediate ancestors, or perhaps the potential was always there, but remained untapped until some enterprising breeder parlayed it to advantage. There are known instances in which specific bitches produced only with one particular dog. In such cases, the desired results are achieved through an ideal blending rather than dominance.

The availability of a true producing bitch is necessarily limited. Whereas all are free to breed to the outstanding sires of the breed, few have access to the producing bitches. Their offspring can and should command top prices; demand always exceeds supply. Their bitch puppies are especially valued, for it is primarily through them that continuity is achieved.

The producing bitch imparts something extra special to her offspring. Though all but impossible to define, this something extra is determined genetically. She is also a good mother, conscientious but not fanatical, calm and possessing an even temperament.

In summary, a basic knowledge of genetics will allow the breeding of better specimens and thus improve the breed. It is not possible to be a successful breeder by hit-and-miss breedings. Hoping that dame Fortune will smile on you is trusting to luck, not scientific principles. Utilizing the contents of this chapter and other parts of this section will enable a conscientious breeder to score and score well in the winner's circle.

The Stud Dog

If one is to be a purist, there are only a few dogs in the country at one time that should be used at stud.

This is to say that only the very finest males should be included in the national gene pool. To breed to just any dog for the purpose of having puppies is self-defeating. The stud dog you choose must be a dog of great merit, one of a bloodline that has been proven to produce top-quality stock. This means progeny that is of proper breed type, of sound structure, of high intelligence, of the requisite sweet, lovable, easily trained temperament.

I would suggest that unless one is a long-time breeder, with a proven record of success, it would be a poor idea to breed to one's own dog. There are great and famous champions out there, and the stud fee is the finest bargain in the dog world. Not only can you produce superior puppies from a great stud, but your puppies will be far more valuable when they carry a famous name as sire.

The Collie is not the avid stud dog that some other breeds can claim. I will admit though that there are exceptions to the rule. There are some male Collies with great libidos but, as a rule, I have found many to be half-hearted in the wooing process. In fact, I have sometimes wondered how the breed would survive without man's intervention.

To introduce your male Collie to a future mate, I suggest the two dogs be put on a lash and allowed to sniff and investigate each other. I do not believe in just letting them play together at liberty. If the female is unwilling, she might damage the male by biting him to keep him away. Most bitches will stand and nearly beg to be bred if they are at the proper time in the season. Some will stand a bit and then wiggle away. Others will encourage the dog then collapse when he mounts her. For all of these reasons it is best to keep both animals on leash, and eventually the male should be trained to accept help. Most will hate to have human hands as part of the process, but, with training, a dog can and will accept help and actually be guided into the bitch.

For purposes of attaining a smooth breeding process, it is best to have a place where the male feels at home. A nice cozy nook away from the other dogs and away from distraction is the best place for wooing. If the dog is bred in the same place every time (at least at first) it will help in reminding him of his duty. Later, he may be willing to breed anywhere, any time, but the beginner should have a familiar spot and as much solitude as can be managed.

There are diseases that can be transferred from one dog to another during breeding. I suggest that both be examined by a veterinarian before breeding. If there is any question, cultures of both dogs may be done.

Many breeders prefer to use artificial insemination (AI) rather than natural breeding. This is a perfectly viable option. The results are nearly as good as they are from nature's way, and the whole thing is much easier than trying to get two dogs together when one or both appears unwilling. If you wish to learn to do the AI yourself, I suggest you get a knowledgeable veterinarian or dog breeder to show you "the ropes." There is a definite technique involved, and this technique can make the difference between a mating that results in puppies and one that does not.

The dog you select to stand at stud should have certain things going for him. First, he should be masculine in appearance and, at least in your appraisal, conform closely to the breed Standard. A major mistake made by breeders is keeping a dog that is overdone in some features in the hope he can overcome a bitch with deficiencies in these areas. It doesn't work that way. It is futile to breed an oversize dog to a small bitch in the hopes of getting average-sized puppies. The hallmark of a good breeder, one who understands basic genetics, is breeding to dogs who conform to the Standard. Extremes should be avoided because they only add complications to a breeding program down the road.

Second, it is important that the stud dog come from a line of Collies that has consistently produced champions on both his sire's and dam's sides. Such a line helps to ensure that he is likely to be dominant for his good traits. A bitch should also come from a good producing line. When a dog is found that has excellent producing lines for three generations on his sire's and dam's sides, there is an excellent chance that he will be a prepotent stud.

The third consideration is appearance. If the male is not constructed right, he is not going to be a great show dog. While the dog doesn't have to be a great show winner to attract the bitches, it helps. There are outstanding examples of non-titled dogs being excellent studs. However, they are somewhat rare.

There is more to breeding than just dropping a bitch in season into the stud dog's pen and hoping for the best.

A subject seldom discussed in the literature about stud dogs is the psyche of the dog. A young stud dog needs to be brought along slowly. If he is a show dog, he most likely has a steady temperament and is outgoing.

Early on, he should be taught to get along with other male dogs, but he should never be allowed to become intimidated. Good stud dogs have to be aggressive for breeding. Dogs who have been intimidated early seldom shape up. However, running, playing and even puppy-fighting with litter mates or other puppies don't have detrimental effects.

Until he is old enough to stand up for himself, the young male should be quartered first with puppies his own age and then introduced to bitches as kennel mates. It's not a good idea to keep him in a pen by himself. Socialization is extremely important. Time for play as a puppy and a companion to keep him from boredom helps his growth and development.

His quarters and food should present no special problems. Serious breeders all feed their dogs a nourishing and balanced diet. Studies in colleges of veterinary medicine and by nutritionists at major dog-food companies have shown that the major brands of dry dog food come as close to meeting the total needs of the dog as any elaborately concocted breeder's formula. Many breeders spice up the basic diet with their own version of goodies, including table scraps, to break up the monotony or to stimulate a finicky eater. However, this is more cosmetic than nutritional and is unnecessary. Dogs are creatures of habit and finicky eaters are man-made. Collies do best on free feeding as they do not overeat.

The most important aspect of being the owner of a stud dog is to make sure he can produce puppies. Therefore, at around 11 to 12 months of age, it's a good idea to have a check on his sperm count by a vet. This will indicate if he is producing enough viable sperm cells to fertilize eggs. Sometimes it is found that while a stud produces spermatozoa, they are not active. The chances of this dog being able to fertilize an egg are markedly reduced. While this problem is usually found in older dogs, it does happen in young animals. Thus, the sperm count examination is important and should be done yearly.

One should also be concerned with a stud dog's general health. Sexual contact with a variety of bitches may expose the dog to a wide range of minor infections and some major ones. If not promptly identified and treated, some can lead to sterility. Other non-sexual infections and illnesses, such as urinary infections, stones, etc., can also reduce a dog's ability to sire puppies. Since it is not desirable for any of these things to happen, stud dog owners need to be observant.

It's a good idea to have your vet check all incoming bitches. A stud-dog owner, however, should insist that the visiting bitch come with a veterinarian's certificate that the bitch is negative for canine brucellosis. While checking for obvious signs of infection, the vet can also run a smear to see when the bitch is ready to breed. The dog should also be checked frequently to see if there is any type of discharge from his penis. A dog at regular stud should not have a discharge. Usually he will lick himself frequently to keep the area clean. After breeding, it is also a good idea to rinse off the area with a clean saline solution. Your vet may also advise flushing out the penile area after breeding, using a special solution.

The testicles and penis are the male organs of reproduction. Testicles are housed in a sac called the scrotum. The American Kennel Club will not allow dogs who are bilateral cryptorchids (neither testicle descended), unilateral cryptorchids, or monorchids (dogs that have only one testicle descended) to be shown.

The male's testicles are outside the body because the internal heat of the body curtails the production of sperm. There is a special muscle that keeps them close to the body for warmth in cold weather and relaxes and lets them down to get air cooled in hot weather.

In the male fetus, the gonads, or sex organs, develop in the abdominal cavity and migrate during gestation toward their eventual position. Shortly before birth they hover over an opening in the muscular structure of the pubic area through which they will descend to reach the scrotal sac. This external position is vital to the fertility of the animal, for production of live sperm can only proceed at a temperature several degrees cooler than normal body temperature. The glandular tissue of the testes is nourished and supported by arteries, veins, nerves, connective tissue and ductwork, collectively known as the spermatic cord. The scrotum acts as a thermostat.

As noted above, there are many involuntary muscle fibers that are stimulated to contract with the environmental temperature, pulling the testes closer to the body for warmth. Contraction also occurs as a result of any stimulus that might be interpreted by the dog as a threat of physical harm, such as the sight of a strange dog or being picked up. This contraction does not force the testicles back up into the abdominal cavity of the adult dog because the inguinal rings have tightened and will not allow them to be drawn back up. The tightening of the rings usually occurs at about 10 months of age.

There are a number of reasons why a dog may be a monorchid or cryptorchid. For example, the size of the opening through the muscles may be too small to allow for easy passage of the testes, or the spermatic cord may not be long enough for the testes to remain in the scrotum most of the time; and, as the proportions of the inguinal ring and testes change in the growing puppy, the time comes when the testes may be trapped above the ring as they grow at different rates. Also, there exists a fibrous muscular band that attaches both to the testes and scrotal wall, gradually shortening and actually guiding the testes in their descent. Possibly this structure could be at fault. The important thing about all of this that it helps the prospective stud dog owner learn about the anatomy of the reproductive organs of the dog.

One should be gentle when feeling for a pup's testicles. The scrotal muscles may contract and the still generous inguinal rings may allow the disappearance of the parts sought.

It's a good idea to get the young stud dog started right with a cooperative, experienced bitch—one of your own preferably. By introducing the young and inexperienced stud to an experienced bitch, his first experience should result in an easy and successful breeding. A feisty, difficult bitch could very well frustrate the youngster, and as a result he may not be too enthusiastic about future breedings. Remember, one wants a confident and aggressive stud dog. There may be difficult bitches when he is an experienced stud, so it's best to bring him along slowly and gently for his first matings.

When the bitch is ready to breed (as your stud gains experience he will not pay too much attention to her until she is really ready) both animals should be allowed to exercise and relieve themselves just before being brought together. It's also a good idea not to feed them before mating. Bring the bitch in first. The place should be quiet and away from noise and other dogs. Spend a few minutes petting and reassuring her. Then bring the dog in on a lead. Do not allow him to come lunging in and make a frustrated leap at her. This can cause her to panic and bite him out of fear.

After a few minutes of pirouetting around together, she throwing her vulva in his face and him trying to lick fore and aft, take off the lead. Allow them to court for a few minutes. She should tell you she is ready by being coquettish and continually backing up into the dog.

Now comes the important time for the future success of the young stud: The dog needs to learn that the owner is there to help and should not back away from breeding the bitch just because someone is holding her.

Plan ahead and make sure there will be a large, nonskid rug on the floor. Place the bitch on the rug and face her rump toward the dog. Pat her on the fanny to encourage the dog to come ahead. Generally speaking, he will. As a rule he will lick her again around the vulva. Some dogs will go to the bitch's head and gently lick her eyes and ears. Encourage him, however, to come to the bitch's rear. If he is unsure of himself, lift the bitch's rear and dangle it in front of his nose.

Encouraged and emboldened, the male will mount the bitch from the rear and begin to probe slowly for the opening to the vulva. Once he discovers it, he will begin to move more rapidly. This is a critical time. Some young dogs are so far off the target they never get near the right opening. If this happens, gently reposition the bitch so he can have a better angle. This may occur any number of times. He may become frustrated and back off. Don't get excited as this is normal in a young dog. He may even get so excited and confused that he swings around and tries to breed her from the front.

Get him back on track. Again, gently get him to move to the bitch's rear and encourage him to proceed. At this time there may be a red, bone-like protuberance sticking out from the penis sheath. This, of course, is the penis itself. When, as a dog continues to probe and finds the opening, he will begin to move frenetically. As he moves in this fashion, a section just behind the pointed penis bone begins to swell. It is capable of great enlargement. This enlargement of the bulbous takes place due to its filling with blood, and it becomes some three times larger than the rest of the penis. In this way the dog, once having penetrated, is tied to the bitch; it is entirely due to the male, the bitch having no part in the initial tying.

When a tie has occurred, the semen is pumped in spurts into the vagina. The bitch then helps to keep the penis enlarged as she begins to have a series of peristaltic waves that cause a slight tightening and relaxing of the vagina. Some males will stay tied for up to one hour and others for as little as five minutes. A five-minute successful tie is just as satisfactory as a longer one because the semen has moved up through the uterus and fallopian tubes to the ovarian capsules by the end of five minutes.

Once the dog and bitch are successfully tied, the male may characteristically try to lift his rear leg over the bitch and keep the tie in a back-to-back position. Other dogs merely slide off the back of a bitch and maintain a tie facing in the same direction. It is always a good idea to have two people involved during the breeding, with one person at the bitch's head and the other at the male's.

Occasionally, a fractious bitch may be sent for breeding. She can be frightened about being shipped or spooked by strange surroundings. Certainly one doesn't want the dog to be bitten by a frightened bitch nor to have one's fingers lacerated. The easiest solution to this problem is to tie her jaws loosely with wide gauze. This muzzle should tie behind her ears to make sure it doesn't slide off. Pet her, reassure her, but hold her firmly during the breeding so she doesn't lunge at the dog.

After the tie has been broken, there sometimes will be a rush of fluid from the bitch. Place the bitch gently in a quiet crate or pen, apart from other dogs, and give her fresh water. It is wise to elevate the bitch's hindquarters for 15 minutes or so. This will keep the semen inside where it belongs. The dog should be petted and praised. Once the dog is fully relaxed, be sure the penis is back in the sheath. Then, he too should be put in a separate, quiet pen with fresh water. It's not a good idea to put him back with a group of male dogs.

How often can the dog be used at stud? If the dog is in good condition he should be able to be used two or three times a week. One cannot expect him to be able to service bitches day after day for any great length of time.

Nature is most generous with sperm. In one good mating a dog may discharge millions, and a copious amount of sperm is produced in dogs who are used regularly. Frequent matings may be possible for a short time, but for good health and good management they should be limited to about three times a week. An individual bitch should be serviced twice—once every other day—for the best chance of conception.

For some breeders, breeding to a stud of their choice is often difficult, especially in countries that have quarantine restrictions. In the United States, the basic cost of shipping and the chances of making connections with a popular stud can produce a great deal of frustration. The use of frozen sperm opens up many new possibilities. At the time of this writing, there are 29 AKC- sanctioned collection stations. There should be many more in the near future.

Collecting sperm from dogs is not like collecting from cattle. One collection from the latter produces enough to inseminate more than 100 cows. The largest amount collected at one time over the many years of research in dogs was 22 vials. Usually two to three vials are used to breed a bitch two to three times.

The estimated time to store enough semen to inseminate 30 bitches differs by age, health, and sperm quantity and quality. Estimate approximately a month for a young dog, approximately three months for a dog of eight or nine years of age or older.

It doesn't take one long to recognize that, in the early stages, those males of outstanding quality will make up the main reservoir of the sperm bank. The collection centers suggest that collection be done at a young age, three to five years.

Limitations in quality and quantity due to old age lengthen the period necessary to store enough sperm for even a few bitches. In addition, the daily routine of a dog's life may limit freezability: The settling down in a new environment, changes in diet, water, or minor health problems. It is also not uncommon to get poor freeze results from a stud dog who has not been used for a month or longer. For the dog, once he settles down, the process of collection is a pleasant experience.

The following information on artificial insemination written by Diann Sullivan is reprinted by permission of *The Labrador Quarterly* (Hoflin Publishing Ltd., 4401 Zephyr St., Wheat Ridge, CO 80033-3299):

> Artificial insemination [AI] has been recognized as possible in dogs for some two hundred years. Semen is collected from the male and introduced into the reproductive tract of the female. When done properly, it is as successful as natural mating. It will not spoil a dog or bitch for future natural breedings and in fact, may desensitize a bitch to accept penetration.

The main reason for AI failure is that it is used all too often as a last resort after trying and failing at natural breedings, when it is too late in a bitch's cycle for her to conceive. The use of artificial insemination as a back-up to a natural mating where a tie was not produced helps assure that as complete a mating occurred as was possible. Bitches who have had a vaginal prolapse and may have scar tissue present after the protruding vaginal wall has been clipped and healed, may reject intercourse due to pain. It is also very useful when the stud dog manager finds he has a spoiled bitch in or one who has had little association with other dogs. Using an AI when natural mating is somehow impossible will provide a satisfactory service versus frustration on everyone's part.

The equipment needed includes one pair of sterile gloves (available through a pharmacy or your doctor), one inseminating rod (through dairy stores or International Canine Genetics), one 12 cc or 20 cc syringe (from stores, pharmacies), one artificial vagina and collection tube (ICG) or the sterile container that housed the syringe, a small piece of rubber tubing to attach the rod to the syringe and a nonspermicidal jelly (K-Y). To sterilize equipment after use, wash thoroughly in warm water and a drop or two of mild liquid dish soap. Rinse well with distilled water and dry completely with a hair dryer to avoid residual minerals that act as a spermicide.

On a safe surface within reach, lay out the package of sterile gloves, not touching the left glove to contamination. Glove your right hand with the right glove. On the sterile paper that the gloves are wrapped in, dispense a little jelly. Attach the collection tube to the smallest end of the artificial vagina (AV). Be sure it is securely in place. Roll down two plus inches on the large end of the AV to make it somewhat shorter. Place the AV and attached tube next to your body. We have the stud dog waiting in a crate within reach until the bitch is securely muzzled and standing ready.

The stud dog handler sits comfortably on a stool facing the bitch's left side. I use my left hand to support her stifle and can hold her tail out of the way with the same hand. Using the right hand, the stud dog helper pats the top of the bitch and encourages the stud dog to "get her." The thumb and forefinger of the right hand grasps the bottom of the vulva to open it for easy penetration of the dog's erect penis, as he is actively mounting. When he is fully penetrated, the right hand can then hold the bitch's hock to add to the support the left hand is giving to her left stifle.

The stud dog may dismount without a tie occurring. If he is fully erect and dripping seminal fluid, the pre-warmed AV is slipped over his penis and held in place with the left hand. The right thumb and forefinger grasp the penis above the bulbous enlargement and apply steady pressure as the penis is pulled down and back for duration of the collection. If a collection is preferred without allowing penetration, the dog is stimulated into erection as he is actively mounting the bitch. Grasping the penis back behind the developing bulbous will produce thrusting at which time the AV is slipped over the enlarging penis. If collection is being done without an AV, the penis is brought down and back and the syringe container tube is carefully held under and away from the tip of the penis. The pressure from the right hand around the bulbous will cause the ejaculation which is carefully caught in the casing. Watch the collection tube fill. When you see a significant third and clear portion on top of the settled, thickened sperm, withdraw the AV.

Put the stud dog away in a kennel or area with enough room for him to safely retract his penis and in a clean environment. The bitch handler should sit comfortably on his stool and left the bitch's rear up over his knee so her rear is tilted up significantly.

Attach the inseminating rod to the syringe securely. Cut the rods to make them easier to handle. Slip the smooth end of the rod into the collection tube and all the way to the bottom. VERY SLOWLY (so as not to rip off those little sperm tails), draw up the seminal fluid into the syringe. Draw up an extra few cc's of air.

Carefully place the syringe and rod back inside your shirt for warmth, and carefully glove the left hand and apply the pre-dispensed K-Y jelly to the left fingertips.

Palm up, carefully insert the left third (middle) finger in and up to where the cervix can be felt. Gently slip your third fingertip just through the cervix. Carefully glide the inseminating rod along the palm side of the third finger to where the smooth tip can be felt by the fingertip. SLOWLY, use the syringe to pass the seminal fluid into the bitch. If you notice leakage, gently pass the finger tip and rod tip in a little further and continue to inseminate. Leaving the third finger in place during insemination acts as the body of the penis to block fluid loss.

Remove your finger after two minutes and continue to massage the vulva every thirty seconds or so, maintaining the tilt of her rear end for at least ten minutes. The massage of the vulva causes her vaginal canal to contract and pull the fluid up.

Crate the bitch for at least one hour after the breeding.

If the dog's sperm count is good and the sperm has good motility, breed three to four days apart to allow for the complete rebuilding of the stud dog's sperm count.

We must each continue to learn new and improved techniques to facilitate healthy pregnancies and practice methods that improve conception rates. Utilizing simple artificial insemination as a back-up to unsuccessful natural matings or as a choice in difficult matings increases the number of successful litters. AI allows the stud dog manager a reliable choice to assist his mating strategy for each bitch. AI is extremely useful in achieving a breeding early in the estrus, near when she may be ovulating. Following with either a successful natural mating or another successful AI every three or four days throughout her standing heat, would help insure that active sperm is available to the ripening ovum.

It is wonderful to receive the phone calls reporting the arrival of a litter that would not exist without the use of artificial insemination. Its reliability is constantly reinforced, and plays a strong role in improving conception rates.

Natural breedings are preferable to artificial insemination. While extenuating circumstances with some bitches may necessitate AI, both the libido in the stud dog and the receptiveness of the bitch are inherited traits. Reputable breeders never want to see the day when artificial means for breeding are the norm rather that the exception.

Frozen and Extended Semen

American dogs have made their presence known throughout the world. Dog breeders in such far away countries as Australia, Sweden and New Zealand have made remarkable strides in successfully introducing new breeds to their countries. There is, however, a major problem in importation of high-quality breeding stock. Stringent quarantine rules make it extremely difficult and financially prohibitive to import quality stock.

There is a solution to this problem. Artificial insemination has been approved by the AKC under certain controlled conditions for use in this country. However, shipping semen over long distances has proven to be a formidable task.

In October and November of 1986, Howard H. Furumoto, DVM, Ph.D. writing in the *ILIO*, Hawaii's dog magazine, cast a new light on the problem. Dr. Furumoto writes:

> Recent research on canine semen preservation and storage offers Hawaii dog breeder's a promising future. The technology and expertise are available today to overcome the hitherto insurmountable barriers of time, logistics, and statutory requirements when considering the importation of new bloodlines.
>
> To properly understand and appreciate the significance of these advancements a short review of the evolution of the two methods of semen preservation are in order.
>
> When approval was granted by the American Kennel Club to legitimize registration of litters conceived by stored semen and artificial insemination, the way was opened for Hawaii's breeders to take advantage of the golden opportunity presented by the new technology. Here at last was an AKC-accredited program which provided the means to circumvent the quarantine requirements and to eliminate the expense, inconvenience, and stress shipping animals to and from destination points. An added attraction for many breeders was the preservation of valuable bloodlines for posterity by the establishment of frozen semen banks.
>
> The original work on frozen semen was done by Dr. Stephen Seager and co-workers at the University of Oregon under the auspices of the American Kennel Club. The widespread interest he created led to a collaboration with the University of Hawaii. The objective was to determine whether or not we could duplicate the results obtained by Dr. Seager and his co-workers with the additional variables of air shipping frozen semen and bitches in estrus cycle. Much to our disappointment the four bitches shipped to Hawaii and inseminated with frozen semen shipped from Oregon failed to become impregnated. Subsequently, other investigators have reported similar negative results.
>
> Because of the unreliable results obtained from the insemination of stored semen, canine theriogenologists began searching for more productive methodologies. Two such pro-

grams came to my attention. One effort was led by Dr. Frances Smith who had obtained her Ph.D. from the University of Minnesota. Her dissertation was based on the successful development of a semen extender which prolongs the viability of spermatozoa for up to seven days after collection without freezing.

Dr. Smith is widely recognized by dog breeders throughout the continental United States for her work with topline breeding stock of various breeds. In her experience she has been just as successful in obtaining pregnancies with the use of the newly formulated extended semen as with natural breeding.

The second source of information led me to Mr. George Govette of the Cryogenics Laboratories in Chester Spring, Pennsylvania. Mr. Gavotte has earned the reputation of being the foremost frozen semen specialist in the country, having successfully registered 44 litters out of the approximately 50 now recognized by the AKC by this method. In addition he has reported successful frozen semen usage in Japan.

Gleaning germane information from both sources, Dr. Furumoto wrote a second article in which he briefly described the methods employed in semen collection, extension, preservation, storage, and preparation for artificial insemination.

He then projected the long-term benefits and potential hazards of these new technologies as they relate to breed improvement:

Semen Collection

Semen is collected for a number of overlapping reasons— for qualitative and quantitative evaluation, for immediate insemination when natural breeding fails or cannot be used due to physical and psychological inhibitions, for extending the volume of serum, for semen preservation and storage and for legal reasons (quarantine restrictions).

To collect semen it is generally helpful to excite the dog with the scent of a bitch in estrus. Ejaculation is usually performed by digital manipulation and the semen is collected in a graduated sterile collecting tube fitted to a funnel- shaped latex sleeve which is held around the penis.

Three distinct fractions are observed from the ejaculate. The scant first fraction is clear and is secreted by the glands of the urethral mucosa; the opaque second fraction is secreted by the testicles and contains spermatozoa; the third and most voluminous fraction is clear and is secreted by the prostate glands.

Qualitative and quantitative evaluations are made after the semen is collected. The volume and turbidity of the semen are noted. Microscopically, the sperm concentration, motility, ratio of live to dead sperm cells and the shape and size are evaluated. Fresh undiluted semen is used for immediate artificial insemination.

Semen Extenders and Semen Preservation

After semen evaluation, semen of good to excellent quality is selected for preservation by one of two basic methods: chilling or chilling and freezing. In both methods a vehicle or media for dilution and maintenance called semen extenders is used.

A great deal of research has been done to determine which media serves as the best semen extender. Various combinations of sterilized skim milk, homogenized milk, egg yolk, glucose, sodium citrate, sodium bicarbonate, potassium chloride and other substances have been used. The tremendous success in conception rate obtained by Dr. Frances Smith is the direct result of her newly developed and tested semen extender.

Fresh undiluted semen maintains its viability for 24 to 48 hours. Beyond this period the viability of the semen may be prolonged for approximately 4 more days by suspending it in special media known as semen extenders and chilling. The viability of spermatozoa may be continued over an indefinite period of years by freezing the semen after it is suspended in a suitable vehicle (semen extender). By a gradual chilling process spermatozoa are conditioned for freezing at -70 degrees Centigrade. The extended semen suspension is then shaped into pellets by placing single drops into super-cooled Styrofoam wells. Enough frozen pellets are placed in each vial to yield about 50 million spermatozoa. Each vial is properly identified and stored at -70 degrees in a liquid nitrogen tank.

An alternative method of preservation is to pipette the extended semen into straws, one end of which is presealed. When the straw is filled the top end is sealed and the semen is conditioned for freezing as with the pelletized semen, frozen and stored.

Preparation for Insemination

The reverse of cooling and freezing is carried out to prepare frozen semen for artificial insemination. A suitable number of pellets or straws are selected to yield 100 to 300 million spermatozoa and gradually thawed to ambient temperature. At this point an evaluation of the thawed semen quality is made. If viability and motility are satisfactory the semen is introduced in the anterior vagina or cervix of the bitch. At least two inseminations usually 24 to 48 hours apart is recommended.

Long-Term Benefits of Extended and Frozen Semen

In the context of foreign countries with quarantine restrictions the greatest advantage to be derived from the use of extended and frozen semen is the by-passing of the transoceanic shipment of stud dogs and their confinement in government quarantine facilities for a specified period of time (10 days beyond the last insemination date). Extended or frozen semen on the other hand may be shipped in special compact containers over long distances.

Another attraction of extended and frozen semen is the flexibility and convenience of synchronizing semen shipment with the optimal breeding period in the estrous cycle of a prospective bitch. This advantage is particularly applicable when long distance shipment of stud dogs and bitches is involved in conventional breeding programs.

Venereal diseases, particularly canine brucellosis and transmissible venereal tumor may be circumvented, simply by the process of screening out potential carriers in the collection process.

By far the most significant benefit to accrue from extended and frozen semen is the concentration of proven or select gene pools for the improvement of the breed to more rapidly attain that elusive goal known as the ideal breed standard. By extending and freezing semen many more bitches can be inseminated with 'matching' semen which would complement the desirable qualities of the sire and dam.

Disadvantages of Extended and Frozen Semen

In addition to the purely technical difficulties of implementing an artificial insemination program which uses extended and frozen semen, the success rate among breeders so far has been very limited.

The greatest concern regarding frozen and extended semen is the potential for intensifying or replicating undesirable gene traits. Just as much as the potential for breed improvement over a shorter period exists, there is also the danger of perpetuating undesirable inheritable traits, i.e., juvenile cataracts, subvalular aortic stenosis, hip dysplaysia, etc. within an abbreviated time frame. Therefore a great deal of selectivity and objectivity must be exercised in the utilization of preserved semen. Any abnormal offspring must be dealt with objectively and decisively and either euthanized or neutered so that the genetic defect will not become established within a given line or breed.

Another area of concern is the requirement for meticulous attention to details of proper identification and documentation. One only needs to refer to AKC regulations on 'Registration of Litters Produced Through Artificial Insemination Using Frozen Semen' to appreciate the complexity of these stringent requirements.

Conclusion

Notwithstanding the objectionable features of semen preservation and storage, the technical and scientific feasibility of their application to canine reproduction have been amply demonstrated. The acceptance of the program depends to a large extent, on the interest and support of dog breeders and the professional and technical competence of Veterinarians to deliver the 'goods' when the chips are down. Ultimately, the success of the program depends on the development of special interest and expertise in the handling of extended and frozen semen from collection to insemination. Success breeds success. Nowhere is this truism more important than in the pioneering use of these techniques.

Each vial is properly identified and stored at -t0

An Update by Dr. H. N. Engel

Conception rates with chilled and frozen semen have increased dramatically with the adjunct of hormonal analysis. The dog, unlike most mammals, ovulates a primary oocyte that needs to undergo an additional meiotic division before fertilization can occur. Consequently, a higher percentage of conceptions occur if fertilization is timed around this latter event.

Ovulation is preceded by a 20 to 40 fold spike in serum luteinizing hormone (LH) which returns to baseline levels within 24 hours. This spike stimulates the release of the ova (eggs) from the ovary. In the dog [bitch], ovulation occurs approximately two days after the pituitary LH surge, no matter how long the dog has been exhibiting signs of estrus. Again, these are primary oocytes (developing eggs) that require an additional two days to undergo their reduction division to produce fertilizable eggs (secondary oocytes). These mature cells can then live for about 48-72 hours. If day 0 is the day of the LH spike, then the optimal time to breed a dog is generally on day 5.

Luteinizing hormone controls the release of another hormone, progesterone, which is produced by the ovary. Normally, progesterone is at extremely low serum levels (below 2 ng/ml). With the beginning rise in the LH peak, progesterone also begins to rise significantly. However, this hormone continues to rise for several days before leveling off. Progesterone remains high whether the dog conceives or not for approximately two months, at which time it drops. This drop in progesterone level occurs around 24 hours before whelping. If the dog is not pregnant, the drop in progesterone may initiate the condition in some bitches known as false pregnancy.

The measuring of serum levels for either of these hormones can provide a more accurate guide to optimize breeding. Bitches should be bred either on day five after the LH peak or on day five after the beginning rise in progesterone levels. In practice, if two breedings can be achieved, it is optimal to breed on day four and day six after the LH spike or progesterone rise. If only one breeding is to be made, then day five is optimal.

Progesterone analysis is generally done every other day beginning after the vaginal cytology exhibits 50 percent cornification. If the progesterone levels indicate no rise one day but have risen two days later, then breedings should be done on days four and six. This works best with natural breedings, fresh semen artifical inseminations (AI) or even inseminations with chilled semen.

Frozen semen generally has only a 24-hour life span after thawing. Consequently, conception is more likely to occur if the insemination can be done on the fifth day after the LH spike. Luteinizing hormone analysis must be done for this determination and these tests need to be performed daily because of the short LH spike interval. Furthermore, frozen semen has poor motility and it is strongly suggested that the semen be surgically implanted into the reproductive tract rather than executing a typical AI.

Another use of hormonal analysis is to calculate the whelping date. The bitch will generally whelp 65 days (plus or minus one day) from the LH peak or from the day of the initial rise in progesterone levels. This can allow the breeder to plan for possible emergencies with their veteinarian. The breeder can also make other personal arrangements, such as getting time off work to be home with the dog. Some breeds usually need to have C-section births. Retrieving premature puppies will be avoided by knowing more precisely the whelping date.

Another determination of serum pregesterone levels can be ascertained a week after breeding to see if indeed the levels are above seven ng./ml. This suggests the dog did ovulate. Some dogs may come into heat but LH levels never get high enough to stimulate ovulation. By detecting that progesterone levels have continued to rise, this indicates ovulation did occur.

Regarding frozen semen, if one decides that they would like to have semen collected from their prize stud dog for freezing, they should work with their veterinarian to take some initial steps. First, the stud dog must have some form of permanent identification. Preferably the dog should be microchiped, but a tattoo will suffice. By all means,the stud dog needs to have been tested negative for canine Brucellosis withing 30 days before collection. In addition, the dog needs to be reexamined no sooner than 21 days after collection to determine that no infections exist. If you have the opportunity to send frozen semen to another country, they may have additional tests that are required prior to collection of the semen. For example, Australia presently requires that the dog be negative for Leptospirosis withis 30 days of collection in addition to the Brucellosis test. By having these tests done prior to collection and the follow-up examination, the frozen semen from that collection can be certified for shipment to other countries.

The Bitch

It would be impossible to overemphasize the importance of the role of the bitch in breeding. Since the male can produce so many more puppies, one tends to think of the male as playing the more important role in development of the breed. Also, the male is available to many more breeders, as he generally stands at public stud. But the bitch is the foundation upon which a breeder builds his stock. The breeder has absolute right to all the produce of his bitch, and that accessibility makes his kennel.

It is up to the breeder to choose the right stud for his bitch. It is also the breeder's fearsome duty to choose the proper puppies from the litters.

Many fine dogs have been lost to the fancy because the breeder, having chosen the right combination, then lets his best one go. In Collies, there are so many changes from early puppyhood to maturity that it is extremely difficult to anticipate the appearance of the dog when grown. For that reason, I always counsel breeders to keep their TWO best from any promising litter. So many strange things can go wrong with one dog. It is far better to hedge your bets by keeping at least two.

It is, in my opinion, non-productive to breed any litter just for the purpose of having puppies. There are enough—no, more than enough—puppies in the world. The only thing needed in the dog world is quality. When a really top-quality bitch is bred to a great producing dog, the resulting litter can be of value. It will be of value to the breeder in advancing his stock, of value as dogs to sell, or of value in setting s step forward for the whole breed.

The bitch not only donates her genes (for good or bad) to the litter. She also must carry the puppies through to parturition, with strong, healthy puppies emerging at the end of her ordeal. She must have a strong mothering instinct so she will clean and cuddle her pups. She must have good nourishing milk in plenitude. She must be not only willing but eager to feed her pups. She must be a careful mother—one who remains aware where her puppies are at all times so she does not step or roll on them inadvertently. The mothering also helps in the development of good temperament in the babies. What is more charming than the sight of a good mother dog nuzzling and playing with her pups when they finally start to be able to interact with her. That playfulness helps build the personality of the grown dog to be.

I have found that the good maternal qualities are very often passed from mother dog to daughter, and on down the line. If I were to buy a bitch to use as a brood bitch, I would want to know what kind of mother her mother was. Did she conceive readily? Did she breed easily? (That is a sign of well-regulated hormonal activity.) Did she whelp easily and without undue stress or length of time? Did she clean and warm the puppies? Did she have good milk? If the dam had all these pluses, it is a good bet that the daughter will have those qualities as well.

It is also important that the bitch come from stock known to produce the qualities that are important in the breed. I would prefer that she be either the daughter or the granddaughter of a great producing stud. I would like the bitch to come from a line in which there are several studs available so her daughters can be easily bred back into the line. If she is to be outcrossed, it would be wise to research which lines have crossed well with her bloodline in the past. No need to go blindly into such an important matter as the selection of a stud for your carefully chosen bitch.

Lastly, I would say do not get stuck in a non-productive situation. If the bitch you have selected does not prove to be a producer of quality, or if she is not a good brood bitch, do not cling to her but replace her. She can be a pet, but in your stock always move upward from every point of view. It is only through your bitches that you can produce great dogs. Hooray for the ladies.

Ch. Loch Larens Theme Song with Dot Gerth Memorial Trophy for Best Bred by Exhibitor. She was the Top Producing Bitch of 1994. Breeder/owners are Barbara Cleek and Don Bickford.

Ch. Highcroft Quintessence pictured at eight years old, the Top Producing Collie Dam in history. She exemplifies the beautiful, correct Collie expression with a normal eye.

Ch. Chelsea Shadowgold (1980) owned by Gayle Kaye.

Ch. Glen Hill Blue Review, litter sister to Glen Hill Dorian Gray. Shown here at eight months, the lovely result of an inbreeding—brother to sister.

Glen Hill ShelanaSwan Lake, dam of several champions. Has champion get of both rough and smooth. Owned by the author and Heidi Mendez.

Ch. Royal Guard I'm Merry Too, dam of champions, at four years old. Bred by Dory Samuels and Connie and Shirley DuBois.

Ch. Kemricks On the Rebound at the Central Jersey Collie Club in 1969 with John Buddie handling and Pat Starkweather judging. This foundation bitch of Clarion Kennels was owned by Judie Evans. (Photo by Evelyn M. Shafer)

Ch. Tartanside Imagination, winner's bitch and BOW at Collie Club of America National Specialty in 1993. She is owned by John Buddie. (Photo by SueS)

The Bitch in Whelp

There are some differences between the average female dog and the Collie bitch. These must be noted to assure the health and safety of the bitch and litter. To begin, the Collie bitch is likely to come into season every eight to ten months rather than the six months typical of most breeds. This is of no concern, it's just that the dogs can't read the books. They don't know just what is expected of them so nature takes its course.

It is sometimes hard to recognize when a bitch comes into season. In most cases, there is very little discharge. I have known many Collie bitches who could pass by their season unnoticed unless the owner took a good look at her at least once a week. It is simple to check. Just lift the tail aside, part the hair and inspect the vulva.

At the beginning of the season, the vulva will be somewhat swollen, and there should be a distinct red discharge. As the season progresses, the area becomes more swollen, and by about 10 days or so the red discharge will change to pale pink or straw color. It should be clear and free running, not thick or mucousy. If there is any question as to the quality of the discharge, it is wise to consult your veterinarian to be sure there is no infection. An infected uterus could kill puppies and the dam as well.

Assuming all is well, the bitch will probably become receptive to the male at about 10 days into the season. However, I have actually known a bitch to breed willingly as late as the 23rd day and have pups. Again, I say the dogs don't read the books. I would say that in most cases in which

Nice, well-balanced heads on two-week-old baby Collie pups.

a bitch misses, it might be due to having bred her at the wrong time. Some bitches will stand for breeding all through the season. Others will stand only a day or two, some will never stand. When the dog and bitch both think the time is right, they are generally right.

In the case of a bitch who will never stand for breeding, it still is possible to breed her by artificial insemination. While that is a perfectly viable option, it has a definite drawback. If the bitch never wants to be bred, she probably has a flaw either in her physical structure or in her hormone system. Think carefully about whether you want to perpetuate that flaw. Will her bitch pups be the same way?

Now, I will assume you have bred your (willing) bitch to a dog of appropriate bloodlines and appearance. She will have a 63-day gestation period. But I do not even say that with absolute assurance. Many a Collie in my experience whelps on or about the 58th day of gestation. In many other breeds that would produce progeny dangerously premature. However, in many Collie bitches that seems to be normal.

Puppies whelped on the 58th day, or on the 61st, are naturally smaller and, should we say, "dumber" than 63rd-day babies. They tend to be slow to learn to nurse. It may be that their sucking instinct is not yet developed.

Anyway, such puppies will need careful attention from the owner. As they are small and not very strong, the mother might lie upon a pup, killing him without even being aware. In the case of very small Collie puppies, I usually take them away from the dam and keep them snug and warm in a box somewhere she cannot hear them. I then bring the pups to the mother for a nursing period many times a day. I recommend staying and watching during this time. You must be sure each puppy gets his full time at a nipple, and that the dam does not get up and trample on them.

If the puppies are not strong enough or developed enough to nurse, you must take over. This means feeding every two hours night and day for at least a week. By that time, the puppies, at least some of them, will be strong enough to take milk from the dam.

Now, back to the time of whelping. I suggest the bitch have a quiet place away from the hustle-bustle of the home. She should have a whelping box at least four-feet square with a railing about three inches off the floor. This is to prevent the mother from rolling on the puppies. Some breeders use a child's wading pool of soft plastic as a whelping box—sure is easy to clean.

When the bitch starts to indicate that she is in labor, she may stand up and hunch over to expel a puppy. More often she will lie down and keep licking her vulva. Suddenly, a puppy will pop out and she will ideally start to lick him and remove the thin membrane that encloses the

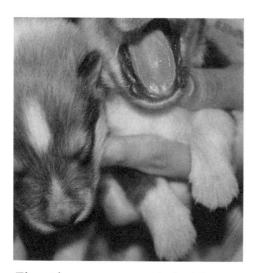

The wide yawn is a sign of a healthy pup.

puppy. This must be cleared from the puppies head immediately or the pup will suffocate. Then she will sever the umbilical cord, and eat the afterbirth. That is all as nature intended.

However, if the birth is easy, the bitch may not even know she has had a puppy. Several times, I have lifted the tail of the mother to find a newborn puppy there. It stays, still wrapped in its "cocoon" still attached to the afterbirth. If that continues, the puppy will die in the sac. You must quickly open the sac over the mouth and head to let the puppy breath. For this reason, along with others, it is important that someone be in attendance while the bitch whelps.

Here is another warning. After the puppies are born they will instinctively snuggle up against the mother's teats and appear to be nursing. But you better check to see if all of them are actually sucking. They can fool you by appearing to be at the nipple when they are not actually taking nourishment. If you find that one or more is only staying close for warmth rather than sucking, I suggest either bottle feeding or tube feeding. A few days of supplemental feeding and usually the pups will grow strong enough and bright enough to feed from momma.

Puppies for the first days need to be kept very warm, some say at least 85° to 90°. If the weather is cold, you can put a heating pad or a hot water bottle in the whelping pen. If the puppies are cold, they can somehow find their way to the source of heat and go to sleep on it. However, they must be able to get away from the heat as well. The heating pad should be kept at medium or low. It is a good idea to wrap it up in a towel in one corner of the box so pups may go to it at will. Too much heat will kill, as will cold. There is an old saying, "a chilled puppy is a dead puppy." They have not yet developed a personal thermostat to control their inner heat.

As the pups are born, I always make sure the airways are open by rubbing with a towel over the mouth and nose. If a puppy seems limp, you may rub it vigorously with a dry towel, and even blow air into its little mouth. I have resuscitated many a puppy over the years in this way. The Collie tends to be smaller and less vigorous at birth than puppies of many other breeds. This may be due to early whelping. The Collie puppy at birth is about the size of a Shetland Sheepdog puppy, so you can see the disparity in size between the Collie puppy and his mother.

Before the whelping, it is excellent practice to cut away the hair from the mother's vulva area, also from her whole belly and under the tail. Many times, I have seen tiny puppies get caught up in their mother's long hair. In fact, I have seen a puppy hanging from the dam as she walked around with the puppy dangling from hair wrapped around the pups neck. Well, I guess I have seen almost everything that can happen to Collies, in my 40 or so years in the breed.

And yet, I have just learned one lesson that should have been brought to my attention long ago—a most important one. If the bitch starts to pass a greenish liquid, and it is not followed *immediately* by a puppy, there is *trouble*. The green discharge means that a placenta has broken. If the pup emerges that is fine. If no pup comes out, rush to your veterinarian, for your litter is in great danger. The green liquid denotes a placenta previa, the placenta has broken too soon. Most veterinarians will give oxcytocin and wait, hoping to force birth to occur. In the recent case I have seen, all the puppies (10) were dead, when the veterinarian finally did a cesarean section. There was a dead puppy, which had poisoned all the remaining puppies. In the future, if it occurs again, I will insist on an immediate section. It was heart rending to see 10 perfectly formed, well developed puppies lined up dead on the operating table. I will never forget it.

Well, to more cheerful things. After the birth is complete, or you think it is, the bitch should go to the vet for an oxytocin shot to clean her out. Sometimes this also includes the delivery of an unexpected puppy. If the shot is not given, the bitch may retain part of an afterbirth, or even a dead

Lovely stop and underjaw on a two-week-old puppy.

puppy. This can endanger the life of the mother. It can also lead to bad milk.

I would suggest that while the veterinarian examines the pups and the dam, you ask him to test the milk. Bad milk from a bitch is not as unusual as you might think. The effects of it usually show up in a weakening puppy and in loose stools from the pups.

If the milk is bad, one faces a nearly man-killing job. The puppies must be hand fed every two hours for several days, then every four hours for another week at least. It is helpful to have the mother continue to clean the puppies. Her licking will help to stimulate elimination. If she does not do it, you will have to stimulate the puppies by rubbing the areas with warm damp cotton balls, after each feeding.

I'll assume all has gone well, and you can restfully and proudly watch mom and litter in one of nature's sweetest scenes. You will not have a thing to do for about four weeks as mom will feed and clean her babies. All you have to do is to change the paper in the whelping box several times a day.

If however, all has not gone well, you may use any one of many formulas. Your veterinarian will probably recommend the use of *Esbilac*, or some other pre-prepared commercial formula. There are also many favorite formulas used by breeders. I personally have had success with the following formula:

> 1 can evaporated milk
> 1/2 cup plain yogurt
> 2 egg yolks
> 1 tablespoon mayonnaise

This formula helps to maintain the proper amount of "good bacteria" in the digestive system, while supplying the desired high-fat content. Bitch's milk carries a very high content of fat which we are trying duplicate.

The way this formula is used is as follows;

> Give three CCs less than the weight of the puppy:
> 8 ounce pup, 5 CCs this is the amount to give

at each feeding

> 12 ounce pup, 9 CCs

Mix the formula in a blender, warm only the amount you wish for each feeding, and refrigerate the rest. Warm to room temperature at each feeding.

You may use either a "preemie" baby bottle to feed, or you may use a tube-feeding method. I personally prefer the tube method, as it is quicker, plus the fact that some pups will refuse the bottle. If you are to tube feed, I suggest you get the equipment from your veterinarian. Also, be sure to have him or her show you how to use it. There are some dangers one can encounter with feeding by tube. But if you feed exactly as directions say, it is no more dangerous than bottle feeding.

It is important to watch the bitch carefully after whelping. Many bitches refuse to eat for a day or two. If that is the case try tempting her with a high meat diet or all meat diet for a few days.

If she continues to lack appetite, I would get to a vet right away, she may be harboring an infection. If not taken care of this can kill bitch and puppies.

Be sure she gets plenty of high-quality food, preferably with a high-fat content. While we are all watching our fat intake and keeping it as low as possible, remember, dogs are a different matter. My late husband Don Starkweather did a study for the Ohio State University as to optimum protein, fat, and carbohydrate balance for the dog. To the surprise of many, the ideal amount of fat was 30 percent. Almost no commercial dog foods contain that high an amount. I prefer a close to 30 percent fat diet for all my dogs, winter or summer, in whelp or not.

I suggest you watch the vulva area for any signs of excess bleeding, black discharge, or mucous. Any of these signs may indicate trouble. Again I say, get her to the veterinarian.

Just about the ideal look for a tri and a sable baby puppy.

Health and Nutrition

The Collie is a dog of all-round good health and disease resistance. As puppies, that is as newborns and baby pups, the dog is somewhat fragile. But, by the time the puppy is weaned and ready to leave the breeder, he will be strong and vigorous. If the dog is kept on heartworm preventive medicine, is kept worm-free, is fed a nutritious diet, he should be able to look forward to a long and healthy life—14 to 16 years.

There are few diseases that affect the Collie in particular. Some Collies at about three to five months of age will develop a slight loss of hair around the eyes and lips. This may or may not be demodectic mange. If the condition remains for more than a month or so, it may be treated with a product called *Mitaban*. This is available from your veterinarian. This mange is probably associated with the stress of passing from puppy to adolescence and should be self-limiting.

If the condition lingers or spreads to other parts of the body, it may turn into generalized mange. If so, you must take the dog to a veterinarian. There are dips that can usually control this condition and hopefully cure it. However, in the case of a dog with a severely depressed immune system, the mange may become generalized. If this occurs, there are rare cases in which the dog may have to be euthanized. At the least, it is always recommended that a dog that has or has had generalized mange should not be bred. This may be an inheritable condition. Some think it probably passes from mother to puppy through lactation. The mode of inheritance, if there is one, has not been determined.

Another more serious skin disorder is called DM or dermatomyositis. This is an inherited disease that affects the skin and muscles. At the beginning, it resembles demodectic mange, with hair loss on the face and legs. Later, it spreads over more of the body and may lead also to muscle weakness. At present there is no known cure for this very serious affliction. This condition is rarely found and is thought to run in certain families of dogs.

As if we did not have enough to worry about, here comes the "new kid on the block." It is a disease that affects only Collies and Shetland Sheepdogs. Isn't that a giant pain? All of the cases on record affect only these two breeds.

This disease is called Familial Canine Dermatomyositis. It is an inflammatory condition mainly affecting the skin and musculature. Dermatomyositis develops mainly in juvenile dogs and consists of dermatitis of the face, ears and tail tip. If also appears over the bony prominences, such as wrists and hocks. It may also produce myositis of the muscles of the jaws and lower extremities.

Dermatomyositis in Collies appears to be inherited as a dominant trait. It has developed in all colors of Collies and both coat lengths. Conclusions regarding the mode of inheritance in Shelties are prevented by limited pedigree analysis and lack of breeding studies. Because of the close relationship between Collies and Shetland Sheepdogs, it would seem that the mode of inheritance is similar in both breeds. Myositis is more common in Collies than in Shelties. At least one parent must have the gene for this disease and half of the litter will carry it.

Cutaneous lesions usually develop between seven weeks and six months of age. Lesions consist of alopecia (loss of hair), scaling, ulceration, crusting, hyperpigmentation and hypopigmentation. Occasionally, oral and footpad ulcers have appeared. In moderately affected dogs, skin lesions may dissolve after three months. Others may have dermatitis for six months. Severely affected dogs may have dermatitis throughout their lives. If minimally affected, dogs may recover without scarring. Others may show hair loss, particularly around the muzzle and the eyes. Estrus or exposure to sunlight may worsen the condition.

Myositis develops after dermatitis. The first sign of myositis is a bilaterally symmetrical decrease of mass of the temporalis muscle. Moderately or severely affected dogs may develop severe generalized symmetrical muscle atrophy.

Severely affected dogs have difficulty lapping water, also chewing and swallowing. This is due to the involvement of the masticatory and esophageal muscles. The growth of moderately to severely dogs is stunted.

For therapy, I quote from *Compendium on Continuous Education for the Practicing Veterinarian*, volume 14 (7), July 1992:

> Because several diagnostic differentials can account for the clinical dermatologic lesions of dermatomyositis, a diagnosis must be established before therapy is instituted. It is often difficult to establish therapeutic efficacy because of the cyclic and often self-limiting nature of canine dermatomyositis. Hypoallergenic shampoos are beneficial. Handling methods that minimize injury should be helpful as cutaneous trauma may play a role in causing dermatitis. Ovariohysterectomy and avoidance of sunlight may help to control dermatomyositis in some dogs.
>
> Glucorticoids may be useful in treating dogs more severely affected...but evidence of effectiveness is inconclusive. For induction of treatment immunosuppressive doses of predisone or prednissolone (1 to 2 mg/kg every 12 hours) are recommended. Once a satisfactory response develops, the

glucorticoid therapy should be tapered to alternate day administration. Repeated doses of glucortcoid therapy may be required for relapses. If dermatologic signs worsen after immunosuppressive therapy begins, the dog should be carefully evaluated because pyoderma, dermatophytosis, and demodicosis can develop after immunosuppressive therapy.

Preliminary results of an ongoing open clinical trial indicate that pentoxifylline (Trental) may be beneficial in the treatment of Canine Familial Dermatomyositis. Pentoxifylline is a rheologic agent in that it alters (increases) microvascular blood flow by lowering blood viscosity, increasing erythrocite deformability retarding platelet aggregation...These factors tend to increase tissue oxygenation.

Dr. Gail Kunkle Diplomate, College of Veterinary Dermatology, College of Veterinary Medicine, University of Florida, has spent years pursuing information on the elusive disease. In the aforementioned veterinary magazine, Dr. Kunkle writes:

> Judging from gathered evidence and data regarding Familial Dermatomyositis in Dogs, this disease process evidently requires a genetic predilection or genetic metabolic defect and then an infectious (probably viral) agent to induce clinical disease. Some investigators believe that the disease is caused by infection, others support an autoimmune pathogenesis. It is possible that both mechanisms are involved. Where dogs are concerned, I believe that most current data indicate that dermatomyositis results from infection.

The only good news I can gather from all this is that the disease is inherited (if inherited) as a dominant. That means that only one parent needs to be the culprit, and the gene will not be able to hide for generations as a recessive ready to poke up its ugly head at any time.

Parasites

Fleas. We must consider that external problem of fleas. There is a relatively new treatment available from veterinarians. This is a pill called *Program.* When administered once a month, the pill will control reinfestation of larva. When starting on this program, the dog should be flea free, and the area where the dog lives must also be flea free. Therefore, it is imperative to wash the dog with flea soap before starting—also treat the house and grounds with insecticide.

For large areas, particularly in the country, it is not feasible to make the land flea free. In that case, one should embark on a long-term attack. The dog must be bathed and dipped about once every two weeks, and the grounds and house must also be treated. Many people have found it worthwhile to have an exterminator to take care of the flea problem. Be sure to hire one that guarantees to keep the property flea free.

Ticks. In some parts of the country ticks are a problem. If invaded by ticks, I have found that spreading 10 percent *Sevin Dust* over the ground will definitely handle the problem. It also may be put on puppies with no ill effects. It must not be put on an adult Collie if you have plans to show. The *Sevin Dust* will take care of the ticks, but will change the white part of the coat to an ugly orange-tan color.

To show how effective the *Sevin Dust* can be, I have a "for instance:" Another fancier raised a litter for me until the puppies were eight weeks old. When she brought them to me they were covered with ticks. An almost unbelievable number crawled on the puppies from one end to the other. Naturally, I was horrified. I asked her why she had not taken care of the infestation. She replied that she had tried without success.

I immediately covered the pups and their area with 10 percent *Sevin.* Voila. Within a couple of hours, there were no live ticks, and they never came back. I must say the puppies were small and weak from the blood suckers. However, I got them soon enough to build them up to normal healthy size and vigor.

The 10 percent *Sevin Dust* is available at gardening stores. It's usual use is to kill garden pests. The great thing about it is that it is an all-natural product. It is so non-toxic it can be used on baby puppies with no damage to the dogs. I have also found *Sevin Dust* to be useful when spread upon dog pens to help control flea infestations.

One thing all of us who raise dogs have found is that fleas apparently mutate. An insecticide that works well at one time may not e effective at another time. Sometimes I think can see the fleas laughing at our efforts. Of course, such fantasizing may mean I have been in dogs too long.

Some chemicals that have been effective are *Diazanon* granules, *Spectracide, Lindane, Dursban,* and *Malathion.* There is a product called *Precor,* which prevents larvae from maturing. This can be used only in the house. For the outside, there is an excellent product called *Toro,* which kills the larvae. However, it can only be obtained by professional exterminators. I am not a professional but have become somewhat of an expert on fleas, since I have lived in Florida. It is flea heaven.

There are several good flea shampoos on the market. I have also found that using a good dish detergent and letting it stay on the dog for 10 minutes or so will kill fleas.

In some areas of the country, it may be necessary to dip the dog. However, I prefer to treat the environment rather than the dog. After all, dips are poisons and I hate to put them on my animals. It used to be that some dips had a residual effect. Now, so far as I can determine, that is no longer so. Perhaps this falls in with the new theory held by genetic scientists. They are now speculating that perhaps mutation or evolution takes place much faster than previously believed.

Over all, the dog's world view is: "Big fleas have little fleas to bite 'em—ad infitim." (Ogden Nash)

The scientific world has been hard at work on the flea problem. They have come up with new solutions which may change the lives of dogs and dog owners for the better.

The product *Advantage* is easily applied. The liquid is presented in pre-measured vials. The application merely involves putting the product on the skin between the dog's shoulders. For small dogs, one vial is enough. For larger dogs it is better to apply one vial between the shoulders and the other on the skin of the rump. This application will work for at least 30 days unless the dog gets wet. If he does get wet another application is required.

Another new development is called *Frontline*. This may be used on puppies, cat, and kittens, as well as adults. The puppies and kittens must be at least eight weeks old. *Frontline* is a spray that is effective for up to three months.

These products are only available from a veterinarian. They may seem expensive at first, but their efficacy will make up for original expense many times over.

Heartworm

At one time it was thought that heartworm was only a problem in the South, and only in hot weather. However, it is now known that heartworm is found all over the United States. This nasty parasite is carried by mosquitoes. The infected mosquito bites a dog and inserts heartworm eggs. The egg enters the bloodstream and is deposited in the heart. The heartworm then grows worm-like until it strangles the dog's heart. This will lead to severe illness and death. There is a treatment for this condition but it is very dangerous to the dog.

Fortunately, there are several preventive treatments for this disease. The one I personally prefer is *Filaribits Plus*. This medication is given daily and prevents not only heartworm but also hook worm, round worm and whip worm This is especially useful in southern climates where parasites are in the ground everywhere. For the Collie owner, it is important to know that **the heartworm preventive *Ivermectin* in incorrect dosage can be fatal to the Collie.** Veterinarians should prescribe exactly the proper dosage, so it should be all right. There are other products that are reliable as well. Just be sure your dog is protected from heartworm no matter what climate or season.

General Health Tips

The other canine parasites, such as hook worm, round worm, whip worm and tape worm will be debilitating to your dog if he is infested. Having periodic worm checks by your veterinarian is crucial. If the dog is not on *Filaribits Plus*, I recommend a checkup for worms every three months or so.

Be sure to have your dog immunized by your veterinarian at recommended intervals.

At the time of writing, there are shots that are five-way. They cover distemper, hepatitis, lepto-spirosis, parainfluinza and parvo. Some veterinarians recommend giving the parvo shot separately and a day later. The important thing is to get those preventative shots into your dog at the proper intervals. Puppies will require a series of immunizations. Again, carefully follow the recommendations of the vet on the shot schedule.

Nutrition

Nutrition of dogs can be maintained at a high level by good, commercial diets. It is not necessary for the owner to be an expert in nutrition, but some background in this science is helpful in understanding the problems that may be encountered in the normal care of your dog.

Dog food is generally prepared in one of two ways—dry and canned. Dry food is usually a blend of cooked cereal and meat. The cereal grains need to be cooked or heated to improve digestibility. Fats are added to increase calories; vitamins and minerals are added as needed. Dry foods contain about 10 percent moisture.

A subject frequently discussed among "dog people" is the addition of supplements to commercially prepared dog foods. Supplements are usually unnecessary because major dog food manufacturers incorporate into their products all the protein, vitamins and other nutrients dogs are known to need. The diet may be specific for a particular life stage, such as adult maintenance or growth, or it may be shown as complete and balanced for all stages of life. When it is fed to normal dogs of any breed, no additional supplements in the form of vitamins, minerals, meats or other additives are needed.

Dry meals are usually pellets, sprayed with oil and crumbled. Biscuit and kibbled foods are baked on sheets and then kibbled or broken into small bits. Expanded foods are mixed, cooked and forced through a die to make nuggets that are then expanded with steam, dried and coated with oil. Food to be expanded must be at least 40 percent carbohydrates or the expansion process will not work.

Soft-moist foods, which are considered dry foods, contain about 25 percent moisture. They can be stored in cellophane without refrigeration due to the added preservatives.

Canned foods come in four types:

1. Ration types are usually the cheapest and are a mix of cereals, meat products, fats, etc., to make a complete diet containing 50 to 70 percent water.

2. Animal tissue may be beef, chicken, or horsemeat. Generally, this type is not balanced although some companies may add supplements. These sometimes are used to improve the palatability of dry foods.

3. Chunk style has meat by-products ground and extruded into pellets or chunks. Some of the cheaper ones have vegetable matter mixed in. A gravy or juice is added.

4. Stews are meats or chunks mixed with vegetables.

Nutritional Requirements

The exact nutritional requirements of any dog are complicated by the wide variation in size, hair coat, activity, etc. Diets can be suggested based on body weight, but the final determination must be based on how the individual responds to the diet. Gain or loss in weight and change in activity level must be observed and some adjustments made.

There are generally two exceptions to the rule that supplements are not necessary when dogs receive a complete and balanced diet. These instances are: to correct a specific deficiency due to the dog's inability to utilize the normal level of a particular nutrient and to stimulate food intake, particularly during period of hard work or heavy lactation. This includes hard-working dogs, such as bird dogs, sled dogs, and bitches with large litters that require a high level of milk production. The addition of 10 to 20 percent meat or meat by-products to the diet will normally increase food acceptance and as a result will increase food intake. At this level of supplementation, the nutritional balance of the commercial product would not be affected.

Water: Fresh and clean water should be available at all times. The amount of water needed is dependent upon the type of food provided, but generally a dog gets 25 percent of its total water requirements from drinking.

Protein: Ten of the approximately 20 amino acids that make up protein are essential for dogs. Dogs must receive adequate amounts of these 10 proteins for good nutrition. The natural sources containing these ten proteins are milk, eggs, meat and soybeans. Sources such as gelatin, flour and wheat are incomplete.

Also important is the ratio of nitrogen retained to the amount of nitrogen taken into the body. In this respect, eggs, muscle meat and organ meat are all good. Some legumes, such as soybeans, are only fair. Most other vegetative proteins are poor. As dogs get older, this vegetative type of food tends to overwork the kidneys. This is especially important with chronic kidney disease in old dogs. More dog food companies are making products for each stage in a dog's life—from puppyhood to old age, and including lactating bitches.

Another important aspect of protein is digestibility. A good quality dry ration has about 75 percent digestibility, while canned foods are up to 95 percent. Some typical figures for digestibility:

Horsemeat: 91%   Meat scraps: 75-86%

Fishmeal: 99%   Soybean meal: 86%

Liver meal: 88%   Linseed meal: 81%

The dog's utilization of protein is dependent upon both the biological value and the digestibility. The digestibility of protein in the dog is related to the temperature to which the protein is subjected during processing. Some dog foods that seem to have proper ingredients at the time they are mixed can give disappointing results. This may well be due to processing at high temperatures or heating for long periods of time.

It is generally recommended that the dietary crude protein for adult dogs be 18 to 25 percent on a dry basis. For example, if a canned food is 12 percent protein and has a 50 percent moisture content, then it is really 24 percent protein on a dry basis. If the protein is of high quality, such as from milk, eggs or meat, the total needed would be less than if it contained substantial amounts of vegetative proteins.

Fats: Fats and oils have an important effect on palatability. A small increase in fat in a diet may greatly increase its acceptability to dogs. Fats supply essential fatty acids, particularly linolenic and arachidonic acids. Other sources are animal fats, corn oil, olive oil and raw linseed oil. A dietary deficiency of the essential fatty acids leads to defective growth, dry hair, scaly skin and susceptibility to skin infections.

The absorption of vitamins A, D, E and K is associated with the absorption of fats. Rancid fat destroys vitamins A and E. Extended use of rancid fats can cause hair loss, rash, loss of appetite, constipation progressing to diarrhea and even death. Commercial dog foods must use an antioxidant to retard rancidity.

The principal danger of excess fat in the diet is that it contains more energy than is needed and leads to storage of fat and obesity.

Carbohydrates: Requirements for carbohydrates in the dog are not known. The dog can utilize as much as 65 to 70 percent in his diet. Because this is the cheapest source of energy, it composes the major part of commercial foods. Carbohydrates are well utilized if properly prepared. Potatoes, oats and corn are poorly utilized unless cooked. High levels of uncooked starch can cause diarrhea. Milk can upset some dogs as some do not have the lactase enzyme needed to digest lactose, the milk sugar. Fresh cow's milk is 50 percent lactose. In some dogs, a ration with as much as 10 percent dried skim milk may cause diarrhea.

Fiber: Fiber is also a part of the carbohydrate portion of the ration. It is only slightly digested. Some fibers absorb water and produce a more voluminous stool. This can help stimulate intestinal action, especially in old or inactive animals. Fiber aids in the prevention of constipation and other intestinal problems. Most foods have 1 to 8 percent fiber. Reducing diets may have as much as 32 percent fiber. Sources of fiber are cellulose, bran, beet pulp and string beans.

Gross Energy: Dogs expend energy in every form of body activity. This energy comes from food or from destruction of body sources. Carbohydrates and fats provide the main source of energy for dogs. Caloric requirements are greater per pound of body weight for small dogs than for large dogs. For example, a 10-week-old puppy weighing 10 pounds would require 650 calories a day. At 12 weeks and weighing 15 pounds, he would need 840 calories a day. Divide the number of calories contained in one pound of feed into the number of calories required by the puppy on a daily basis to determine how much to offer the puppy initially. Using the example: At 10 weeks, he requires 650 calories a day; divide this by 690 (the number of calories in one pound of a popular dry puppy food) and the answer is approximately 1 pound.

There are various theories on how often to feed a dog. The Gaines Basic Guide to Canine Nutrition establishes this schedule: Up to five months, feed three times daily; from five months to one year, feed twice daily; from one year on, feed once daily.

Divide the amount of food needed each day into the appropriate number of feedings to determine the amount of food to give the puppy at each feeding. For example, because a 12-week-old puppy requires three feedings, divide the puppy's one pound of food into three servings of one-third pound each.

Russell V. Brown, writing in the February 1987 issue of *The Basenji*, points out:

While caloric needs vary with age and activity, a rule of thumb is that for dogs of 5 to 65 pounds the need is X(33-1/4 X) = kcal/day.* In this case "X" is the body weight in pounds. A 20-pound dog would work out as 20(33-20/4) = 20 (28) = 560 kcals per day. For dogs over 65 pounds, the formula is 18X = kcal/day. The following adjustments are recommended:

a. Age adjustments

    1. add 10% for dogs 1 year of age

    2. add 30% for dogs 6 months of age

    3. add 60% for dogs 3 months of age

  b. Activity variable

    1. add 25% for moderate activity

    2. Add 60% for heavy activity

c. Pregnancy and lactation

    1. from conception to whelping—increase 20%

    2. at whelping—increase 25%

    3. 2nd week of lactation—increase 50%

    4. 3rd week of lactation—increase 75%

    5. 4th week of lactation—increase 100%

* Kcal is the scientific term for what laymen call calorie.

Some owners find that the portion-control methods, such as the feeding schedule above, are inconvenient. They opt for the self-feeding method, which is also called the free-choice method. Free choice ensures that the puppy's feed consumption correlates with his rate of growth. The idea behind free-choice feeding is that it provides reasonable assurance that the puppy is obtaining all he needs for growth, even though these needs are essentially changing.

Free-choice advocates believe that dogs know quite accurately what their needs are and eat accordingly. Free choice works especially well for the pup who dawdles over his food for hours. A slight variation on the free-choice method is to feed the pup all he can eat in a specified time, usually 20 minutes. The pup would be fed for those time periods a certain number of times a day. This timed method may not be suitable for the slow or picky eater (or the glutton). Studies have indicated that free-choice eaters tend to turn out heavier by some 23 percent and that these weight differences were mostly in body fat. Collies are more likely to be too thin rather than too fat.

Regardless of the feeding method used, food should be served lukewarm or at room temperature. If the food is prepared with an ingredient that can spoil quickly, such as meat or milk, be sure to serve fresh food only.

Estimating Caloric Content

In determining how much to feed a dog, use the following:

a. Dry food usually contains about 1360 calories a pound.

b. Canned food can be estimated at 475 calories a pound.

Minerals. Calcium and phosphorus are needed in a ratio of 1.2 parts calcium to 1 part phosphorus. A deficiency causes rickets and other less serious diseases. Young and old dogs need additional calcium. Common sources are bone meal, skim milk and alfalfa leaf meal. Sources of phosphorus are bone meal and meat scraps. Vitamin D is necessary for proper utilization of the calcium and phosphorus.

Magnesium is needed for bones and teeth, and bone meal is a good source. Sodium chloride should be in the diet as 1 percent salt. Sulfur and potassium are needed and are usually in the foods dogs eat. The best sources of iron are liver and eggs. A strict vegetarian diet will cause iron deficiency. Trace minerals are contained in milk, liver and egg yolks for copper, fish for iodine, and most foods contain cobalt, manganese, and zinc.

Vitamins. Vitamin A is important to vision, bone growth and skin health. Deficiency may cause lack of appetite, poor growth, excessive shedding, lowered resistance to disease and infection. Severe deficiency can cause deafness. On the other hand, too much is harmful and can cause birth defects, anorexia, weight and bone problems.

Vitamin D deficiencies are most often found in large breeds. Deficiencies cause rickets in the young and softening of the bones in adults; they also cause irregular development or eruption in teeth. Sources of Vitamin D are sunlight, irradiated yeast, fish liver oils and egg yolks. Too much Vitamin D can cause anorexia, calcification and other problems.

Vitamin E deficiency may involve reproductive and lactation problems. It may be involved in muscular dystrophy. Natural sources are corn oil, wheat germ oil, fish and egg yolks. It seems to be of some value topically in the healing of wounds.

Vitamin K is involved in blood clotting. It is found in egg yolks, liver and alfalfa. Most dogs can synthesize enough in the intestines.

Thiamine deficiency causes anorexia, weight loss, dehydration, paralysis and convulsions. Overheating during the processing of dog food destroys Thiamine. It is also commonly destroyed if dry food is stored in a hot location, such as a feed store without adequate cooling facilities. Best natural sources are raw liver, wheat germ and brewer's yeast. High-carbohydrate diets, particularly bread and potatoes, increase the need for thiamin. Fats may decrease the need.

Riboflavin, niacin and pyridoxine are all B vitamins found in liver, wheat germ, leafy vegetables, yeast and mild. Riboflavin deficiency can cause dry scaly skin, muscular weakness, abnormal redness of hindlegs and chest due to capillary congestion, anemia and sudden death. Niacin deficiency can lead to pellagra or black tongue with oral ulcers. Pyridoxine deficiency can also cause anemia.

Chlorine deficiency causes fatty liver. Best sources are liver, yeast and soybean oil.

Biotin deficiency causes posterior paralysis and seborrhea. Raw egg whites contain a substance that ties up biotin. A diet of all raw egg whites should not be fed. Natural sources are liver and yeast.

Vitamin B-12 is important for blood formation. Dogs used in heavy work need a good supply. Dogs produce B-12 in their intestines and when given foods that have enough B-12 they can function adequately. Large doses of antibiotics may stop this synthesis. Best sources are liver, milk, cheese, eggs and meat.

Vitamin C deficiency may cause delayed wound healing and scurvy-type lesions of the mouth and gums, loose teeth, bloody diarrhea and tender joints. Generally, the bacteria in the gut produce sufficient Vitamin C. However, intestinal problems can affect the amount produced.

The 7.5 percent protein in bitches' milk is equivalent to 30 percent dry dog food, but is probably all digestible. Dry dog food protein is only about 80 percent digestible unless it comes from a meat or fish source. A pup must consume twice as much cow's milk to the protein of bitches' milk, but would then get three times as much lactose sugar that it has difficulty digesting. As a result, pups frequently have diarrhea on cow's milk. Non-fat dry milk is even worse, for without the fat the percentage of lactose is even greater.

Weaning Puppies

It's a good idea to feed puppies a diet of 115 calories for each pound of their body weight three to four times a day. Begin to wean them at four to seven weeks of age. Seven to 10 days should see the puppies no longer dependent on their mother. Often, the dam will begin to wean the puppies on her own. During the weaning process, take the dam away during the day for gradually longer periods of time. Feed the puppies three times a day. Puppies often gulp a lot of air when learning to eat solid foods. Slow them down by spreading the food out on a large pan. Chopped meat and small kibble may be better than finely ground meal because it passes through the intestines more slowly, causing fewer digestive problems.

Feeding Older Puppies

The first step in any puppy's feeding program is to weigh him. From birth through six months, the breeder should weigh and record each pup's growth weekly.

The next step is to determine the diet to be fed. This depends, in large measure, on the stage of growth the puppy has reached. Young puppies require twice as much energy per unit of body weight as an adult dog. But feeding the rapidly growing puppy twice as much food of the adult variety is not the answer. The diet must include a protein with high net protein utilization value. This is because the puppy's digestive tract is immature and cannot fully digest and utilize the energy and nutrients that adult foods include. The total need for all nutrients is double for a puppy, and the nutrients must be in an easily digestible form.

When acquiring a puppy from a breeder, be sure to find out the details of his feeding program. The breeder should provide you with the type of food the puppy is used to, the feeding times and the amount of food to be fed. Whether you agree with the program or not, duplicate it for several days until the pup is accustomed to his new surroundings.

After the puppy is settled, don't hesitate to change food or feeding methods if there is a need to do so. Using the information above, use good judgment in selecting the commercial dog food best suited to his size and needs. Make the change in his diet gradually so as not to cause diarrhea. Dry food is the most popular because it is normally most convenient, feed efficient and economical.

Be sure to choose a high-quality dog food. Not only will it be better for the dog's health, but it will also require less food to meet his nutritional needs. Don't be mislead by how much the puppy eats; it's the performance of the food that counts. Lower quality food is also less digestible and will result in the puppy eating more to compensate. The increased food eaten will further reduce the digestibility of the food.

Don't try to save money by feeding maintenance or low-quality foods. The puppy will end up with a pot-bellied appearance, slower growth, poor muscle and bone development and less resistance to disease and parasites.

Regardless of the form of commercial dog food used, Donald R. Collins, DVM, author of *The Collins Guide to Dog Nutrition*, believes every growing puppy should have liver in his diet. Liver is a good source of most of the good things an animal needs. It can be fed chopped, raw, or slightly braised. To avoid diarrhea, feed small amounts at first and gradually increase to no more than 10 percent of his total diet.

Catering to a dog's nutritional needs is one thing; catering to his desires is another. Do not permit a puppy to dictate his food preferences. This reverses the positions of authority and can cause training problems as well. It could also create nutritional deficiencies.

The goal should be that by the time a pup has reached maturity, his digestive system should be capable of handling all the foods he will eat during his adult life. This program should help him reach the average height and weight for the Collie's standard.

Material for the content for much of this chapter is drawn from three main sources: 1) "Nutrition and Feeding of Basenjiis," by Russell V. Brown, appearing in the February 1987 issue of *The Basenji*; 2) "Feeding Your Puppy," by Ann Bierman, appearing in the March 1987 issue of *Golden Retriever Review*; and, 3) "Supplementation—May be Hazardous to Your Pet's Health," by R.K. Mohrman, published in the March/April 1980 issue of the *Great Dane Reporter*.

PART V.

STANDOUTS IN THE COLLIE WORLD

Ch. Glen Hill Campus Cutie, famous winner and producer. The Best American Bred at the Collie Club of America National Specialty Show. (Photo by June Napoli)

1. Ch. Tartanside Th'Critics Choice.

2. Ch. Twin Creeks True Grit.

TOP ROUGH COLLIE SIRES

CH. TARTANSIDE TH'CRITICS CHOICE	68
CH. TWIN CREEKS TRUE GRIT	57
CH. TWIN OAKS JOKER'S WILD	53
CH. TWIN CREEKS POSTSCRIPT	52
CH. TARTANSIDE THE GLADIATOR	44
CH. TWO JAYS HANOVER ENTERPRISE	44
CH. SILVER HO PARADER	37
CH. PARADER'S BOLD VENTURE	35
CH. TARTANSIDE APPARENTLY	31
CH. GINGEOR BELLBROOK'S CHOICE	28
CH. VENNESSEE'S MIDNIGHT EXPRESS	25
CH. PARADER'S COUNTRY SQUIRE	24
CH. PARADER'S GOLDEN IMAGE	24
CH. SEALORE'S GRAND APPLAUSE	23
CH. TWIN CREEKS GRAND MASTER	23
CH. BRANDWYNE DESTINY'S ECHO	22
CH. TARTANSIDE HEIR APPARENT	22
CH. TEL STAR'S COSMIC CAPERS	22
CH. EXECUTIVE RIDE THE HIGH WIND	21
CH. FURY'S THE SPIRIT OF LEGENDS	21
CH. CUL MOR'S CONSPIRATOUR	20
CH. TWIN CREEKS TUFF GUY	20

• •

PEDIGREE OF CH. TARTANSIDE TH'CRITICS CHOICE

                              Ch. Tartanside The Gladiator

          Ch. Tartanside Heir Apparent

                              Ravettes Tar N'Feather

Ch. Tartanside Th'Critics Choice, whelped 1982

                              Ch. Briarhill Glen Hill Sky High

          Ch. Briarhill Midnight High

                              Highefield's A Tisket A-Tasket

• •

3. Ch. Twin Oaks Joker's Wild.

4. Ch. Twin Creeks Postscript.

5. Ch. Tartanside The Gladiator.

PEDIGREE OF CH. TWIN CREEKS TRUE GRIT

                              Ch. Vi-lee's Myster Mac
          Ch. Lochlomuns Interlock
                              Lochlomun N'Lee Aires Virgo

Ch. Twin Creeks True Grit, whelped July 27, 1976

                              Ch. Ransom's Regency
          Ch. Lee Aire's Amazing Grace
                              Ch. Lee Aire's Live Wire

• •

PEDIGREE OF CH. TWIN OAKS JOKER'S WILD

                              Ch. Twin Creeks Postscript
          Ch. Executive's Table Stakes
                              Ch. Caven's Executive Affair

Ch. Twin Oaks Joker's Wild, whelped 1983

                              Ch. Twin Creeks Post Script
          Ch. Twin Oaks Executive Affair
                              Ch. Executive's Quest To Glory

• •

PEDIGREE OF CH. TWIN CREEKS POSTSCRIPT

                              Ch. Lochlomun's Interlock
          Ch. Twin Creeks True Grit
                              Ch. Lee Aire's Amazing Grace

Ch. Twin Creeks Postscript, whelped March 10, 1980

                              Ch. Twin Creeks True Grit
          Ch. Twin Creeks Nitty Gritty
                              Bon Bar's Forget Me Not

• •

6. Ch. Two Jays Hanover Enterprise.

7. Ch. Silver Ho Parader.

8. Ch. Paraders Bold Venture.

PEDIGREE OF CH. TARTANSIDE THE GLADIATOR

                    Ravette's Wayside Traveler
    Ch. HiVu The Invader
                    Glen Hill Cloth of Gold
Ch. Tartanside The Gladiator, whelped May 3, 1969
                    Ravette's Wayside Traveler
    Tartanside Tiara
                    Tartanside HiVu Classic

• •

PEDIGREE OF CH. TWO JAYS HANOVER ENTERPRISE

                    Ch. Paraders Bold Venture
    Ch. Paraders Country Sprire
                    Fairhaven's Golden Saleen
Ch. Two Jays Hanover Enterprise, whelped July 13, 1966
                    Ch. Cul Mors Conspiratour
    Ch. Cul Mors Highland Holly
                    Budh're Shiel Bri

• •

PEDIGREE OF CH. SILVER HO PARADER

                    Ch. Honeybrook Big Parade
    Ch. Silver Ho Shining Arrow
                    Silhouette of Silver Ho
Ch. Silver Ho Parader, whelped January 15, 1943
                    Heatherton Pal
    Lodestone Bandoliera II
                    Landmark Lady

• •

9. Ch. Tartanside Apparently.

10. Ch. Gingeor Bellbrookes Choice.

PEDIGREE OF CH. PARADERS BOLD VENTURE

Ch. Silver Ho Parader

Ch. Parader's Golden Image

Sterling Starsweet

Ch. Paraders Bold Ventue, whelped 1950

Ch. Silver Ho Parader

Paraders Cinderella

Parading Lady

• •

PEDIGREE OF CH. TARTANSIDE APPARENTLY

Ch. Tartanside The Gladiator

Ch. Tartanside Heir Apparent

Ravettes Tar N'Feather

Ch. Tartanside Apparently, whelped 1981

Ch. Wayside Grand Slam

Ch. Tartanside Fairwind Fantasy

Two Jays Medea O'Fairwind

• •

PEDIGREE OF GINGEOR BELLBROOKES CHOICE

Paraders Future Sensation

Bellbrookes Master Pilot

Paraders Bold Duchess

Ch. Gingeor Bellbrookes Choice, whelped 1960

Tomahawk of Lincair

Gayheart's Golden Miss

Bellbrookes Golden Glow

Ch. Silver Ho Parader (Photo courtesy of Gayle Kaye)
Ch. Gingeor Bellbrooks's Choice (1963). Photo courtesy of John Buddie)

TOP PRODUCING DAMS

TOP ROUGH DAMS

CH. HIGHCROFT QUINTESSENCE	14
STARR'S DARK CRYSTAL	10
BRAEDOONS HALLELUJAH	9
CH. TARTANSIDE FAIRWIND FANTASY	9
CH. ALTEZA THE SILVER LINING	8
CH. KENDRAS HEARTHROB	8/1 SMOOTH
WILTSHIRE-LEEAIRE SILHOUETTE	8
CH. CAINBREAKE CLEAR CALL	7
CH. PEBBLEBROOKS SWEET 'NUFF	7
CH. SHAMONT SABRINA	7
CH. STARR'S BLUE JEANS	7
CH. TARTANSIDE AMIMATION	7
CH. EDEN EDITH OF BELLHAVEN	6
CH. EXECUTIVE'S QUEST TO GLORY	6
CH. HALBURY JEAN OF ARKEN	6
HANOVER'S LOVE SONG	6
HIGHEFIELD TISKET A TASKET	6
CH. MYRIAH'S WESTWEND	6
CH. PALARY'S STAR SPANGLED	6
PARADICE'S BRELLY BY GOLLY	6
RENWICKS ROSEY FUTURE	6
CH. RAGALINE'S BLUE INTUITION	6
CH. BELLHAVEN SEEDLEY SNOWDROP	5
CH. BELLHAVEN SEEDLEY SOLUTION	5
CH. BONBARS SANDY GIRL	5
CH. BRANDWYNE BAYBERRY MISS	5
CH. BRIARHILL MIDNIGHT HIGH	5
CH. BRIARHILL QUICKSILVER	5
CANDRAY CORNICHE	5
CANDRAY LUMINESSE	5
CLARION MISTY MORN	5
DAKOTA'S OH SUSANNA	5
CH. EXECUTIVES BUY ME BLU RIBBONS	5
CH. FONTAINES CARA MIA	5
CH. GLEN HILL BLUE DRESS	5
CH. HIVU MADRESFIELD MOLLY	5
CH. HIGHEFIELD DEBUTANTE	5
CH. JANCADA PROMISES PROMISES	5
CH. KITSAPS SHADOW O'SHANE	5
CH. KITTREDGE SOCERESS	5
LIZDON MERRY FROLICKER	5
CH. LOCHLAREN THEME SONG	5
CH. LOU RA YOUNGHVAEN ARISTOCRAT	5
CH. MARVA'S CRACKLIN' ROSE	5

CH. NYMPH OF ARKEN	5
PARADING LADY	5
CH.PATRICIANE BLUE MIST	5
CH. PEBBLEBROOKS TWIN CREEKS AFFAIR	5
RENWICKS ROSEY FUTURE	5
CH. SHEPERD'S HEIRESS O'PHILAMOUR	5
CH. SHE ME TWO-DOTS VELVET SAGE	5
CH. SONTAWS TRUDY FAIR	5
CH. TARTANSIDE IMAGINATION	5
TOKALON MATINEE STAR	5
TOKALON PEACHES BROWNING	5
CH. TRAILWINDS SUNSHINE BRIGHT	5
TWIN CREEKS JOIUS PIN UP	5
CH. TWIN CREEKS LOVE STORY	5
CH. TWIN CREEKS NITTY GRITTY	5
CH. TWIN CREEKS TAR BABY	5
CROWN ROYAL MIDNIGHT MOOD	5
CLARION MISTY MORN	5
GLEN HILL PIPI LONGSTOCKING	5

• •

1. Ch. Highcroft Quintessence.

2. Starr's Dark Crystal.

3. Braedoon's Hallelujah.

PEDIGREE OF CH. HIGHCROFT QUINTESSENCE

Ch. Tamarack Hot Line

Twin Creeks Hot Property

Ch. Twin Creeks Stolen Property

Ch. Highcroft Quintessence

Ch. Sujim's Mr. Onederful

Sarallyn's Adventuress, CDX

Sarellyn's Sundown Lady, CD

Bred and owned by Don and Leslie Jeszewski

• •

PEDIGREE FOR STARR'S DARK CRYSTAL

Ch. Tartanside The Gladiator

Ch. Tartanside Heir Apparent

Ravett's Tar N'Feathers

Starr's Dark Crystal

Ch. Karavel Sudden Wyndfall

Ch. Starr's Blue Jeans

HiVu Silver Mystery

Bred by Pam and Louis Durazzano, owned by Dan Cardoza and Pam Durazzano

• •

PEDIGREE FOR BRAEDOON'S HALLELUJAH

Ch. Twin Creeks Aristocrat

Ch. Overland A Different Drummer

Overland A Christmas Feature

Braedoon's Hallelujah

Ch. Two Jays Hanover Enterprise

Braedoon's Glory Glory

Glentoran Tamberlane

Bred by Nancy Gustafson and Donna Burchard, owned by Rita Stanjczik

3. Ch. Tartanside Fairwind Fantasy.

5. Ch. Tartanside Animation.

5. Ch. Starr's Blue Jeans.

PEDIGREE FOR CH. TARTANSIDE FAIRWIND FANTASY

Wayside Warhawk

Ch. Wayside Grand Slam

Wayside Two Jay Tempo

Ch. Tartanside Fairwind Fantasy

Ch. Two Jay's Free Spirit

Two Jay's Medea O'Fairwind

Fairwind's Prelude

Bred by Jim Frederiksen, Jim Noe, Bobie Bayne. Owned by John Buddie

• •

PEDIGREE FOR CH. ALTEZA THE SILVER LINING

Ch. Carrico's Boy Blue

Carrico's Blue Note Supreme

Carrico's Mona Lisa

Ch. Alteza The Silver Lining

Windswept Major Jet

Alteza Witchery

Brandwyne Miss Winsome II

• •

PEDIGREE FOR CH. KENDRAS HEARTHROB

Lochlane's Handsome Devil

Ch. Hawick's Heartbreaker

Hawick Hawthornden By Design

Ch. Kendras Hearthrob

Lochlane's Handsome Devil

Ch. Lochlane The Devil's Double

Lochlane's The Devil's Darlin'

• •

PEDIGREE FOR WILTSHIRE-LEEAIRE SILHOUETTE

		Ch. Teecumsee Temptation
	Ch. Ransom's Regency	
		Ch. Ransom's Rapture
Wiltshire-Leeaire Silhouette		
		Ch. Bay Mar's Coming Attraction
	Ch. Lee Aire's Live Wire	
		Ch. Lee Aire's A Real Happening

Bred by Edith Catney. Owned by Gail Wilkes & Joann Thomas

• •

CH. CAINBREAKE CLEAR CALL

• •

CH. PEBBLEBROOKES SWEET 'NUFF

• •

PEDIGREE FOR CH. SHAMONT SABRINA

		Ch. Wickmere War Dance
	Ch. Wickmere Battle Chief	
		Bonnie Dawn Mactavish
Ch. Shamont Sabrina		
		Wickmere Royal Guardsman
	Ch. Wickmere Cotillion	
		Wickmere Tarantella

Bred/owned by Linda Sanders

• •

PEDIGREE FOR CH. STARR'S BLUE JEANS

		Lick Creeks Hellza Poppin
	Ch. Karavel Sudden Wyndfall	
		Wyndfall's Majesty New Dawn
Ch. Starr's Blue Jeans		
		HiVu Silver Smith
	HiVu Silver Mystery	
		Ch. HiVu Madresfield Molly

• •

PEDIGREE FOR CH. TARTANSIDE ANIMATION

Ch. Applause Parader Persuasion

Ch. Sealore's Grand Applause

Starr's Dark Crystal

Ch. Tartanside Animation

Ch. Tartanside The Candidate

Tartanside Caress

Ch. Eaton's Tartanside Colleen

Bred/owned by Pam & Louis Durazzano

TOP SMOOTH COLLIE SIRES

CH. BLACK HAWK OF KASAN	78
CH. FOXBRIDE'S MCLAUGHLAN	39
CH. LISARA'S MERRYTIME RAINMAKER	25
CH. ARYGGETH'S LISARA LIAISON	22
CH. STORMS T N T	20
CH. FIREHAWK OF KASAN	18
CH. JIM PAT COPPER DUST O'MERRYTIME	18
CH. SCANDIA BAYBERRY NIGHT HAWK	17
CH. KING'S VALLEY BLUE ENCHANTOR	17
CH. CRYSTAL BEAR OF KASAN	16
CH. STORMS COMMAND PERFORMANCE	16
CH. STORMS GRAND SLAM	16
CH. CUL MORS BOW STREET RUNNER	15
CH. LISARA'S MERRYTIME DRAMBUIE	14
CH. MCMAURS DIAMOND JIM	14
CH. NATURAL EXPLOSION	14
CH. CHARMANTS ALL THAT JAZZ	14

ROUGH SIRES OF SMOOTH CHAMPIONS

CH. SUJIM'S MR. ONEDERFUL	20
CH. SUNKIST MIDNIGHT FLYER, CD	16
MARNUS PROMISED LAND	13
CH. BLUE BARON OF ARROWHILL	10
HONEYHILL HARVESTER	10
CH. ROYAL ROCK MINSTREL BOY	10
ASIL'S THE MEADOWS TWICE AS BLUE	9
CH. TWIN CREEKS TRUE GRIT	8
CH. FURY THE SPIRIT OF LEGENDS	7
CH. VENNESSEE'S MIDNIGHT EXPRESS	7
CH. CUL MORS CONSPIRATOUR	6
CH. SEALORES GRAND APPLAUSE	5
CH. TARTANSIDE TH'CRITICS CHOICE	5
CH. TWO JAYS HANOVER ENTERPRISE	5
CH. TARTANSIDE THE GLADIATOR	5
CH. IMPROMPTU RICOCHET	4
CH. EXECUTIVE RIDE-THE-HIGH WIND	2
CH. GINGEOR BELLBROOKES CHOICE	2
CH. TWIN OAKS JOKER'S WILD	2

1. *Ch. Black Hawk of Kasan.*

2. *Ch. Foxbride's McLaughlan.*

3. *Ch. Lisara's Merrytime Rainmaker.*

4. *Ch. Aryggeth Lisara Liaison.*

SMOOTH SIRES OF ROUGH CHAMPIONS

Ch. Aryggeth Lisara Liaison   2
Ch. Lisara Merrytime Rainmaker   1

● ●

PEDIGREE OF CH. BLACK HAWK OF KASAN

Arrowhill Ace High

Ch. High Man of Arrowhill

Arrowhill Janie Of Crag Crest

Ch. Black Hawk of Kasan, whelped May 13, 1966

The Bogie Man of Drelms

Ch. Kasans Fine and Fanci

Ch. Mal Bonn's Blue Saphire

Owner: Sandra K. Tuttle, Kasan Collies

● ●

PEDIGREE FOR CH. FOXBRIDE'S MCLAUGHLAN

Ch. McMaur's Diamond Jim

Ch. Charmant's All That Jazz

Charmant's Cracklin' Rose

Ch. Foxbride's McLaughlan, whelped 1987

Ch. Deep Rivers Time Lord

Foxbride's Fairly Obvious

Ch. Wagon Stars Total Recall

Owned by Dehaven & Debbie Batchelor

● ●

PEDIGREE FOR CH. LISARA'S MERRYTIME RAINMAKER

Ch. Sunkist Midnight Flyer, CD

Ch. Lisara's Blueprint

Ch. Lisara's Afterknight Delight

Ch. Lisara's Merrytime Rainmaker, whelped 1985

Ch. Windrifts Blue Knight

Ch. Lisara's Afterknight Delight

Ch. Lisara's Cover Girl

Bred by Carmen & Larry Leonard
Owned by Carol Ann & Fran Coleman

• •

PEDIGREE FOR CH. ARYGGETH LISARA LIAISON

Ch. Braegates In The Blues

Ch. Lynridge Shades of Night

Ch. Clarion's Caberet

Ch. Aryggeth Lisara Liaison, whelped 1983

Ch. Sunkist Midnight Flyer

Am/Can Ch. Lisara's Morning After

Ch. Lisara's Afterknight Delight

Bred by Carmen & Larry Leonard
Owned by Dona & George Haggerty

• •

CH. STORMS T N T
• •

CH. FIREHAWK OF KASAN
• •

CH. JIM PAT COPPER DUST O'MERRYTIME

CH. SCANDIA BAYBERRY NIGHT HAWK

• •

CH. KING'S VALLEY BLUE ENCHANTER

• •

CH. CRYSTAL BEAR OF KASAN

• •

9. Ch. Kings Valley's Blue Enchanter

TOP SMOOTH DAMS

Ch. Jancada Tender O'Kings Valley	14
Ch. David's Pride Hanover Special	18
Ch. Lisara's Seaiew Nightingale	13
Ch. Lisara's Afterknight Delight	13/ 1 rough
Ch. Verler's Charmer of Lick Creek	13
Ch. Crossheart's Camlin Caper	13
Ch. Glocamera Evermore of Emboy	12
Ch. Jancade The Windbird	12
Ch. Cul Mor's Birken Shaw	11
Ch. Adam Acres Dark Side O'Th Moon	11
Ch. Mel-Bars Brandwyne Bobbi, CD	10
Ch. Franchel's Sweeat Charity	10
Ch. Storms Starlit Skies	10
Ch. Lisara's Hanky Panky	10
Ch. Crossheart's Bobbi Sox	9
Ch. Kimberee On The Road Again	9
Ch. Ledge Rock Simply Smashing	9
Ch. Windameres Firstmover	9
Ch. Lisara's Morning After	9/ 3 rough

1. Ch. Jancada Tender O'Kings Valley

PART VI.
APPENDIX

Biographies of Contributors

Dr. Cindi Bossart graduated from the University of Pennsylvania School of Theriogenology (Reproduction). She is a member of the International Canine Genetics Network.

Cindi has bred and shown dogs for 19 years and is presently breeding Collies.

Campaign and Standing: Ch. Alfenlock the Silver Laser

     1994 #5 Collie All-Breed Canine Chronicle

     1994 #6 Collie Breed Canine Chronicle

     1994 #3 Top Ten Invitational Collie Club of America

John Buddie began the Tartanside kennel operation in 1962 with the show bitch, Ch. Glen Hill Emperor's Double Up, purchased from the book's author. Some of the top sires of the breed have originated from this kennel. John has spent 25 years as a professional handler. He has been writing about Collies for more than 25 years and his articles have appeared in some of the most prestigious magazines on dogs. He is the co-chairman of the CCA National Archives and was co-editor of the 1994 CCA Yearbook. John is also a teacher of gifted students at the Eisenhower Middle School.

Harold N. Engel, DVM, PhD, is a professor at the College of Veterinary Medicine, Oregon State University.

He is a registered veterinarian with International Canine Genetics, Inc.

Gayle Kaye has been interested in Collies for more than 25 years. Even though living in the metropolitan area of San Jose, her Chelsea kennel has produced a respectable number of major, specialty-winning Collies. Three of the best-known champions emerging from this small kennel are: Ch. Chelsea Shadowgold, Ch. Chelsea Ice Castles and Ch.

Chelsea Castles In The Sky. She is co-chair of the CCA National Archives. She has been an author of a series of articles for Collie publications. Gayle has also contributed as editor of CCA Yearbooks. Her latest undertaking was as editor of the *American Collie Champions*, volume IV.

Carol Knock is a registered veterinary technician, all-breed dog and cat groomer, dog trainer, behaviorist and retired high school animal management technology teacher (Trumbull County Joint Vocational School in Warren, Ohio). She has been a member of the CCA for 30 years and is now serving as chairman of the National Obedience Committee. She has shown her Collies and achieved more than 30 titles. She has had UDs in the United States and Canada and has earned a tracking certification. Carol currently co-owns a dog obedience-training business and has helped train thousands of students to train their dogs. She co-authored an obedience video marketed nationally and internationally and is currently working on a book about obedience.

Jean Levitt is president and public relations director for the American Working Collie Association. As public relations director, she represents Assistance Dog Partners worldwide focusing on educating the general public on the benefits of assistance dogs—guide, hearing and service—for disabled persons. Jean's career as a Radio City Rockette, dance therapist and television host was interrupted by a disability received as a result of a car crash in 1988. She is partnered with her second assistance dog, Sir Austin," a champion blue merle, rough-coated Collie Service Dog, bred by Markos' Collies. Jean is also an award-winning writer on dogs.

Lois Russell has been conducting dog obedience classes at all levels for all breeds and mixed breeds for 25 years. She has researched what differentiates one breed from another, particularly as far as temperament and learning facilities are concerned. In 1988, the AKC requested that she organize a competitive herding program for dogs in the Herding Group. This project entailed additional research to her ongoing studies for the obedience classes, and it is from this research that she uncovered the key role that the Collie played during the 18th and 19th centuries as a drover's dog in Great Britain. She has served as president jof the American Working Collie Association and has been a district director of the Collie Club of America for 10 years.

Doris Werdermann has been a strong supporter of the smooth Collie since the late sixties and has owned and bred several top dogs—the best known being Ch. Dorelaine Smooth Domino. She is the past president of the CCA and the Collie Club of Long Island and is one of the founders of the Tri-County Collie Breeders Association of Southeastern New York and the Collie Club of Long Island. Doris is a judge who speaks at both national and local breed judges' study groups and was the chairman of the successful 1995 National Educational Seminar in Tennessee. She wrote the history of the smooth Collie for the CCA breed book, *The New Collie*, which became a milestone for the smooth Collie in 1983.

GLOSSARY OF TERMS

Bitch: A female dog.

Breeder: The person whose name appears on the papers as owner of a bitch at the time she is bred.

Brood bitch: A female dog that is used to produce puppies.

Champion: An American Kennel Club registered dog that has won 15 championship points, including two major (three or more points) shows, under three different judges.

Collie Club of America (CCA): The national organization that represents the Collie nationally.

Collie Club of America Specialty Show: Also called CCA Specialty or the National Specialty. This is the show that is put on by the National Club and is the largest show of Collies each year. Wins here carry enormous prestige.

Collie, rough: A collie with long thick coat.

Collie, smooth: A Collie with a short, harsh, tight-fitting coat.

Conformation: This is the type of competition in which the dogs are evaluated against each other. There is a Standard for each breed, and the dogs are compared against the Standard. This is the type of competition in which championship points are awarded. Most dog shows around the country and around the world are based on this type of show.

Dog: A male dog.

Expression: A term used particularly in Collies to describe the look of the dog's face, preferably a sweet look.

Feathering: The long coat that hangs on the back of the front legs and under the body of a well-coated Collie.

Hocks: The part of the hindlegs that reaches from the ground to the next joint above (should be straight and parallel, but sometimes will be weak and pointing outward.)

Match show: A show that offers no championship points but is more or less a training show for novice dogs or beginning handlers.

Natural ears: A term used to describe the Collie ear, which rises up from the head, then tips over gently. This is sometimes referred to as the "tulip ear."

Obedience competition: This may be held in a separate event or, in conjunction with a point or match show. Obedience Competition is judged on the performance of a certain pattern of behavior which has been predetermined by AKC. This includes such things as heeling, sitting on command, coming on recall, and much more. Dogs must be trained to certain commands in order to enter this competition.

Owner: The person or persons shown as owners on the American Kennel Club registration paper.

Placements: At conformation shows, sometimes the titles of placements are abbreviated. Here are the meanings of those terms:

> Ch., Champion (has earned enough points for its Championship)
>
> BOB, Best of Breed (BOV rough and smooth compete for BOB)
>
> BOV, Best of Variety (smooth, rough coated)

BOS, Best Opposite Sex (to the animal awarded BOV)

BOS to BOB, Best Opposite Sex to Best of Breed

BOS to BOV, Best Opposite Sex to Best of Variety

BW or BOW, Best of Winners (Best between Winners' Dog and Winners' Bitch)

WD, Winners' Dog (best male in competition, wins points)

RWD, Reserve Winner's Dog (second best male, wins no points)

WB, Winners' Bitch (best female in competition, wins points)

RWB, Reserve Winner's Bitch (second best female, wins no points)

Point show: An American Kennel Club show at which championship points may be awarded.

Puppy: A dog under a year of age.

Ruff: The long part of the collie coat that stands up behind the head and around the neck of the well coated collie.

Show Superintendent: The organization that handles the logistics of putting on a show, and which receives the entries. There are many of these all over the country. You must contact one to get on a list of those receiving entry forms.

Skirts or pants: The profuse hair that adorns the area from below tailset to the hocks of the Collie.

Specialty Show: A show that is entered only by dogs of one breed. These shows are usually large, and wins there carry great prestige.

Stifle: The part of the hind legs that reaches from the underbody to the hocks. This should be well bent.

Stud: A dog that is purposely bred to produce puppies.

Whelp: To give birth.

INDEX